T0338411

Securitisation Swaps: A practitioner handbook

Founded in 1807, John Wiley & Sons is the oldest independent publishing company in the United States. With offices in North America, Europe, Australia, and Asia, Wiley is globally committed to developing and marketing print and electronic products and services for our customers' professional and personal knowledge and understanding.

The Wiley Finance series contains books written specifically for finance and investment professionals as well as sophisticated individual investors and their financial advisors. Book topics range from portfolio management to e-commerce, risk management, financial engineering, valuation and financial instrument analysis, as well as much more.

For a list of available titles, visit our website at www.wileyfinance.com.

Securitisation Swaps:
A practitioner handbook

MARK AARONS

VLAD ENDER

ANDREW WILKINSON

WILEY

This edition first published 2019
© 2019 Mark Aarons, Vlad Ender, Andrew Wilkinson

Registered office
John Wiley & Sons Ltd, The Atrium, Southern Gate, Chichester, West Sussex, PO19 8SQ, United Kingdom

For details of our global editorial offices, for customer services and for information about how to apply for permission to reuse the copyright material in this book please see our website at www.wiley.com.

Library of Congress Cataloging-in-Publication Data

Names: Aarons, Mark, 1975- author. | Ender, Vlad, 1974- author. | Wilkinson,
    Andrew, 1979- author.
Title: Securitisation swaps : a practitioner's handbook / Mark Aarons,
    Vlad Ender, Andrew Wilkinson.
Description: Chichester, West Sussex, United Kingdom : Wiley, 2019. | Series:
    Wiley finance series | Includes bibliographical references and index. |
    Identifiers: LCCN 2018041666 (print) | LCCN 2018048782 (ebook) | ISBN
    9781119532347 (ePub) | ISBN 9781119532309 (Adobe PDF) | ISBN 9781119532279
    (hardcover) | ISBN 9781119532309 (ePDF) | ISBN 9781119532330 (ebook)
Subjects: LCSH: Derivative securities—Handbooks, manuals, etc.
Classification: LCC HG6024.A3 (ebook) | LCC HG6024.A3 A2325 2019 (print) |
    DDC 332.64/57—dc23
LC record available at https://lccn.loc.gov/2018041666

A catalogue record for this book is available from the British Library.

ISBN 978-1-119-53227-9 (hardback) ISBN 978-1-119-53234-7 (ePub)
ISBN 978-1-119-53230-9 (ePDF) ISBN 978-1-119-53233-0 (Obook)

10 9 8 7 6 5 4 3 2 1

Cover Design: Wiley
Cover Image: © chain45154 / Moment / Getty Images

Set in 10/12 pt, TimesLTStd-Roman by SPi Global, Chennai, India.

Printed and bound by CPI Group (UK) Ltd, Croydon, CR0 4YY

To Suzanne, Alex, Will and Jacqui with love and gratitude
– M.A.

To Irena and Anna – you gave me support and love when I needed it
– V.E.

To Amy, who never fails to shine a guiding light for me
– A.W.

Contents

About the Author

Mark Aarons was Head of FICC Structuring at the National Australia Bank from 2010 to 2017, where he built a leading securitisation swap business in both Australia and the UK. Mark is currently Head of Investment Risk at a leading Australian funds manager and is also an Adjunct Associate Professor in the Centre for Quantitative Finance and Investment Strategies at Monash University. He has degrees in Law and Science from Monash University and a PhD in Mathematics jointly from the Max Planck Institute for Gravitational Physics and the Free University of Berlin, Germany. He resides in Melbourne with his wife and three children.

Vlad Ender is a director at Kauri Solutions, a financial markets consulting practice. Prior to founding Kauri Solutions in 2015, Vlad spent eight years at National Australia Bank's London office. He served as an Executive Director in the FICC Structuring team, providing bespoke derivatives to NAB's clients, including innovative solutions for asset and liability swaps to support RMBS and covered bond issuance by some of the largest UK issuers. Before joining NAB, Vlad was a partner at a New Zealand IT consultancy delivering tailored solutions to the financial sector. Vlad holds an MBA from London Business School and a Masters degree in Computer Science from Charles University, Prague.

Andrew Wilkinson is currently a senior legal counsel in Australia where he specialises in bespoke derivatives and securitisation. Previously, Andrew spent a decade in London working through the financial crisis and beyond for leading law firms Linklaters LLP and Weil, Gotshal & Manges. Through this period Andrew worked on some the most complex and innovative transactions in the market, providing advice to securitisation and covered bond issuers and arrangers across UK, Europe and Asia. He has extensive experience in structured finance, securitisation and derivatives across all asset classes. Andrew holds a Masters of Banking and Financial Services Law from the University of Melbourne and Bachelors degrees in Law and Arts from Monash University.

Foreword

I first met Mark in London in March 2007. He had taken a transfer from head office in Australia to join our UK Market Risk team as a model validation quant. Mark's timing was impeccable – the start of the global financial crisis and one of the most extraordinary chapters in the history of financial markets was only a few months away. By September, depositors were queuing outside Northern Rock and within a year Lehman Brothers would collapse. These events, and those that followed, would shape our careers and lead to the book you hold today.

Shortly after Mark started, chatter about the new 'risk guy' began to emerge. Mostly that he might have a personality, but also that he was a problem-solver, someone eager to learn and work with front office to get things done. It didn't take long for him to make an impression on me either with his enquiring mind and intellect (who gets a maths PhD and a law degree?).

The collapse of Lehman's was the defining moment of the crisis, when the sheer scale of the credit and liquidity binge was finally laid bare for all to see, leaving the financial universe staring into the abyss. It was at this point that I was tasked with taking over the bank's capital markets structuring portfolio. That team had avoided CDOs and CLOs (not the bank however, where we had billions of dollars of CDOs in an SPV) but there was still correlation, credit and funding risk not being captured or valued and requiring serious work to sort out. With that transpired one of the easiest decisions I have ever had to make: just over a year after starting in Market Risk, Mark moved to front office to manage the portfolio.

A few months later Mark and I had a meeting with the Head of Secured Funding of our UK retail bank. Historically we had had little relationship with them, not having the capability to price or book their balance guarantee swaps. That meeting proved to be the genesis of this book. The swap provider to their master trust programme had given notice and no one else would step in (at least not for a price that was anywhere near reasonable). It was left to the parent bank as the AA-rated entity, and more specifically to us, to find a solution. We were going to have to solve the complex quantitative and operational challenges necessary to price, risk manage and book the trades, which this book so comprehensively discusses.

Given the amount and complexity of work involved, Vlad was the ideal additional person to bring on board to work with us on the task at hand. Vlad had started as a programmer consulting to the New Zealand subsidiary of ours a few years earlier. After moving to London, he had shown great aptitude in building the systems for the nascent inflation swap business. His curiosity and smarts led him to take a keen interest in the structuring and risk management side of that business where his value was soon realised by Sales and Trading.

Over the following months and years, I watched Mark and Vlad break down and solve each of the various challenges discussed in this book. Along with other colleagues, they created a suite of analytics, wrote the code, built interfaces to core bank systems, developed risk and finance policies, worked on the transaction documents with legal counsel, influenced myriad stakeholders to support us and then took it all through the hierarchy of risk committees. All these years later, I can still picture Vlad sitting at his desk in London, headphones on, trying to work out how we would ever get the accompanying basis swap into our systems.

The rest is history. Approvals were granted and our first UK securitisation swap took place shortly after. This new capability, when allied to our AA rating at a time when the incumbent, lower-rated swap providers were pulling out, was to prove a compelling proposition. Over the following years we built out a strong distribution capability and went on to close numerous notable and high-profile transactions, both for our own issuance and as a third-party swap provider in both the UK and Australia. Throughout this period there was no guide book or paper we could find to teach us how to price balance guarantee swaps. To the best of my knowledge there still isn't – which is what makes this book so invaluable.

Around the same time I met Mark, a young lawyer was also embarking on a similar journey. Andrew arrived in London from Australia in early 2008 to join the structured finance team of a leading law firm, just in time for the financial crisis. As the crisis began to take hold Andrew found himself right in the middle of it, whether it be advising financial institutions to access the emergency liquidity measures introduced by Bank of England or working on the Lehman Brothers administration itself. As the focus shifted from deal origination to restructuring, Andrew was on the frontline, working on many innovative solutions to address the issues arising from the crisis. This proved to be the perfect breeding ground for when he later came to work with Mark back in Australia to help navigate the complex legal and regulatory framework, which has since burgeoned around both securitisation and derivatives.

On reflection, there are several points to make. Firstly, we came to appreciate the elegance of securitisation and to distinguish it from the seemingly non-existent credit standards of sub-prime securitisation. Amongst other benefits, securitisation allows non-bank lenders to flourish and provide finance to many who are viewed as 'non-conforming' by high street banks. Secondly, and where this book is of such value, secured financing treasury teams often do not have the ability to price or challenge swap pricing. Instead, the focus is on the headline coupon or floating margin. What really matters is the landed cost of funds inclusive of swap execution cost. For that to occur, each of the features of the swap have to be priced and negotiated. I would also commend this book to those in bank securitisation relationship teams – the ability to understand and challenge their traders swap pricing is now at hand!

In my experience, quantitatively talented people are not that unique. What is unique however is when, together with that, they also have ambition, resilience, wit and, most importantly, the ability to distil complex quantitative topics into simple, concise and easily understandable points. It is these attributes that enabled us to take complex risk features through a conservative risk environment and it is the same attributes that make this book so compelling. I may be biased, but Mark, Vlad and Andrew have done an outstanding job in the quality and breadth of content and its sheer accessibility.

Chauncy Stark
Sydney, July 2018

Acknowledgements

As many authors before us have observed, writing a book has turned out to be a significantly larger task than first imagined. It is a good thing that many authors only realise this in hindsight, else there may be considerably fewer books! It is therefore with great pleasure that we acknowledge the following people for their invaluable assistance to us over this journey, for their thoughtful comments and expert insight across quantitative finance, securitisation origination, derivatives and securitisation law, product control, risk management and structuring. We sincerely thank: Craig Stevens, David Addis, Dmitry Pugachevsky, Glen Rayner, Jamie Ng, Jenny Schlosser, Michael Liberman, Robert Phillips and Rohan Douglas. Any errors that remain are solely our own. We would also like to thank Alan Brace for permission to quote his mixed measure result in Chapter 5 and Quantifi for providing analytics for an XVA example in Chapter 7.

We also wish to thank many of our former/current colleagues and friends for assisting the build out of a successful securitisation swaps business. Particular thanks are due to Chauncy Stark and Lee Kelly for their vision, leadership, support and business acumen; Tony Kelly, Grant Armstrong and Andrew Downes for their outstanding skill, dedication and good humour; Jacqui Fox and Sarah Samson for their fantastic collaboration and leadership in building Australia's top-rated securitisation origination business; and Dennis Craig for his high calibre expertise and support. We also acknowledge our other wonderful colleagues in the departments of Risk, IT, Legal, Finance, Treasury, Operations and Front Office and our many clients across financial institutions in Australia and the United Kingdom.

CHAPTER 1

Introduction

There are literally trillions of dollars of face value of swaps embedded in securitisation and covered bond structures globally. These embedded swaps – which we shall call *securitisation swaps* – have several highly distinctive features that make them quite different from other derivatives. Despite these differences and the sheer size of the market, securitisation swaps have long been neglected in both the practitioner and academic literature.

Amongst the participants of structured funding markets the emphasis is (rightly) on the funding task for originators and the relative value proposition for investors. Much attention and discussion are lavished on the size of the coupon on residential mortgage-backed securities (RMBS), asset-backed securities (ABS) and covered bonds and whether it is tighter or wider than recent comparable issuance. Yet for originators the key metric is not the coupon but rather the landed cost of funds, that is the cost of funding once all expenses, including swap fees, are included.[1] This is almost never publicly disclosed – but that certainly does not diminish its central importance. In this vein, securitisation swaps deserve more prominence as they are, in many cases, a material proportion of the overall funding cost.

In addition to impacting the landed cost of funds, securitisation swaps incorporate new risks and complexity into structured funding transactions. For instance, a credit rating downgrade of the swap provider can, in certain circumstances, lead to a downgrade of the associated bonds without any change in the creditworthiness of the underlying loan pool. Securitisation swaps can also be a significant impediment to restructuring deals,[2] which can blindside investors who aren't fully aware of the consequences of having swaps embedded in structured funding deals.

It therefore makes good sense for practitioners to understand how securitisation swaps are priced, what risks they carry and how the price and risk varies across the

---

[1]For banks, who must hold credit risk capital against loans on their balance sheet, the landed cost of funds should also include the cost of capital *savings* from transferring securitised loans off their balance sheets. This does not apply to non-bank originators.

[2]For example, the Federal Reserve Bank of New York's Maiden Lane III portfolio of legacy AIG assets faced these problems. See https://tinyurl.com/y9bmg7c6.

myriad structuring options. As for any financial instrument, the pricing depends on the qualitative and quantitative nature of the risks being transferred. So, understanding the risk management of securitisation swaps by those who provide them is useful knowledge. It is the authors' contention that having a deeper understanding of the structuring, pricing and risk management of securitisation swaps will be of great benefit to everyone involved in structured funding, whether directly or as a service provider.

What makes securitisation swaps different? Securitisation swaps are different because they are inextricably linked to the inner workings of the underlying structured funding. The dynamics of the underlying loan pool and cash flow waterfalls – which are usually highly tailored – need to be incorporated in to the modelling of the swaps. This is in contrast to derivatives used by corporations, fund managers and other entities to manage risk. For example, consider a fund manager who owns USD200 million of offshore assets and hedges them back to domestic currency with foreign exchange (FX) forwards. It doesn't matter if the offshore asset is a portfolio of stocks or a power station, the FX forward is a simple currency risk management overlay, which can be easily bolted-on. In contrast, securitisation swaps are not bolted-on, but *embedded*.

The embedding of swaps in securitisation and covered bond structures is designed to remove market risk from funding deals. When underlying cash flows change, whether due to prepayment rates in the loan pool, a trigger feature in a cash flow waterfall or the originator hasn't called its bonds at a call date, any associated securitisation swap will have its cash flows altered in lockstep. This de-risking of structured funding enables the issuance to receive a very high credit rating – often AAA – from credit rating agencies. In turn, these very high ratings enable structured funding to be a highly efficient form of funding for banks and non-bank lenders.

Imagine if a securitisation swap was not in place on a structured funding issuance into, say, US dollars (USD) from a sterling (GBP) denominated loan pool. The currency volatility would expose the US investors to significant potential loss without any deterioration in the credit risk of the underlying pool of assets. For example, in 2008, GBP plunged 30% in value from buying around 2.00 to 1.35 USD in a matter of months. Removing this currency risk is an absolute necessity for any issuer hoping to achieve a AAA rating on such bonds. Likewise for interest rate risk and other market risks. But market risk can only be *totally* removed if the swap provides a *perfect hedge* – and this requires the swap cash flows to be in total alignment with the underlying cash flows from the structured funding vehicle.

Of course, the converse of the de-risking of structured funding deals is that the provider of the swap is assuming those risks. It goes without saying that anyone assuming such complex cross-asset risks needs to have significant expertise or else they could incur very material financial losses and risk management pain. This is equally true no matter whether the swap provider is also the originator or whether it is a third-party provider.

The risks from providing a securitisation swap are complex because there are multiple moving parts. Not only are the underlying cash flows subject to change, but markets are moving at the same time, specifically spot FX rates, interest rates and basis curves. The good news and key message of this book is that rigorous modelling and a wide variety of risk-mitigating structures can tame these complex risks. In this regard, the swap structuring techniques described in this book, and the legal mechanisms to incorporate them into deals, are just as important as the quantitative modelling. A thorough understanding of risk-mitigating structures for securitisation swaps should be an important part of the toolkit for anyone involved in structured funding.

We devote an entire chapter to each of the three key distinctive risks of securitisation swaps. Chapter 5 is dedicated to **swap prepayment risk**. This is the risk of simultaneously adverse moves in both loan pool prepayment rates and market risk factors. Swap prepayment risk is more complex than prepayment risk since it is concerned with the consequential impact of prepayment risk *together with changes in market risk factors* on derivatives valuation.

Chapter 6 concentrates on **swap extension risk**. This is the risk that the weighted average life (WAL) of the underlying ABS, RMBS or covered bond may extend, causing associated securitisation swaps to also extend. Extension events can be caused by originators not calling their bonds as expected (for securitisations) or by an issuer event of default (in the case of covered bonds). Extension risk is concerned with a single low probability, high impact event. In contrast, swap prepayment risk is concerned with a series of high probability, low impact events.

Chapter 7 is devoted to **downgrade risk**. Downgrade risk arises from swap providers having to comply with strict obligations linked to their own credit ratings. These obligations are defined by the rating agencies and arise from the fact that swap providers are usually rated lower than the structured funding they are supporting. The obligations are designed to de-link the swap provider's rating from that of the structured issuance. Downgrade risk consists of two underlying risks: (i) the risk of posting collateral one-way if its own credit rating falls to a prespecified trigger level; and (ii) the risk of being forced to novate out of a swap if its credit rating falls to a (lower) prespecified trigger level. Both events can be costly. The risk of posting collateral also entangles securitisation swaps with Basel III liquidity regulation and requires a new derivative valuation adjustment (yet another XVA!) to account for it.

This book is intended for a wide audience – for everyone involved in structured funding in some capacity. This includes originators, sponsors and arrangers, investors, swap providers, rating agencies and regulators. Relevant staff at swap providers includes derivative structurers, sales, traders, quants, risk managers, lawyers, product controllers and system developers. This book focuses primarily on swaps in structured funding transactions where the underlying debt is residential mortgages in predominantly floating rate markets (such as Australia and the UK), auto loans or credit card receivables. Nevertheless, much of the content of this book will still be broadly applicable, with some modification, to other underlying asset classes such as corporate loans, commercial real estate and student loans, and to other jurisdictions.

The book can be referred to in discrete parts or read cover-to-cover. Readers with a strong background in securitisation can skip Chapters 2 and 3 and begin with the discussion on swaps in Chapter 4. Readers with a derivatives background, but little or no securitisation knowledge, should start at Chapter 2 where they can learn about securitisation quickly, with the material tailored to build a foundation for *securitisation swaps* specifically. Worked numerical examples are available in a spreadsheet on this book's website at www.securitisationswaps.com.

Overview of Structured Funding

Never invest in a business you can't understand.

— Warren Buffet

FUNDING

Banks, building societies and non-bank lenders are in the money business. Money, in all its forms, is for these institutions what inventories are for other businesses. As such, these institutions must raise money. A profitable institution will then loan the money out to borrowers at a higher average interest rate than the aggregate cost of its funding. The difference between these two rates is known as the *net interest margin* (NIM) and it is a key metric for all for-profit financial institutions.

Banks need money for a multitude of reasons: for capital, liquidity and regulatory purposes. Interestingly enough, banks do not need to raise money to fund loans at inception. Alan Holmes, who managed the Federal Reserve System Open Market Account, wrote in 1969 that 'in the real world banks extend credit, creating deposits in the process, and look for the reserves later'.[1] Thus, in the process of writing loans banks are able to independently create money themselves in the form of deposits. In contrast, shadow banks require funding in order to be able to extend credit as they are unable to take deposits.

Whether or not the cash raised is used to fund loans, the term *funding* is still used ubiquitously in the financial services industry to describe the raising of money and will be used in this book as well.

All funding instruments have a cost to the issuer. The whole-of-life cost is comprised of two components: the market cost of funds and transaction costs.

The market cost of funds is the sum of the various risk premia that investors require as compensation for taking risk, including the term credit, interest rate, liquidity and

---

[1] See [AH] at page 73.

complexity premia. It is the cost of funding prior to the inclusion of any transaction costs.

The market price of risk is the return in excess of a benchmark rate,[2] such as a relevant bond yield, that the market wants as compensation for taking on credit and other risks. A credit index, such as iTraxx Senior Financials, can provide an indication of this level. The market price of risk is a highly dynamic feature across securities markets and, in times of market stress, can blow out by several orders of magnitude.

There are two main drivers of the perceived credit risk attaching to a funding instrument: seniority and tenor. The more senior the instrument, the greater the chance the investor will be repaid in the event of an issuer default. Longer-term funding instruments generally cost more as investors require higher compensation for the extended loss of liquidity, the increased risk of default and greater uncertainty that longer time horizons inherently produce.

Transaction costs comprise an inception issuance cost and running costs. The inception cost depends on the complexity of the instrument and how tailored it is to particular investors' requirements. Standard market instruments, such as bank bills and short-term repurchase agreements ('repos') have very low inception issuance costs due to their generic, 'cookie cutter' nature. On the other hand, new capital instruments, long-term debt and especially secured, complex or bespoke funding instruments will involve a great deal of work to put together, which is reflected in higher costs. Running costs will vary depending on how much reporting and disclosure is required and the level of active management the funding requires and whether external parties such as *special purpose vehicles* (SPVs) are involved.

One would expect that a financial institution should try to obtain the cheapest possible funding available to it, but that could expose the institution to unwanted risks and restrict its business model. For example, the cheapest funding in the market is generally a short-term repo. A repo is a form of short-term, structured funding, whereby the seller of a security agrees to buy it back at a specified time and price. However, a repo involves having a stock of high-quality collateral available to be repurchased in the market. Before the Global Financial Crisis (GFC) many AAA-rated instruments were accepted in the repo market as high-quality collateral. However, the repo market has developed so that only collateral issued by certain governments or some supranational organisations will be accepted as high quality. Furthermore, as some governments pare back the volume of their debt issuance, the availability of collateral and hence the size of the repo market has declined, leading to this cheap source of funding drying up.

Similarly, unsecured short-term interbank loans, another staple of cheap funding prior to the GFC, have also declined in importance. This has contributed to an overall decline in the centrality of IBOR rates, which were the rates at which banks would

---

[2] Strictly speaking, in Mathematical Finance, the market price of risk is the excess return divided by the standard deviation of returns. In this context, we are only concerned with the excess return.

offer unsecured lending to one another. No bank will offer the same rate on unsecured lending to all of its peers now.

More generally, the GFC has shown very dramatically that overreliance on any form of short-term funding can be extremely dangerous. A significant number of financial institutions failed during the GFC when short-term funding evaporated. While excessive leverage, poor credit quality and rating agencies were also major contributing factors, lack of liquidity was, arguably, the most important culprit.

Thus financial institutions must consider more factors than simply cost when designing their funding plan. The stability and diversity of their funding mix are critical factors to ensure resilience during periods of market stress. Indeed, various new Basel III regulatory reforms – for example, the Liquidity Coverage Ratio (LCR) and the Net Stable Funding Ratio (NSFR) – have compelled institutions to extend the tenor and diversity of their funding. As a result, the issuance of more costly instruments is an even more important part of the funding mix of every financial institution.

FUNDING INSTRUMENTS

Financial institutions, like all corporations, may be funded via a mix of debt and equity. However, financial institutions generally have a much higher proportion of debt funding than other corporations, which is likely why they have developed a larger array of debt funding instruments, with myriad characteristics, purposes, advantages and disadvantages. Broadly speaking, we can identify the following four attributes of funding instruments:

1. *Seniority*. This defines an investor's priority in claiming assets in the event that a financial institution fails. Equity confers ownership rights but the lowest seniority. Debt ranks higher but is graded from senior to subordinated. Deposits have the highest seniority.
2. *Tenor*. This can range from very short-term funding like on demand deposits, through short-term bills, long-dated bonds and finally equity that is perpetual.
3. *Security*. Unsecured or secured by a segregated pool of assets. Structured funding includes repos; single-recourse debt instruments such as asset-backed securities (ABS), residential mortgage-backed securities (RMBS) and collateralised loan obligations (CLOs); and dual recourse debt instruments such as covered bonds.
4. *Complexity*. This ranges from very simple instruments such as common equity, term deposits or senior unsecured bonds to highly structured and/or tailored instruments such as convertible bonds, ABS and RMBS.

Figure 2.1 shows the most common forms of funding instruments and relative levels of risk that can be attributed to them.

Lowest risk

AAA-rated senior secured debt
- Covered bonds
- Securitised debt (ABS and RMBS)

Deposits
- At-call deposits
- Term deposits

Senior unsecured debt
- Bank bills
- Senior unsecured bonds

Subordinated debt
- Lower and upper tier 2 (unsecured)
- Lower tranches of securitised debt

Hybrids
- Convertible bonds
- Convertible preference shares

Equity
- Ordinary and preference shares

Highest risk
- Lowest tranche of securitised debt

FIGURE 2.1 Relative levels of risk to investors from various funding instruments.

Note that securitised debt is listed several times in Figure 2.1 as the *tranching* process (described below) can create a number of debt securities with very different credit risk.

SECURITISATION

The Securitisation Process

Securitisation is the process by which non-tradeable debt, such as residential mortgages, auto loans and credit card receivables, is converted into a tradeable debt security issued to investors. The principal and interest from the underlying contractual debt is used to pay the investors. In principle, any receivable with regular, predictable cash flows can be securitised.

Investors buying securitised debt are assuming the credit risk on the pool of underlying debt and are compensated accordingly via the credit spread they receive in the bond coupons. They are not assuming any direct credit risk on the institution that originated the underlying debt.[3] This is known as *bankruptcy remoteness*. It means that even if the institution that wrote all the underlying mortgages defaults, the securitised debt built from those mortgages can continue to repay investors.

In order to achieve bankruptcy remoteness, a legal separation is required. Some terminology is needed to clearly define this. The *originator* is the institution that originated the underlying debt; that is, it is the bank that wrote the mortgage or the finance company that provided the auto loan. The *issuer*, on the other hand, is the legal entity that has issued the securitised debt to investors and is responsible for its repayment.

The legal entity used to issue the securitised debt is called a SPV. In common law jurisdictions,[4] SPVs usually have the legal form of a trust, although companies may also be used. In reality, the SPV is simply a holding vehicle used to achieve legal separation from the originator. Note that certainty of law is a key fundamental requirement for the securitisation process to work. Although this is a given in developed market jurisdictions, it cannot always be assumed elsewhere.

The process works as follows:

- The originator establishes an SPV.
- The SPV purchases receivables from the originator, funded by a loan from the originator.
- The SPV issues one or more bonds to investors that are secured against the principal and interest cash flows it has purchased from the originator, and uses the proceeds to repay the loan from the originator.
- The trust pays a company, called a servicer, to *service* the assets, that is, to collect payments, manage arrears and resolve defaults. In the UK and Australia this is usually the originator. In the USA it is commonly a third party.
- The trust uses the money it receives from the servicer to pay expenses and investors. Excess spread may be returned to the originator.

Figure 2.2 illustrates the basic structure.

Structured Funding Participants

Originator/Seller The originator, sometimes also called the seller, is the entity behind the securitisation or covered bond that is responsible for originating the assets and owning the income stream from the receivables being securitised. For example, in a securitisation backed by residential mortgages, the bank that underwrites and advances the mortgage loans will be the originator. Therefore, the obligations arising with respect to securitised assets are originally owed to the originator before the

---

[3]If the originator is also a swap provider, then investors will have a credit risk exposure to the originator via its capacity as swap provider.
[4]These include: Australia, Canada, Hong Kong, New Zealand, Singapore, UK and USA.

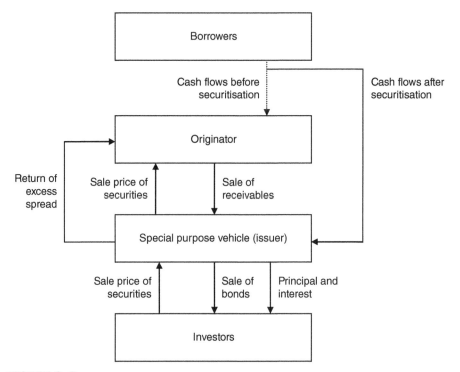

FIGURE 2.2   Cash flows of a securitisation.

transfer to the issuer takes place. Originators can include banks, building societies, non-bank lenders, captive financial companies of the major car manufacturers, insurance companies and other financial institutions. Occasionally, the seller may be a third party who buys the pool with the intention to securitise it thereafter.

There are a number of non-mutually-exclusive reasons why an originator may choose to securitise its assets rather than holding them, including: to achieve a lower cost or alternative source of funding; to accelerate cash receipts and remove assets from on-balance sheet; to engage in regulatory capital arbitrage.

Issuer   In a securitisation transaction, the issuer will hold the assets and issue the securities. The issuer will normally take the form of a newly created SPV that is structured to be bankruptcy remote. In practice, this means that the issuer:

- has no shareholders or employees;
- is a new company with no existing creditors that could potentially raise competing claims with noteholder in the event of an insolvency event; and

▪ has limited constitutional objects, which restrict it from undertaking any business other than issuing notes within the context of a securitisation.

The SPV commonly takes the legal form of a trust, though may also exist as a corporation, partnership or a limited liability company.

In a covered bond transaction, the issuer is the financial institution issuing the bonds.

Servicer The servicer is the entity that services the assets, including collecting the principal and interest payments from the underlying pool. More often than not the originator of the loans will continue to act in the role of servicer on the basis that this will involve no change to the documented payment collection procedures and that enforcement and recovery procedures will already be established to deal with customers in default. From the perspective of the borrower of a loan this means that it is often very difficult to tell if a loan has been securitised. The servicer is typically compensated with a fixed servicing fee.

Trustee In a structured funding transaction the primary duty of the trustee is to protect the interests of the noteholders and to administer the duties of the SPV within the documentary framework. Because the trustee acts in a fiduciary capacity this means that it is legally obliged to act in the best interests of the noteholders and preserve their rights within the transaction.

The trustee performs a fundamental role, which can be broken down into two distinct areas of responsibility: the notes and the security. It is important to distinguish between the capacities of the note trustee and the security trustee. The note trustee holds the issuer's covenant to pay on trust for the noteholders, whereas the security trustee holds the benefit of the security interests on trust for all of the secured parties, that is, the noteholders and other various transaction parties (including the swap counterparty) that may also be granted security.

In some transactions these roles may be separated so that there is a separate note trustee and a security trustee, but in other transactions the same trustee may perform both of these functions with no distinction being made between these obligations. It should be noted that where the trustee role is combined there may be obligations towards the noteholders (under the notes) and the noteholders and other transaction parties (under the security) that could give rise to a potential conflict of interest, which would need to be addressed within the documentation.

For the sake of ease and convenience here we have split out the note trustee and security trustee to give a better idea of the different roles but note that it is not unusual for these to be combined into a single trustee role.

Note Trustee The note trustee represents and co-ordinates the group of noteholders, which in turn provides the issuer with a single point of contact. One of the main advantages of the trust structure is that a single trustee can be utilised to deal with a multitude of different investors. As a trustee, the note trustee holds certain duties and responsibilities that are enshrined in legislation and the general principles of equity under the common law.

The note trustee role is largely administrative and the acting note trustee will be empowered to agree certain minor or technical amendments without consultation with the wider group of noteholders. This can alleviate some of the administrative burden associated with the transaction. However, while there are various discretions to act, in practice, it is extremely unlikely that the note trustee will take any material actions unless it has received instructions to do so (which in a bond transaction may involve convening a meeting with a quorum of noteholders) and unless it has been indemnified against any cost, expenses or liabilities that it may incur as a result of taking such action. Because the role of the note trustee is relatively mechanical and limited in scope, the fees earned by a note trustee for acting in the role are generally quite low.

Security Trustee An issuer will grant security over all of its assets and an undertaking in order to secure its obligations to noteholders and certain other transaction parties (which become collectively known as the 'secured creditors'). The only transaction parties who tend not to be secured creditors are the arranger and managers who take their fees on day one and then have little involvement in the remainder of the securitisation. The security is not granted to each secured creditor on an individual basis but rather to the security trustee, who will hold that security on behalf of all of the secured creditors. Again, this provides the issuer with a single point of contact and makes the management of the security interests easier.

The security trustee is responsible for enforcing the security and distributing the proceeds of the security. Because there may be numerous secured creditors with different priorities and size of claims against the security there may need to be a pre-determined method for how the security trustee takes instructions (an 'inter-creditor arrangement'), which can vary depending on the size and complexity of the transaction. The security trustee will distribute proceeds following the enforcement of security in accordance with the post-enforcement priority of payments (also known as the post-enforcement waterfall). This process allows any available cash to cascade down to the relevant parties dependent on their ranking in the waterfall, which is commercially negotiated considering a number of factors, including overall amount and size of risk that the party is taking within the transaction.

As with the note trustee, the security trustee is also usually paid a relatively low fee, which reflects the fact that the role of the security trustee is intended to be largely administrative and that the security trustee is not being paid to assume significant risks. As the fee is quite low, the security trustee will generally not take any issue against the issuer without being indemnified for any expenditure or liability it may be exposed to.

Arranger and Managers The arranger function in a securitisation is normally performed by an investment bank. The lead arranger will be instructed by the originator to structure and price the funding transaction on its behalf. Importantly, it is the lead arranger who will manage the relationship with the rating agencies. The lead arranger will typically be assisted by other appointed managers, who market the notes to prospective investors on investment roadshows. The role of the lead arranger and managers is to subscribe for the securities offered by the issuer and then distribute these to the investors, upon which the role the lead arranger and the other managers play in the transaction concludes. This is sometimes why the arranger and joint managers are referred to as the underwriters.

Third Parties

Account Bank As money is being paid to and from the issuer throughout the life of a transaction it will need to maintain bank accounts and the account bank provides these. In a securitisation there may be many different bank accounts, including a principal and interest cash flow collection account into which most of the money it receives is paid. Other accounts may include reserve accounts that are set up for credit enhancement (CE) purposes, principal and income receipts accounts, a liquidity account and swap collateral accounts for use in connection with any underlying swaps. To perform the function of account bank, a financial institution will be required to have a sufficiently high and stable credit rating under the relevant counterparty criteria.

Cash Manager The cash manager is responsible for managing the issuer's accounts and instructing the account bank in relation to specific day-to-day cash movements between the various transaction accounts. That is, the cash manager will generally give instructions for payments to be made of the requisite calculated amounts (as calculated by the cash manager or an appointed calculation agent) to the various reserve accounts or to the payment agents in order to make distributions to investors under the notes. As the role does not involve the same level of skills and expertise as the servicer or the existence of any pre-existing relationship with the underlying borrowers, this function can be performed by a third party and it is not uncommon for the account bank to also perform the role of cash manager.

Swap Counterparty(ies) In a securitisation transaction the issuer may utilise swaps to smooth out its cash flows – for example, where the income from the receivables does not match the amounts it is required to pay out under the notes. There are a variety of different swaps that could be included within a specific securitisation transaction, however the most common are swaps used to hedge the currency risk (where bonds may be denominated in a currency that is different from the assets) and the interest rate risk (where the issuer may hedge the difference between fixed and floating rates of interest).

The swap counterparty may be the originator of the assets, and in many cases the treasury function of originating financial institutions will assume this role because they routinely manage the associated market risks of funding trades. However, the swap counterparty can also be a separate third-party financial institution. One of the key aspects is that the swap counterparty must hold an appropriate credit rating to support the rating of the notes. Since the onset of the financial crisis and the downgrade of many financial institutions this has meant that there are a smaller number of appropriately rated financial institutions who are willing to act as a swap counterparty within a securitisation transaction. See the sub-section on The Competitive Landscape for Third-Party Swap Providers for a full discussion of this topic.

Corporate Services Provider Because the issuer is established as a bankruptcy remote SPV, it is the corporate services provider who will generally be responsible for the day-to-day running of the issuer. When an issuer is established as a corporate SPV, a separate company will need to be incorporated. The corporate services provider provides a number of administrative services, including the provision of independent company directors and the performance of all company secretarial functions including maintenance of a registered office, arranging company meetings and the preparation and submission of all company filings with regulatory authorities. This also includes the maintenance of books and preparation of management accounts and annual accounts for audit purposes as well as liaising with the tax advisors to the issuer for the submission of tax returns.

Liquidity Provider The liquidity provider is typically a financial institution (which may be a manager on the transaction or other third-party bank) that provides short-term cash cover to the issuer to deal with cash flow volatility. Any liquidity arrangements applicable to a securitisation transaction will generally be documented in a separate liquidity facility, which is used by the issuer to cover the risk of the timing mismatch between principal and interest receivables, and payments due to noteholders. A liquidity provider is generally required to have a sufficiently high and stable credit rating to provide such services to the issuer.

Paying Agent The paying agents for a securitisation perform exactly the same function as they do on any other bond issue, which is to channel money received from the issuer's accounts to the noteholders. Securitised bonds typically accrue interest at a floating rate, in which case an agent bank will also be required to calculate the rate of interest for each interest period and, in practice, that role will be performed by one of the paying agents. If the bonds are issued in registered form, a registrar and transfer agent will also need to be appointed to hold the bond register and facilitate transfers of the bonds. The roles and responsibilities of the agents are set out in an agency agreement.

Investors Investors buy the securities issued by the issuer and, according to the terms and conditions of the notes, will be entitled to receive the principal and interest payments based on the cash flows generated by the underlying assets. Investors in securitised assets are generally a blend of pension funds, insurance companies, hedge funds, banks and to a lesser degree high net-worth individuals.

Rating Agencies A credit rating agency is an independent company that assigns and monitors ratings that assess the creditworthiness of issuers and the underlying assets in a securitisation. Interestingly, the rating agencies are not a contracting party to any legal documentation and will usually be engaged by the originator and arranger to act in a third-party capacity to rate the notes being issued. A rating is an opinion on the ability of the issuer to meet its financial obligations when they fall due – for example, making payments under the notes to investors. When determining a rating, the rating agency will take into consideration the terms and conditions of the notes, the creditworthiness of other transaction parties, such as swap providers, and other structural features (including any economic or legal weaknesses) and how these are addressed. Rating agencies also provide criteria for the purpose of counterparties seeking to enter into derivative transactions linked with a securitisation.

The market for ratings is currently dominated by a few major players, including Standard & Poor's, Moody's, Fitch and DBRS. The rating agencies wield significant power in the structuring process as it is virtually impossible to offer notes in the market without a rating being allocated. While the rating process and the interpretation of a rating is different across the various rating agencies, the following general factors are typically considered when determining a rating:

- Quality of the pool of underlying assets in terms of repayment ability, maturity diversification, expected defaults and recovery rates.
- Abilities and strengths of the originator/servicer of the assets.
- Soundness of the transaction's overall structure; for example, timing of cash flow (or mismatch) and impact of defaults.
- Analysis of legal risks in the structure; for example, effectiveness of transfer of title to the assets.
- Ability of the asset manager to manage the portfolio.
- History of the assets and originator/servicer so there is sufficient data to draw conclusions about the future performance of the assets.
- Quality of credit support; for example, nature and levels of CEs.

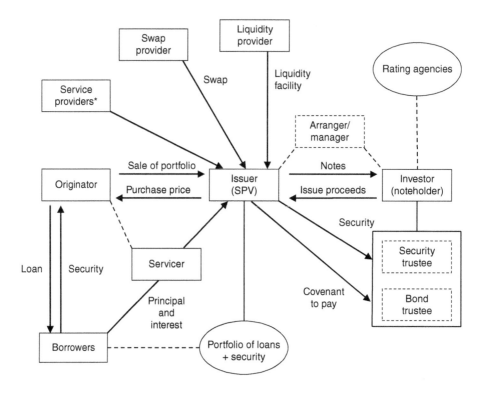

*Service Providers: Cash Manager,
Account Bank, Paying Agent, Corporate
Service Provider

FIGURE 2.3   Overview of structured funding participants.

Figure 2.3 provides an overview of all participants in a structured funding transaction.

Asset and Cash Flow Transformation

In a securitisation, the SPV essentially facilitates the pass-through of cash flows to investors and is structured to make minimal profit. Importantly, the SPV also facilitates the transformation of those cash flows. The purpose of cash flow transformation is to create a range of securities that match the disparate needs of many investors at the same time and from the same loan pool. For example, the weighted average life (WAL) of a typical residential mortgage can range from seven to ten years, whereas some investors may only wish to purchase three-year bullet securities. In general, there are five types of transformation that can occur within SPVs:

1. Credit risk
2. WAL
3. Timing of cash flows
4. Interest rate cash flows
5. Currency

The first three types of transformation are affected via *tranching*. The last two types of transformation require derivatives – specifically interest rate or cross-currency swaps.

Tranching involves splitting the cash flows of the receivables into different tranches, which have different credit risk. Junior tranches absorb credit losses first, whereas senior tranches are *credit enhanced* by the presence of subordinated tranches, and can therefore have a very high credit rating. Different bonds are issued for each tranche.

Tranching typically also involves duration transformation, which entails converting the principal cash flows into short, medium and longer-dated tranches. This is achieved by a *cash flow waterfall* – specified in the legal documentation establishing the SPV – which directs some or all principal and interest cash flows to specified tranches in priority over the other tranches (Figure 2.4). Note that, in theory, duration transformation and credit transformation can be separate processes. In practice, it is very commonly the case that the short-dated notes also have the greatest CE and long-dated notes tend to have the lowest CE.

Sometimes the cash flow waterfall changes when certain trigger events occur. For instance, when a senior tranche is paid down to a specific level (e.g. for a given level of CE to be attained), the waterfall may switch to direct cash flows pro rata to other, less senior, tranches. These triggers are important to help balance the various needs of investors, but they add complexity to the overall structure.

The certainty of cash flows can also be transformed via the cash flow waterfall. For example, prepayment risk can be greatly reduced by creating *scheduled amortisation* tranches that, under all but extreme circumstances, offer investors a prespecified amortisation schedule rather than one subject to the random whims of prepayment volatility in the asset pool. This will be discussed in detail in Chapter 3.

Swaps are required to transform interest rate cash flows and, if required, to change the currency of cash flows. Interest rate transformation is a critical component of almost all securitisations and can take several different forms. Fixed-rate mortgages or loans generally need to be converted to a standard floating interest rate, for example three-month London interbank offer rate (LIBOR), for investors. Similarly, mortgages that reference a different floating interest rate, such as an overnight rate (tracker mortgages) or an institution's own standard variable rate (SVR mortgages) need those cash flows converted to a standard floating interest rate. Because the timing of the underlying cash flows is uncertain due to prepayment risk, and because the tranching process is highly transformative, the swaps embedded within securitisations are, in general, highly complex. Navigating this complexity is the purpose of this book.

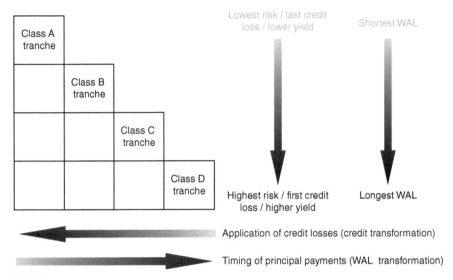

FIGURE 2.4   Tranching of a securitisation: credit and duration transformation via a cash flow waterfall.

Summary of Securitisation

To recap the above discussion and reinforce the key points, the salient features of securitisation can be summarised as follows:

1. *Conversion* of non-tradeable debt into tradeable debt.
2. *Aggregation* of many small debt obligations into an appropriate size for wholesale capital markets.[5]
3. *Transformation* of the risk profile via tranching/cash flow waterfall and swaps.
4. *Bankruptcy remoteness* from the originator via an SPV structure.
5. *Upfronts* future cash flows to provide funding for the originator.

Master Trusts

The structure we have described above is called a *standalone* securitisation. It is used for exactly one issuance (which typically involves multiple tranches at the same time). The underlying pool of assets usually remains static, save for the maturing of the loans over time, through natural expiration, prepayment by the borrower or default. It is possible for a standalone securitisation structure to be revolving.

---

[5]Aggregation also allows the law of large numbers to smooth out idiosyncratic risk from individual debt obligations.

As with any structure, it has its advantages and disadvantages. The primary advantage is that the structure is, relatively speaking, simple. Since the pool of assets is static, it is simple to estimate the expected (zero prepayment) amortisation profile of the pool and assess its credit risk.

At the same time, there are numerous drawbacks:

- Setting up an SPV is not a cheap exercise, and doing so for every bond issuance can be expensive.
- Setting up an SPV is not a quick exercise, and doing so impedes the originator's speed-to-market.
- It is more difficult to create certain securitisation structures, such as scheduled amortisation or bullet notes.
- Some asset classes, such as credit card receivables, are so short-dated that duration extension is required – and this cannot be achieved with a static pool of assets.

To address these issues, a more complex structure called a *master trust* has been developed. Master trusts combine a single, *revolving* pool of mortgages with an off-the-shelf issuance programme, not dissimilar to the medium term note (MTN) programmes used by bank treasuries to issue senior unsecured bonds. This means that the trust can be reused repeatedly by the originator to issue notes. All that the originator has to (potentially[6]) do for each new debt issuance – called a *series* – is to add new collateral to the pool and have the rating agencies assign a rating (Figure 2.5). This allows for much faster and agile issuance than standalone SPVs.

Unlike standalone SPVs, master trusts have two beneficiaries: investors and the sponsor. Their interests are referred to as the *funding share* and the *seller share* respectively. The funding share consists of the proportion of assets required to back the issued debt. The seller share is for the benefit of the sponsor and does not provide any direct CE to the funding share. However, principal receipts from the seller share can be allocated to the funding share to transform the amortisation profile. This *time-subordinates* the seller share, but does not cause direct credit subordination.[7]

The most common style of note issued from a standalone SPV is a *pass-through* note. As its name suggests, the cash flows (after costs) are directly passed on to the investors. The cash flow waterfall still transforms the credit risk and duration of the underlying debt, but it does not seek to transform the uncertainty of those cash flows, in particular the uncertainty caused by individual borrowers deciding to prepay their loans early. At the aggregate pool level, this creates prepayment risk, which makes the amortisation schedules of the pass-through notes somewhat unpredictable. This means

---

[6]The originator may add collateral well in advance of a new issuance, resulting in substantial over-collateralisation of the bonds, but allowing for very quick issuance.
[7]Given that credit risk increases with tenor, time-subordination indirectly increases credit risk.

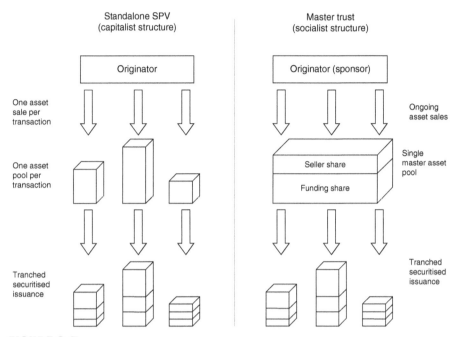

FIGURE 2.5 Comparison of standalone SPVs and master trusts.

that investors require a higher risk premium to hold such a debt. Some investors may be reluctant or even unable to hold pass-through notes at all.[8]

In addition to causing problems for investors, prepayment risk can be a major headache for those risk-managing associated swaps. As we will see in Chapter 5, higher prepayment risk increases swap costs considerably. When an originator wishes to issue securitised debt to offshore investors in foreign currency, a cross-currency swap is normally required to hedge the currency exposure. Cross-currency swaps with prepayment risk can be very expensive. Reducing the prepayment risk via the use of controlled amortisation structures, or even bullets, can save a lot of money and materially reduce the landed cost of funds. Master trusts are very well suited to this purpose because of the existence of the seller share and the ready availability of additional principal receipts. Replicating this in standalone SPVs requires cash buffers, which cost more and require tailoring for each issuance.

Each time debt is issued, the notes form a distinct *series*. Often series are enumerated by the year of issuance and the sequence with each year, for example, 2018–1, 2018–2 and so on. When multiple series of debt is issued from the same SPV, the way

---

[8]For example, European insurance regulation (Solvency II) imposes significantly higher capital costs for bonds with prepayment risk.

each series interrelates with all the other series matters. For instance, does the B note of a previous series provide CE to the A note of a later series? There are two possible approaches: the so-called *capitalist* and *socialist* structures.

Under the socialist structure, all issuance of the same seniority ranks *pari passu* (i.e. ranks equally in terms of credit risk) across the whole structure. Under the capitalist structure, each series is segregated. Lower-rated notes from one series only provide CE to higher-rated notes from the same series. The socialist structure has become the dominant method employed in UK RMBS master trusts since its inception under Northern Rock's Granite master trust in 2005. The socialist structure is arguably more efficient since it allows *de-linkage* – that is, tranches can be issued at different times, rather than each series having a complete capital structure as required in capitalist structures.

Securitisation and the GFC

Securitisation gained a very bad name during the GFC where, in some instances, the assets backing the debt – notoriously sub-prime mortgages – proved to be of much poorer credit quality than investors expected. This was caused by a confluence of factors, including a lack of transparency into the underlying assets, poor underwriting standards, rating agency deficiencies in assigning high ratings and financial markets awash with liquidity looking for a home. We would argue that these problems were much more prevalent in the USA. In Europe, the UK and Australia stronger practices and controls ensured that their securitised issuance was much more robust than in the USA. Furthermore, it would seem that this was very much a problem confined to certain asset classes. Prime and near-prime RMBS, auto ABS and credit card ABS programmes globally remained robust, in stark contrast to sub-prime RMBS and collateralised debt obligations (CDOs).

An important historical example is the case of Northern Rock, which was the first UK bank to suffer a bank run since 1866. Northern Rock was heavily reliant on its Granite RMBS programme for funding. Despite the failure of the bank, the bankruptcy remote SPV continued to perform as designed.[9] At its worst the AAA-rated tranches of Granite fell to 60 % of face value but within six months had recovered most its original value. The BBB tranche also suffered very significant falls, to under 10% of face value. While the rate of recovery for the lower-rated tranches was slower, by late 2014 the BBB prices had converged to the AAA prices at close to full face value.

All investor-available classes of debt were repaid in full by early 2016. From the above we can see that the only investors who lost money on Granite were those who sold during the panic in 2009, where some tranches were trading as low as single digits. These were balanced by the purchasers of those same tranches who, presumably, made a great deal of money as their price rebounded sharply.

---

[9]See https://www.bondvigilantes.com/blog/2015/12/21/tough-as-granite-an-rmbs-case-study for a full account.

The Granite example is important as it demonstrates the robustness of the UK master trust structure during a period of extreme stress.

COVERED BONDS

Covered bonds are a very old form of debt – preceding the development of securitisation by over two centuries! They were first issued in Prussia in 1769 and have a singularly remarkable track record: there has never been a covered bond default in history.[10] This is especially remarkable given the volume of outstanding covered bond issuance from Greek, Portuguese, Spanish, Italian and Irish banks as the GFC unfolded.

Partly as a result of this track record, in recent years the number of common law jurisdictions where covered bonds are issued has increased substantially (Table 2.1).

Other jurisdictions where covered bond issuance has occurred include the Nordic and East European countries, Turkey and South Korea.

The strength of the credit quality of covered bonds is primarily due to their dual recourse nature. While covered bonds are a senior obligation of the issuer, investors also have an additional guarantee provided by high-quality bank assets that are ring-fenced from bank creditors. These ring-fenced assets are called a *cover pool*. There are two basic structures for the cover pool: on-balance sheet and off-balance sheet. The on-balance sheet structure is used in Germany and many other European jurisdictions and is characterised by the cover pool remaining on the issuer's balance sheet. In these jurisdictions, bankruptcy law restricts creditors from making any claims over the cover pool. The off-balance sheet structure is used in common law countries and a small number of European countries such as the Netherlands. In this

TABLE 2.1 Inception covered bond issuance and regulation in common law countries.

Country	Year of first issuance	Year of legislation or regulation
Australia	2011	2010
Canada	2007	2012
New Zealand	2010	2011
Singapore	2015	2013
UK	2003	2008
USA	2006	n/a

---

[10]See, for example, http://www.ebrd.com/publications/law-in-transition-2016-covered-bonds .pdf.

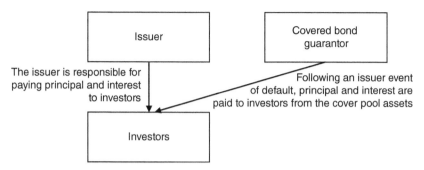

FIGURE 2.6   Covered bond payment obligations.

case the cover pool is segregated in an off-balance sheet SPV. We shall assume the second structure throughout this book. However, most of the material is applicable in both cases.

The SPV entity that holds the cover pool is called the covered bond guarantor (CBG). Following an issuer event of default, covered bonds are designed to achieve uninterrupted principal and interest repayments due to the cash flows provided by the cover pool (Figure 2.6).

In some respects, the cover pool is similar to a master trust, as it is a single, revolving pool backing multiple series of debt issuance. However, the requirements in relation to cover pools are often much stricter than for securitisations. For example, if the bonds are issued under UK or Australian law,[11] the cover pool must over-collateralise the debt by a specified minimum level. Since covered bond pools aren't tranched, this over-collateralisation provides CE in the absence of other subordinated tranches. There may also be other regulatory requirements, such as a maximum loan-to-value (LTV) ratio of the assets and restrictions on other metrics, such as the percentage of the balance sheet that can be used for covered bonds.

Covered bonds are always structured as bullets up until their expected maturities. This is not the case for many other forms of securitised debt (with the exception of credit card receivables) as there are usually amortising tranches in RMBS and other ABS issuance. This means that the cover pool must be periodically replenished by the sponsor as the underlying assets pay down and mature, prepay or default. It is also not uncommon for the issuer to remove assets from the cover pool and substitute them with new ones based on various criteria, such as arrears.

There are three types of covered bond structures, distinguished by their cash flows following an issuer event of default: hard bullet, soft bullet and conditional

---

[11]Not all jurisdictions have explicit covered bond regulations. In such cases, a contractual structured product can be created, which in most respects is equivalent to a regulated covered bond.

pass-through (CPT). We shall describe these structures in more detail in the section on Covered Bond Structures.

DOCUMENTARY FRAMEWORK

A securitisation is a complex financial transaction that involves a variety of parties performing different functions. Befitting the complexity is an intensive documentary framework, which can initially be confronting for swaps practitioners who are used to dealing within the standard ISDA documentary framework. However, the securitisation documents bear many similarities to those documents that would be entered into for an ordinary secured bond issuance or a standard unsecured corporate bond issue, with some specific modifications such as limited recourse and non-petition language, which is used to protect the bankruptcy remote status of the issuer.

In order to understand the framework, it is helpful to break out the documentation into its various parts so that the purpose each document serves in the overall transaction becomes clear.

Offer Document

The offer document[12] is a marketing document made available to investors for the purpose of selling the bond issuance and is sometimes also referred to as the 'disclosure document'. It is essential that the offer document disclose all material information about the bond offer in order to enable a potential investor to make an informed decision whether or not to purchase the bonds. In the context of a securitisation or covered bond this means information about the underlying assets, the transaction structure, the transaction parties, the cash flows and the security and any other CEs that might be applicable.

The offer document will set out a summary of the terms and conditions of the notes, it will describe the receivables to be transferred and, if receivables income is to be reinvested in purchasing further receivables from the originator during the life of the transaction, it will usually also include a description of the originator's business and its prospects for continuing to generate the required level of receivables in the future. Risk factors for investors will feature prominently, and these will include particular factors such as default by the underlying debtors, a description of the portfolio and any associated concentration risk, and the specific risks relevant to the type of receivable. Note that swap providers will face additional risks that are not always explicitly disclosed in any offer document, which are further discussed throughout this book.

The offer document will also describe the main parts of the transaction (e.g. servicing, cash management, hedging and liquidity arrangements and trust and

---

[12]The offer document may be known by various other names including the prospectus, the offering circular, and the information memorandum.

security arrangements) as well as how income flows within the transaction and to noteholders. There will also be a description of any CE features. While the offer document is comprehensive in disclosing the transaction to investors, it is important to recognise that the offer document itself is not a legal contract.

Subscription Agreement

The subscription agreement is the principal contract between the issuer and the managers, which is entered into before any of the other transaction documents are signed (the date on which the subscription agreement is entered into is known as the 'signing date'). Pursuant to the subscription agreement, the issuer agrees to issue the notes on the issue date and the managers agree to subscribe for the notes at a specified price (typically par). This ensures that the issuer obtains the predicted issue proceeds and has sufficient funds to purchase the receivables at the predetermined price.

The issuer is required to give representations and warranties to the managers, including: confirming that the offer document contains all material information in the context of the offer; that the statements in the offer document are true, accurate and not misleading; and that there are no material omissions from the offer document. In return the managers will covenant not to breach any selling restrictions when marketing the bonds.

Sale Agreement

An issuer will use the proceeds from the note issuance to purchase the underlying receivables that will form the asset pool. For example, in the case of an RMBS transaction the receivables take the form of mortgage payments and the sale agreement[13] would be referred to as the 'mortgage sale agreement'.

The key purpose of the sale agreement is to effect the transfer of the receivables from the originator to the issuer and it is a pivotal document for ensuring that the transaction constitutes a 'true sale'. Key provisions of the document include: the obligation of the originator to sell and the issuer to purchase the receivables; the calculation of the purchase price, representations and warranties of the originator relating to the receivables being sold and any other conditions precedent to the transfer.

Trust Documentation

As noted previously, it is possible to distinguish the role of the trustee into separate categories relating to the notes and the security and this is also relevant for the trust documentation. We have set out in this sub-section the relevant documentary obligations pertaining to both the note trust and the security trust.

---

[13]The sale agreement may be known by various other names including the loan sale agreement and the receivables purchase agreement.

Note Trust The issuer and the note trustee will enter into a trust deed that constitutes the notes and contains the issuer's covenant to repay principal and interest to the noteholders. The note trust deed will set out which decisions can be taken by the note trustee on behalf of noteholders and which may require noteholder consent. This means that the note trust deed will contain all of the mechanical provisions for calling a meeting of noteholders, along with the terms and conditions of the notes, which will be legally binding on the issuer, and the various forms of the notes (e.g. temporary global, permanent global and definitive), which would all typically be set out as schedules to the note trust deed. Other key provisions in the note trust deed include the issuer's covenant to pay and the noteholders 'non-petition' clause.

Covenant to Pay The issuer's covenant to pay all amounts due under the notes is held on trust by the note trustee for all noteholders. This undertaking is required because notes do not tend to be issued to noteholders in definitive form. This means that an individual noteholder will not be in possession of any documentation that evidences proof of any entitlements to any payments due under the notes.

Non-petition Clause The non-petition clause prevents individual noteholders from pursuing action against the issuer (other than as part of a class of noteholders) or independently of the note trustee. Usually its terms provide that noteholders may not take any action independently of the note trustee to enforce the terms of the notes unless the trustee has failed to act within a reasonable time and when directed by noteholders.

Security Trust Security is always granted by the issuer in securitisations. It is granted to secure the performance of the issuer's obligations to noteholders under the notes and to the other transaction parties to secure the issuer obligations under the other transaction documentation. It is essential at the outset of a transaction to identify the nature and identity of the property that is to be secured, including the jurisdiction of incorporation of the grantor of the security, the law governing that property and the place where that property resides. It is then possible to build the security interests around this basic information.

Depending on the relevant jurisdiction, the security can be granted by way of a fixed and/or floating charge, a lien and/or assignments by way of security over all of the issuer's chargeable property that comprises its right to the receivables income and all of the contractual rights it holds against the various transaction parties under other documents.

The security interests and the waterfall provisions may be included in different documents. However, in some cases, where there is a single trustee acting as both note trustee and security trustee, the security interests and waterfall provisions may be contained within the various note trust provisions within a single trust deed. In other cases there may be a note trust deed and a separate security document in the form of a deed of charge.

Servicing Agreement

The servicing agreement sets out the terms of the appointment of the servicer to administer the receivables or other assets constituting the security. The main duty is to collect amounts due under the underlying receivables contracts and payment processing but the servicing agreement will also cover service standards and collection actions (including default management and enforcement) and the preparation of monthly reports.

Because the servicer is generally also the originator, in practice the underlying borrowers will continue to make payments into a collections account, which is then transferred to the issuer on a regular basis, often at the end of each business day. This process is known as a 'cash sweep'. In order to protect against the risk of the servicer becoming insolvent while in possession of the collected monies, the servicer will declare a trust over the collections account (or that portion of the collections account which is relevant to the securitisation) in favour of the issuer. In some transactions a back-up servicer may also be appointed who is able to step in as a replacement servicer should the original servicer be unable to perform its servicing duties or if it no longer holds the requisite rating to perform the function.

Swaps

Over-the-counter ('OTC') swaps are a key component of securitisation and covered bond transactions. The issuer holds receivables that are generating income and has also issued notes that require payments to noteholders. The currency, interest rate and timing of those two sets of cash flows won't necessarily match one another. To deal with this potential mismatch, the issuer is able to enter into one or more swaps whereby it will take the money it receives from the portfolio and swap it for the money it needs to meet its payment obligations under the notes. There are two main risks that are hedged in a securitisation or covered bond transaction: the currency (FX) risk and the interest rate risk.

There are two main types of swap that are typically entered into in a securitisation swap: asset swaps and liability swaps, which are discussed further in Chapter 4. Each swap entered into in a securitisation transaction will be a bilateral agreement between the issuer and the swap provider using standard ISDA documentation, namely a master agreement with schedule and a credit support annex ('CSA'), together with one or more confirmations. However, to make the swaps 'securitisation ready', the following modifications will need to be adopted:

1. *Restricted termination events and events of default.* Termination events and other events of default are generally restricted so that the swap provider will only have the right to terminate the swap in the event of: (i) the issuer's failure to pay; (ii) issuer bankruptcy; (iii) issuer merger without assumption of liabilities; and (iv) illegality.

2. *Ratings downgrade triggers.* In order to obtain a rating for the notes, credit rating agencies require that the swap provider comply with its rating criteria. While rating criteria can differ from agency to agency, it is a universal requirement that the swap provider must maintain a certain minimum rating in order to support the rating of the notes. This means that upon any downgrade of the credit rating of the swap provider there will be an obligation embedded into the swap documentation to take one of the following remedial actions in line with the relevant rating agency criteria: (i) to provide collateral to the issuer; or (ii) to provide a guarantee from a suitably rated entity to the issuer of the swap provider's obligations under the swap.

3. *Tax gross up.* There are certain modifications to be made in the event that a withholding tax is imposed on payments. If these payments are to be made by the issuer then, typically, there will be no gross up requirement as the issuer is unlikely to have any funds available to pay such gross up. This means that the issuer would pay any amounts to the swap provider net of any withholding tax. Conversely, if the withholding tax is applicable on the payment from the swap provider to the issuer the swap provider may be obliged to gross up these payments on account of the withholding tax. If the obligation to gross up payments for withholding tax is removed from the swap documentation then this should be clearly disclosed to investors in the offering document.

4. *Limited recourse and non-petition.* This standard securitisation wording states that the issuer's creditors, including the swap provider, will only have recourse to the issuer's secured assets. Further, the swap provider will be restricted from petitioning to wind up the issuer regarding amounts that may be deemed owing to it under the swap. In a securitisation, only the security trustee is able to petition for the winding up of the issuer.

5. *Principal.* The principal schedule of a swap is very often linked to (i) the principal of a tranche of notes in the case of a liability swap or (ii) the principal of a pool of assets in the case of an asset swap. In a 'standard' swap, the principal is fixed and explicitly stated in the confirmation. Not so for securitisation swaps. The exception to this is bullet swaps (prior to any extension event), which can be covered bond liability swaps or RMBS/ABS liability swaps.

Ancillary Service Provider Documentation

Agency Agreement   The agency agreement is a mechanical document that sets out the powers and responsibilities of the paying agents within a transaction. The provisions of this agreement are similar to other corporate bond issues; however the documentation is subject to limited recourse and non-petition language as per other securitisation documentation.

Account Bank Agreement   The terms of the account bank's appointment and any instructions to operate the various accounts are documented in an account bank agreement. This will contain a bank account mandate from the issuer to set up all of the required accounts and any operating provisions.

An account bank agreement should include a waiver by the account bank of set-off rights it may hold, which is intended to preserve the priorities of payment that have been agreed between the different secured creditors (if set-off were available to the account bank then it may be able to leapfrog other secured creditors in the payment waterfall). Other standard terms include limited recourse and non-petition clauses that limit the amounts due to the account bank and restrict its right to petition for the winding up of the issuer in the event of the non-payment of its fees. It will also document any fees payable to the account bank and any requirement for the account bank to maintain a minimum rating, which can be relevant for the rating of the notes.

Cash Management Agreement The appointment of the cash manager is documented in the cash management agreement, which will normally include provisions for the cash manager to invest sums standing to the credit of the issuer's accounts in highly-rated short-term investment (known as authorised investments or eligible investments) if to do so would earn the issuer a higher return. Any authorised investments must mature (or be able to be liquidated) prior to the next payment date.

As the cash manager is responsible for the distribution of cash the cash management agreement may also include one or more pre-enforcement payment waterfalls, which contain the directions for distributing available receipts prior to the occurrence of any enforcement event. The cash management agreement will also include the provisions for any fees payable to the cash manager and the usual limited recourse and non-petition clauses.

Corporate Services Agreement The corporate services agreement sets out the terms and conditions relating to the appointment of the corporate services provider. It is standard to include the parameters of the administrative functions that the corporate services provider is expected to perform, along with the fees payable.

Liquidity Facility A liquidity facility acts like a short-term financing or bridging loan to compensate for any timing mismatches between the incoming receivables and outgoing payments to investors. In order to maintain the desired rating of the notes, the issuer must pay any principal or interest amounts due on the notes on time. This is because the ratings provided by the rating agencies are an assessment of the issuer's ability to repay the investor. However, there is a risk that the issuer may suffer from short-term cash flow problems, which can arise in a number of situations not related to an actual default or downgrade of the credit quality of the portfolio, including things like delayed payments on the receivables, technical problems or administrative error.

Cash flow volatility for an issuer can become a serious issue very quickly, potentially resulting in an event of default under the notes if distributions to investors cannot be made on time or there is a technical insolvency of the issuer on the basis that its liabilities exceed its assets. However, a liquidity facility is only a short-term measure and is not used to cover defaults within the underlying asset portfolio.

A liquidity facility will be committed, so that the liquidity provider is bound to advance funds when requested to by the issuer. It generally contains features found in other short-term revolving loan agreements and will roll over at the end of each year on the same terms. Because the liquidity provider is not paid to assume any credit risk in the deal it will generally sit senior to the noteholders and the other transaction parties in the payment waterfalls.

Legal Opinions and Due Diligence Reports In a securitisation transaction it is standard for a law firm (normally issuer/originator counsel) to provide a written legal opinion addressing certain matters of law relevant to the transaction. The transaction legal opinion must be from the jurisdiction of the issuer and requirements may vary between jurisdictions. For example, where the transaction involves a Rule 144A issuance there are additional legal due diligence reports that are required such as the 10b-5 letter.

The transaction legal opinion will generally opine on matters such as:

- the due capacity and authority of the issuer to enter into the transaction;
- the legal, valid, binding and enforceable nature of the obligations of the issuer under the transaction documentation;
- the true sale of the receivables from the seller to the issuer;
- an analysis of the insolvency risk associated with the transaction; and
- the validity of any security granted and any recharacterisation risk that may be applicable to the security.

The transaction legal opinion may also be accompanied by a separate tax opinion dealing solely with tax risks. It also not uncommon for legal firms to undertake loan file due diligence on the underlying loan documentation and provide a due diligence report to satisfy the issuer as to the transferability and enforceability of the loans being purchased.

Legal opinions are only addressed to the transaction parties (such as the originator, issuer, trustee, arranger and managers) but there is typically a provision that enables the opinion to be shared with rating agencies for review. From the perspective of the rating agencies, the legal opinion is a key document.

Auditor Comfort Letters Auditor comfort letters are prepared by the issuer's auditors and addressed to the originator, issuer, arranger and managers. Auditor comfort letters are particularly important in terms of providing reassurance to the arranger and managers about information set out in the offering document relating to the underlying assets. The auditors check and confirm this information is correct in a process that is known as the 'tick and tie'. This is a key means of mitigating any liability that may arise through inaccurate disclosure to the investors.

Auditor comfort letters are usually binding on the auditors but it is common for the auditor to seek to limit its liability. Auditor comfort letters may also be shared with rating agencies; however they will not be addressees nor will they be able to rely on the information set out in the auditor comfort letters.

STRUCTURED FUNDING MARKETS

We will use the term *structured funding* throughout this book to collectively describe direct securitisations such as ABS and RMBS as well as dual recourse instruments with a securitised guarantor; that is, covered bonds. The reason for using this collective term is that, as far as the use of swaps is concerned, they have a great deal in common and it is expedient to have an overarching term.

The size of the structured funding market is vast. The global volume of all securitisation bonds outstanding in Q3 2017 was around EUR9.3 trillion[14] (of which half is US agency MBS) and the global volume of all covered bonds outstanding in 2016 was EUR2.5 trillion.[15] To put these numbers into perspective, their combined size is comparable to the GDP of China.

The importance of structured funding varies considerably across different countries, as does the type of structured funding. Europe has a long history of covered bonds, hence there is more than double the outstanding volume of EUR-denominated covered bonds than RMBS. The USA has no covered bond market – instead its structured funding market is dominated by agency RMBS. The UK has developed sizeable securitisation and covered bond markets, although outstanding UK RMBS is three times the size of outstanding UK covered bonds, which was more recently introduced in the UK (in 2003). In Australia the outstanding size of both securitisation and covered bonds is roughly equal. However, in Australia securitisation is much more important to non-bank lenders than it is to the big four banks.

Structured funding is one of the most complex classes of funding instruments and as a result the transaction costs for an issuer are amongst the highest. This complexity comes from multiple sources: the legal structure; tranching and triggers; the construction and ongoing maintenance of the asset pool; and – the key topic of this book – the use of complex swaps that aim to reduce the overall risk to the investor. At the same time structured funding can have a lower market cost of funds than other instruments of comparable tenor, as the debt is secured and the majority of issuance very highly rated.

---

[14]See https://www.sifma.org/wp-content/uploads/2017/12/Europe-Securitisation-Quarterly-2017-12-15-AFME-SIFMA.pdf page 11.
[15]See www.securitisation.com.au/Library/General%20Market%20and%20Product%20Material/ECBC-Fact-Book-2017_Web.pdf page 588.

RISKS

There are many risks inherent in structured funding that impact all market participants. However, the manner in which these risks can impact the different participants varies depending on their role.

This section will describe the risks for issuers and investors, where relevant, with a particular emphasis on the risks that a swap provider faces.

Credit Risk

The most clearly identifiable risk with structured funding is credit risk – the risk that the obligor (or the guarantor, if the obligor has already failed) will not pay the money it owes to investors. After all, that is the main risk to which investors in structured debt are seeking exposure and the main basis on which the securities are priced.

Due to the complexity of structured funding, it is not sufficient to only examine the credit quality of the underlying loan pool, although that is fundamentally necessary. Further analysis must consider the impact of OC, CE via tranching and any originator dependence such as call options or the topping-up of revolving pools.

Swap providers face an even more complex form of credit risk. Firstly, they must understand clearly where they rank in any cash flow waterfall. Sometimes they may be senior to the investors, sometimes *pari passu*, and sometimes possibly somewhere below. The documents need to be read thoroughly. Secondly, since swaps are market instruments, their mark-to-market (MTM) can vary widely over their life. If the swap is out-of-the-money to a swap provider when a default event occurs, then there is no credit risk whatsoever for the swap provider at that point in time, even though there certainly is for the investors! Conversely, if the swap is in-the-money to a swap provider when a default event occurs, then there is indeed credit risk for both swap providers and investors, who will both have a claim to the same pool of assets.

Market Risk

Market risk is the risk of loss from moves in market rates such as FX, interest rates and single and cross-currency basis. For example, if interest rates increase, an investor receiving fixed interest coupons will suffer a market loss, that is, their asset becomes less valuable. While buy-and-hold investors can usually ride through such market losses, it does impact portfolio volatility and, during times of market stress, can result in actual loss if the buy-and-hold strategy is abandoned.

Investors can also be exposed to market risk losses if they hold foreign-denominated debt that is not currency hedged by a swap provider.

Ultimately, the party exposed most to market risk in structured funding is the swap provider. Indeed, swap providers exist precisely to take on this market risk to the benefit of the other parties. However, because of the simultaneous presence of other risks – in particular prepayment risk and extension risk – market risk becomes significantly more complex to manage than is the case for standard 'plain vanilla' swaps. At a high level, the reason for this is that prepayment and extension risk create uncertainty in the timing and size of cash flows. When market movements are overlaid on top of that timing uncertainty, the risk management challenge becomes seriously hard and/or expensive and forms one of the main reasons why this book was written.

Liquidity Risk

Liquidity risk is the risk that market depth will become shallow and prevent transactions from occurring without significant price impact. For investors needing to sell structured bonds in the secondary market when liquidity is low, this means being forced to sell below fair market value and realising a loss. For issuers needing to sell structured bonds in the primary market to raise funding when liquidity is low, this means paying a wider coupon and absorbing a higher cost of funds. And for swap providers needing to novate out of a securitisation swap, this means taking a MTM loss upon exit.

Liquidity risk for investors is highly market dependent. Some markets have a much higher proportion of buy-and-hold investors than investors willing to trade. Furthermore, liquidity for investors can be quite variable depending on a variety of factors including market sentiment, supply and demand dynamics, idiosyncratic credit factors, changes to regulation and central bank intervention.

Liquidity risk for swap providers is usually high at the best of times. As will be discussed in Chapter 7, the number of eligible swap providers for highly-rated issuance is quite small. This reduces the number of participants considerably. If a swap provider really needs to novate out of a securitisation swap, they will either have to be patient to realise a fair price, or take a substantial loss if they're in a hurry.

Prepayment Risk

Prepayment risk is the risk that principal owed on a debt obligation is returned early. In one sense this is the opposite of credit risk: not only has the money been repaid, it has been repaid ahead of schedule. Given that credit risk can cause loss, one might therefore think that prepayment risk is a good thing. In fact, *unexpected* prepayment can also cause loss and so prepayment risk needs careful attention.

If prepayment can be accurately predicted, it can be relatively benign. One helpful aspect of bundling a large number of debt obligations together is that prepayment gets averaged out. While it is extremely difficult to predict prepayments at the individual loan level, at the pool level prepayment rates are generally range-bound over time.

For originators and investors, prepayment risk creates uncertainty as to when their principal will be returned. This means that the yield-to-maturity is unknown in advance. Many structures have been developed to reduce prepayment risk for (some) investors and hence widen the investor base. These structures are discussed in detail in Chapter 3. However, mitigating prepayment risk has other costs, or results in higher prepayment risk for other parties. It is therefore unavoidable that prepayment risk will need to be modelled.

For swap providers, prepayment risk creates an even more complex type of risk: *swap prepayment risk*. This is the risk of simultaneous adverse moves in both prepayment and market rates, which is discussed in detail in Chapter 5. With sufficient modelling, good judgement in choosing and structuring deals and conservative pricing and risk management, taking on swap prepayment risk can be a profitable exercise for a swap provider while simultaneously providing a significant benefit to both issuers and investors. However, without good management, assuming swap prepayment risk can subject the risk taker to material downside risk.

Extension Risk

A common feature of securitisations that have long-dated underlying assets is the originator call option. This is an option for the originator to redeem the debt in full on a given date or a specified percentage of the pool size. These call options allow the construction of shorter-dated tranches, which can suit certain investors. Investors invariably expect such calls to be exercised in all but the most extreme scenarios. Given this widespread expectation in the market, backed by the rarity of non-call events, an actual non-call event could catch investors and the wider market off guard.

If an originator does not exercise its call option, the debt will extend in duration and investors will need to wait a lot longer than they may have originally expected to receive their principal back. This is called extension risk. Investors are usually compensated for this by receiving an increased coupon following the first possible call date. This increased coupon also acts as an incentive to the originator to exercise the call, failing which their cost of funds increases. However, if credit spreads have blown out sufficiently, it could be cheaper for an originator to let its debt extend. Reputational risk is also critical in this decision, and few originators would want the market to doubt their intention to call their bonds. Such doubt could result in higher funding costs as investors require a higher coupon as compensation for that perceived risk.

For swap providers, extension risk creates an even more complex type of risk: *swap extension risk*. Since rating agencies require swap providers to swap cash flows to legal final maturity if required. An extension event can leave swap providers completely unhedged at very short notice if they have not factored in a potential non-call event. Without careful pre-deal structuring, pricing and risk management, taking on swap extension risk is akin to picking-up pennies in front of a steam-roller. Swap extension risk is discussed in detail in Chapter 6.

Downgrade Risk

Downgrade risk is the risk that an instrument or entity has its credit rating downgraded by one or more rating agencies. For investors, downgrade risk is realised if their bonds are downgraded in which case their price will likely fall. For investors with constrained mandates, downgrade risk can also mean they have to sell the bonds, which forces an actual realisation of the price drop. In one sense downgrade risk is closely related to credit risk. However, downgrade risk focuses on specific events *prior* to default due to a change in rating, whereas credit risk focuses on the risk and consequences of an actual default event.

There is a very particular type of downgrade risk that swap providers to rated structured funding transactions must assume. If a swap provider is downgraded to a specific credit rating, it has to post collateral one-way to its SPV counterparty. This can be expensive and, if the swap is long-dated, any extension can give rise to continuous operational burdens. Additionally, if the swap provider is downgraded to another, lower, credit rating then it may have to novate out of the swap. Depending on the circumstances of such a forced novation, this could be a very costly exercise. Should a swap provider not be in compliance with its posting of collateral or novation obligations, the related structured debt will likely be downgraded by a rating agency. This is a key point some investors may gloss over: highly-rated structured bonds are subject to downgrade risk not only from the credit risk of the underlying loan pool, but also from other parties involved in the structured funding, such as swap providers. This is also a risk to the originator: no institution wants its debt downgraded due to a swap provider on one of its funding programmes not meeting the required standard. Downgrade risk is dealt with in detail in Chapter 7.

Operational Risk

Operational risk is the risk of loss caused by a failure in the actual handling of a structured funding transaction. Such a failure could occur before, during or after the issuance, all the way until the debt is fully discharged.

Since structured funding transactions are complex and have multiple parties, there are many potential points of failure. Cash flows need to be collected, calculated, distributed and paid on time. Swaps need to be correctly booked to ensure, amongst other things, that tranche cash flows and derivative cash flows line up. Collateral may need to be posted. Fraud can occur, systems can go off-line and procedures can fail when staff are absent.

In general, very few operational risks can be completely mitigated. However, a professional standard of risk management demands that operational procedures and controls receive a high degree of attention.

Legal Risk

The overriding concern in a structured funding transaction is to ensure that there will be sufficient cash flow through the structure to meet payments due to investors under the notes. All of the risks set out in the immediately prior sections are factors that could undermine the integrity of the cash flows. Rating agencies will be looking at these risks when they come to rate the notes and they will require certain structural features to be incorporated as a condition of assigning a given rating to a specific tranche of notes. While these risks are common in most jurisdictions, the legal risk factors are much more diverse, often depending on the development of the law in that jurisdiction.

Rating agencies will require that these legal risks be outlined and explained in the transaction legal opinion. As discussed above, the transaction legal opinion outlines areas of legal uncertainty and will confirm the effectiveness of the structure of the transaction, including a description of any residual legal risk. Some of the key legal risks common across jurisdictions include the effectiveness of the true sale mechanism and the risks associated with insolvency.

True sale is a key aspect of securitisation since it allows the credit risk of the assets to be isolated and can result in the notes being rated higher than the originator. The transaction legal opinion will examine the mechanics associated with the transfer of the receivables (or the 'true sale') in order to assess whether there is any legal risk that this process could be recharacterised as a security interest.

In an insolvency, a liquidator or administrator will owe its duties to the general body of creditors and this includes maximising the assets available for distribution. If it appears to the liquidator or administrator that the originator's interests in the receivables are not consistent with an outright transfer to the SPV, then this opens an avenue for the transfer to be challenged.

The insolvency risk in structured finance transactions is important to the ratings analysis, particularly regarding any risks associated with the SPV being wound up. The legal opinion will address aspects of the transaction that may be vulnerable in an insolvency event, including:

1. The risk of technical insolvency if payment flows are impaired for any reason
2. Investors' rights in an enforcement situation, with particular regard to any expected distribution of the limited assets of the SPV issuer
3. The effectiveness of any security and any right of claw-back specifically allowed under insolvency law
4. The ability (or not) of an SPV issuer to contract out of aspects of a jurisdiction's insolvency laws
5. The effectiveness of limited recourse and non-petition clauses and of subordination arrangements in pre-enforcement and post-enforcement scenarios.

The transaction legal opinion should also address due capacity and authority of the relevant parties executing the documentation to ensure that the rights and obligations set out there will be enforceable. For this reason, the transaction legal opinion is extremely important to rating agencies and any swap provider should ensure that it is included as an addressee in order to mitigate any legal risk that could be attached to the structured funding transaction.

CHAPTER 3

Asset-Backed Debt Structures

Follow the money...

Securitisation swaps are deeply embedded inside the asset-backed structures they support. They aren't just bolted on in the way other derivatives usually are. For example, a fund manager who wishes to enter into a currency hedge for an offshore asset might use a foreign exchange (FX) forward. This FX forward will take the same form no matter whether the asset is a portfolio of equities or a power station. In contrast, the cash flows of securitisation swaps must precisely match the cash flows generated by the underlying asset pool within the securitisation or covered bond structure: it must be a perfect hedge. Without this lockstep alignment, the securitisation swap will not remove the market risk from the asset-backed structure, which will invariably result in a lower credit rating and hence a higher cost of funding for the originator. Thus, in order to model securitisation swaps, it is critical to 'look through' and understand some key features of the underlying structure.

This chapter will cover the spectrum of common underlying structures in order to lay a foundation for the detailed securitisation swap modelling covered in Chapters 5–7. There are many more aspects of securitisation and covered bond structuring, which will not be covered; the sole focus here is discussing what is needed to model the swaps.

The starting point for understanding asset-backed structures is with the underlying debt obligations. Residential mortgages, auto loans, credit card receivables, commercial mortgages and corporate loans all have very different maturity profiles. This has consequences for choosing the appropriate asset-backed structures to overlay. We will take a bottom-up approach, following the money from the individual loans and loan pools, then investigating how they are transformed via cash flow waterfalls.

LOAN POOL DYNAMICS

There are four types of principal repayment formats for the underlying loans in a securitisation or covered bond:

1. *Fully principal amortising loan.* This is the most common type of principal repayment and is used for residential and commercial mortgages, auto and equipment loans and student loans. If interest rates are constant, this type of loan will involve a constant periodic repayment over the life of a loan. The proportion of the periodic loan repayment that pays down the loan principal increases over the life of the loan until the initial loan principal is fully repaid.

2. *Partial principal amortising loan.* This is similar to 1, except that the loan terminates when the principal has amortised to a given percentage of the initial loan principal – for example, 30%. The final repayment of principal is called a *balloon payment*. These are typically used in auto and equipment loans and some commercial mortgages.

3. *Zero amortisation loan.* This is more commonly known as an interest-only (IO) loan. No principal is repaid until the end of the loan (a 'bullet' structure). Alternatively, these loans can convert to a principal amortising loan at the end of a fixed period of time. These are used in some residential mortgages.

4. *Scheduled amortisation loan.* This loan follows a bespoke paydown structure and can be simple or complex. These loans are used in some commercial mortgages.

The amortisation schedule for a fully principal amortising loan is given by the following well-known formula:

$$P_i = P_0 \cdot \left[1 - \frac{(1+r)^i - 1}{(1+r)^n - 1} \right] \cdot (1-p)^{i \cdot \tau} \tag{3.1}$$

where:

P_i is the loan principal outstanding at the start of the ith period
r is the interest rate (for the period, not annualised)
p is the constant prepayment rate (CPR) (annualised)
τ is the length of time, expressed as a fraction of a year, of each of the n payment periods, which are assumed to be of equal tenor.[1]

Derivation of Eq. (3.1)

Assume that an n period loan is fully repaid with constant monthly payments c. As a result, the principal amortisation over any single period follows the equation

$$P_i = P_{i-1} \cdot (1+r) - c \tag{3.2}$$

---

[1] So, if the payment periods are monthly, then $\tau = 1/12$.

After n periods, there is zero principal left to repay,[2] that is,

$$0 = P_n = P_0 \cdot (1+r)^n - c \sum_{i=0}^{n-1} (1+r)^i$$

Solving the above equation for c and using the geometric series identity $\sum_{i=0}^{n-1} x^i = \frac{x^n - 1}{x - 1}$ gives:

$$c = \frac{P_0 \cdot r \cdot (1+r)^n}{(1+r)^n - 1} \tag{3.3}$$

which is the formula for the constant monthly payments. Recursively nesting Eq. (3.2), using the geometric series identity once again and substituting in Eq. (3.3) yields:

$$P_i = P_0 \cdot (1+r)^i - c \cdot \sum_{j=0}^{i-1} (1+r)^j$$

$$= P_0 \cdot (1+r)^i - c \cdot \frac{(1+r)^i - 1}{r}$$

$$= P_0 \cdot (1+r)^i - \frac{P_0 \cdot r \cdot (1+r)^n}{(1+r)^n - 1} \cdot \frac{(1+r)^i - 1}{r}$$

which simplifies to Eq. (3.1) with zero prepayment, that is, $p = 0$. The prepayment term $(1-p)^{i \cdot \tau}$ is the *definition* of how constant prepayment impacts amortisation. □

Figure 3.1 illustrates how the principal amortises according to Eq. (3.1) for a 30-year loan with a constant 5% p.a. interest rate, with different levels of prepayment. As can be seen from the graph in Figure 3.1, even a seemingly small 5% annual prepayment rate dramatically changes the amortisation profile of a 30-year loan. Intuitively – and very roughly speaking – paying off an additional 5% of the outstanding loan principal every year means paying off somewhere in the order of an additional 50% of the outstanding loan principal after ten years. Viewed that way, the impact is perhaps a little less surprising.

One simple and commonly used metric for quantitatively comparing the paydown profiles in Figure 3.1 is the *weighted average life* (WAL). The WAL is the average time it takes for each dollar of principal to be repaid. For a bullet profile, where the entirety of the loan principal is paid back at the same time (i.e. at maturity), the WAL is simply

---

[2] For loans with a balloon payment B at the end, $P_n \neq 0$. The derivation proceeds in the same way, with an additional term containing B.

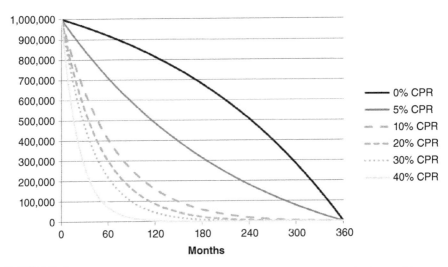

FIGURE 3.1 Monthly paydown schedule of a 30-year principal amortising loan with an interest rate of 5% p.a. with different annualised CPRs.

the tenor. Hence one may also think of WAL as the tenor of an 'equivalent' bullet loan. WAL is defined as follows (we give two equivalent formulae[3]):

$$WAL = \sum_{i=1}^{n} \frac{\Delta P_i}{P_0} t_i = \sum_{i=0}^{n-1} \frac{P_i}{P_0} \Delta t_i \qquad (3.4)$$

where:

   n is the number of repayment periods in the loan
   t_i is the ith loan repayment time (the loan starts at t_0)
   P_i is the ith outstanding loan principal (P_0 is the initial loan principal)
   ΔP_i is the amount of loan principal repaid at time t_i i.e. $\Delta P_i = P_{i-1} - P_i$
   Δt_i is the year fraction $\Delta t_i = t_{i+1} - t_i$

The total interest paid over the life of the loan is $WAL \times P_0 \times r$ where, for the avoidance of doubt, r is the annualised interest rate, not the period interest rate. Clearly, if WAL decreases as a result of an increase in prepayment, the loan originator will receive a smaller total amount of interest.

---

[3]If one thinks of WAL as the (normalised) area under the principal amortisation curve, then the first formula computes the area via summing the area of *horizontal* rectangular strips (height ΔP, width t) while the second formula computes the area via summing the area of *vertical* rectangular strips (height P, width Δt). Needless to say, the area is the same either way!

It is instructive to compute the WALs for the example in Figure 3.1: the WAL of the 0% CPR profile is 18.7 years whereas the WAL of the 5% CPR profile is 11.3 years. The WAL of the 20% CPR profile is 4.2 years. This calculation can be done numerically via spreadsheet, or analytically by substituting Eq. (3.1) into Eq. (3.4) to arrive at:

$$WAL = \tau \cdot \left[\frac{\alpha^n - 1}{\alpha - 1} + \frac{1}{\beta^n - 1} \cdot \left(\frac{\alpha^n - 1}{\alpha - 1} - \frac{\alpha^n \beta^n - 1}{\alpha \beta - 1} \right) \right] \qquad (3.5)$$

where we have defined $\alpha = (1 - p)^\tau$ and $\beta = 1 + r$ in order to condense the equation.

It is instructive to compare the impact of prepayment on a 30-year loan, such as a residential mortgage, to the impact of prepayment on a 7-year loan, such as an auto loan (Figure 3.2).

Optically, the impact of a 5% prepayment rate on the 30-year loan is much larger than on the 7-year loan. Why? The shorter the loan, the larger the scheduled payments must be so that the loan is fully repaid in the shorter time span. As a result, the relative impact of unscheduled payments versus scheduled payments is reduced for shorter loans. From this simple fact we can already deduce that a swap on an auto loan pool will be cheaper than a swap on a residential mortgage pool for 'the same amount' of underlying prepayment risk.

By way of comparison with the 30-year loan, the WAL of the 0% CPR profile of the 7-year loan is 3.7 years whereas the WAL of the 5% CPR profile is 3.3 years. The WAL of the 20% CPR profile is 2.4 years.

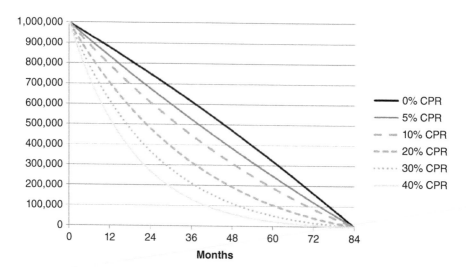

FIGURE 3.2 Monthly paydown schedule of a 7-year principal amortising loan with an interest rate of 5% with different annualised CPRs.

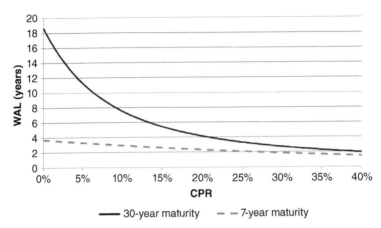

FIGURE 3.3 WAL (in years) as a function of CPR for two principal amortising loans with different maturities.

The graph in Figure 3.3. shows this visually. The vertical axis is WAL in years and the horizontal axis is the CPR. Figure 3.3 was computed using Eq. (3.5)

The steeper gradient on the 30-year loan compared to the seven-year loan shows it has much great WAL sensitivity to prepayment. In both cases, this sensitivity declines as CPR increases.

Pool Amortisation

Figures 3.1 and 3.2 model single loans where the borrower *partially* prepays a constant proportion of the outstanding principal every month. In reality, prepayment most often occurs via *full* prepayment. Nevertheless, the graphs (Figures 3.1 and 3.2) look similar to a loan pool where a constant proportion of the total outstanding pool principal is prepaid every month. The reason is that the zero prepayment amortisation profile (the 'contracted schedule') of a large pool of loans usually looks just like the schedule of a single loan. This is because originators and arrangers choose a diverse set of loans with well-distributed metrics, such as remaining tenor, so as to avoid any concentrations that would cause sharp changes in the amortisation profile.

SECURITISATION STRUCTURES

Standalone Structures with Pass-Through Tranches

The original and simplest securitisation structure is a standalone special purpose vehicle (SPV) issuing pass-through notes. This structure is capable of generating notes with a wide variety of WALs to simultaneously satisfy the myriad investment horizons and risk appetites investors will have. In order to illustrate how this structure works, consider the three residential mortgage-backed securities (RMBS) examples that follow. The first example is rather simplified. New, realistic features will be added as the examples progress; the third and final example is broadly similar to some actual commercial transactions.

EXAMPLE 3.1:

FiCo is a finance company issuing $1bn of prime RMBS via the *FiCo RMBS Trust* 2018-1 SPV. The SPV will issue six classes of notes as follows:

Class	A1a	A1b	A2	B	C	D
Principal	$100 m	$550 m	$240 m	$50 m	$40 m	$20 m
WAL	0.25 yrs	2.05 yrs	6.03 yrs	9.72 yrs	12.65 yrs	18.29 yrs

The WAL is calculated on the assumption of a 21% CPR. The principal receipts are distributed via the cash flow waterfall below.

On each payment date the manager shall pay in the following order of priority:

1. first, *pari passu* and rateably to the Holders of the Class A1a notes until the principal is reduced to zero;
2. next, *pari passu* and rateably to the Holders of the Class A1b notes until the principal is reduced to zero;
3. next, *pari passu* and rateably to the Holders of the Class A2 notes until the principal is reduced to zero;
4. next, *pari passu* and rateably to the Holders of the Class B notes until the principal is reduced to zero;
5. next, *pari passu* and rateably to the Holders of the Class C notes until the principal is reduced to zero;
6. next, *pari passu* and rateably to the Holders of the Class D notes until the principal is reduced to zero.

Assuming the pool principal pay down is proxied by a single 30-year principal amortising residential mortgage with interest paid monthly at 5%, the tranche principal amortisations are:

(Continued)

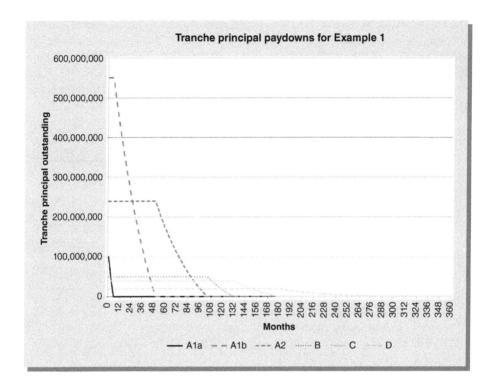

Tranche principal paydowns for Example 1

EXAMPLE 3.2:

As per Example 3.1 except that after two years, the waterfall changes to allocate principal receipts pro rata (proportionally) across the remaining tranches. This *sequential-to*-pro rata *trigger* is used to (i) cap the otherwise ever-increasing credit enhancement of the A1b tranche[4] and (ii) reduce the WAL of the A2 and lower tranches.

Class	A1a	A1b	A2	B	C	D
Principal	$100 m	$550 m	$240 m	$50 m	$40 m	$20 m
WAL	0.25 yrs	3.44 yrs	5.83 yrs	5.83 yrs	5.83 yrs	5.83 yrs

---

[4]The credit enhancement of tranche X is the aggregate principal of all the tranches below tranche X as a proportion of the total pool. These lower tranches absorb credit losses before tranche X. The greater the proportion of these lower tranches as a percentage of the pool, the less likely it is for tranche X to suffer any credit losses.

The post-trigger cash flow waterfall is below.

On each payment date the manager shall pay in the following order of priority:

1. first, *pari passu* and rateably to the Holders of the Class A1a notes until the principal is reduced to zero;
2. next, *pari passu* and rateably to:
   a. the Holders of the Class A1b notes until the principal is reduced to zero;
   b. the Holders of the Class A2 notes until the principal is reduced to zero;
   c. the Holders of the Class B notes until the principal is reduced to zero;
   d. the Holders of the Class C notes until the principal is reduced to zero;
   e. the Holders of the Class D notes until the principal is reduced to zero.

The tranche principal amortisations are:

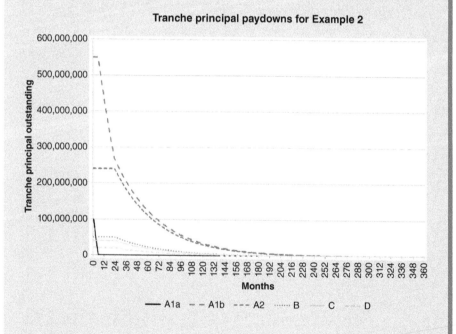

Tranche principal paydowns for Example 2

EXAMPLE 3.3:

As per Example 3.2 except that all the outstanding bonds may be called by FiCo after four years. If FiCo doesn't call the bonds as expected by investors, the coupon on the bonds will step-up. Assuming FiCo does call the bonds as expected, the tranche metrics are as follows:[5]

Class	A1a	A1b	A2	B	C	D
Principal	$100 m	$550 m	$240 m	$50 m	$40 m	$20 m
WAL	0.25 yrs	2.33 yrs	3.55 yrs	3.55 yrs	3.55 yrs	3.55 yrs
Rating	AAA	AAA	AAA	AA	BB-	NR
Spread	+60	+130	+170	private	private	private

The tranche principal amortisations are:

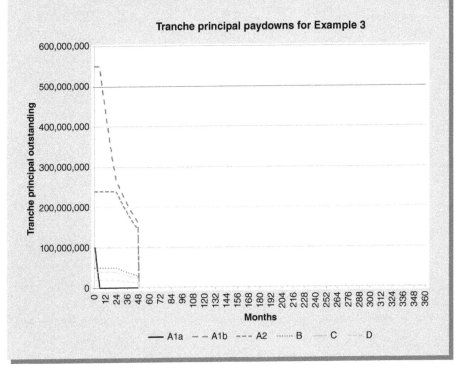

Tranche principal paydowns for Example 3

---

[5]This example has additional ratings and spreads for each tranche unlike the previous two examples, which are purely illustrative and not comparable to real market transactions.

The above examples are equally applicable to standalone auto asset-backed securities (ABS) structures as standalone RMBS structures, albeit with shorter WALs on the notes given the shorter WALs of the underlying loans.

Standalone Structures with Bullet Tranches

There are classes of investors who don't want any prepayment risk in their fixed income portfolios. Sometimes this is a preference of the portfolio manager, sometimes this is mandate-driven, and sometimes it is because of regulation – for example, penalties for prepayment risk in Solvency II, the European Union's harmonised insurance regulations. The structuring and inclusion of a bullet note into the tranche structure can bring these investors into securitisation deals from which they would otherwise be excluded. A further reason why bullet notes might be included in some securitisations is to significantly reduce the cost of swapping the notes into a foreign currency.

Given these advantages, one might ask why securitisation structures don't structure more, or even all, of the notes as bullets. The answer is that the prepayment risk in the underlying loan pool cannot be made to simply disappear. Cash flow waterfalls re-allocate prepayment risk between different tranches, but they cannot change the overall amount of prepayment risk. And they certainly can't eliminate it. We discuss this in more detail in the sub-section on Tranche Conservation Laws.

Bullet notes come in two varieties: *hard bullet* and *soft bullet*. In the case of hard bullets, investors have a much greater probability of being repaid (the word 'guaranteed' is often used – we shall refrain). There are two ways hard bullet notes are repaid in standalone structures:

1. Via a refinancing note backed by a redemption facility.
2. Via the accumulation of principal receipts.

A refinancing note is a new note that is issued in the market to pay back the original investors in the initial bullet note. The successful issuance of a refinancing note depends on market conditions. If reissuance fails, or is overly expensive, the redemption facility, usually provided by a bank, can be used to fund the principal repayment. Both structures have cost components associated with them. Banks will charge a fee for the redemption facility. Likewise, the accumulated principal receipts will need to be stored in a bank account, which will earn a rate of interest below that of the note, creating negative carry. This reduces the overall yield in the structure, from which investors are collectively paid.

In the case of soft bullets, the originator has discretion to not call the notes, in which case they become pass-through. In this case, the notes will pay a stepped-up coupon to investors. Chapter 6 deals with the extension risk generated by this possibility. When originators do call the notes as investors expect, they are generally funded by a refinancing note.

Unless principal is accumulated to fund the redemption, the inclusion of a bullet note increases the rate of amortisation of all the other tranches since the pool principal receipts are diverted to the other tranches. This means that the credit support of a bullet note in a sequential paydown decreases over time. In contrast, the credit support of a pass-through tranche in a sequential paydown increases over time.

Standalone Structures with Controlled Amortisation Tranches

Controlled amortisation occupies the middle ground between bullets and pass-through tranches. Controlled amortisation tranches have a pre-defined principal schedule that will be realised as long as prepayment rates remain above a given rate, which is typically very low. We shall call this minimum prepayment rate the *breakeven* prepayment rate. If the breakeven prepayment rate is low, then investors will have higher confidence around the timing of cash flows, with only residual risk that the principal receipts will be inadequate to fund the scheduled amortisations. Likewise swap providers will have higher confidence that they understand the timing of the cash flows, which will substantially reduce their hedging costs. Indeed, most RMBS tranches issued in foreign currency are controlled amortisation as including a currency swap for pass-through RMBS tranches is very expensive.

Since prepayment is volatile (see Chapter 5 for a more in-depth discussion), controlled amortisation tranches need a mechanism to smooth the principal receipts over time. This is achieved via trapping and releasing cash when required. Specifically, there are two accounts for this purpose:

1. A Guaranteed investment certificate (GIC) account for collecting excess principal receipts if prepayment is higher than a given threshold.[6]
2. A reserve facility to draw from when (i) prepayment is low and insufficient to fund a scheduled amortisation and (ii) the GIC account has already been drawn down to zero. This is called a controlled amortisation facility (CAF).

The larger the CAF, the lower the rate of prepayment that can be suffered before the controlled amortisation schedule will be broken. If the CAF was the size of the controlled amortisation tranche it is supporting, then the prepayment could go to zero and the schedule would be maintained. However, CAFs are not free, as they need to be funded. Nevertheless, funding a CAF can still be cheaper than paying a swap provider to swap a pass-through tranche into a foreign currency, so long as the overall structure is optimised. Optimisation involves correctly sizing the controlled amortisation tranche to bring in sufficient new investors to achieve the desired volume and price tension. Also,

---

[6]This is the CPR of the controlled amortisation schedule itself.

the CAF can be optimised by amortising the CAF size as the tranche itself amortises. This minimises the CAF funding costs while still maintaining a constant breakeven prepayment rate.

Tranche Conservation Laws

Cash flow waterfalls conserve the total amount of principal receipts at each point in time since every dollar put into the waterfall is allocated somewhere. In closed pools, where the size of principal receipts can be forecast for the entire life of a deal, this conservation law can be neatly expressed as follows:

$$WAL_{pool} = \sum_{j=1}^{m} \frac{P_j}{P} WAL_j \qquad (3.6)$$

where:

P_j is the initial principal of tranche j
P is the initial principal of the entire loan pool
WAL_j is the WAL of tranche j
WAL_{pool} is the WAL of the entire loan pool
m is the number of tranches

In other words, the weighted average WAL of the tranches equals the WAL of the entire loan pool.

EXAMPLE 3.4:

In Example 3.1, the WAL of the single 30-year loan with 21% CPR is 3.96 years. The weighted average WALs of the tranches is: $(0.1 \times 0.25) + (0.55 \times 2.05) + (0.24 \times 6.03) + (0.05 \times 9.72) + (0.04 \times 12.65) + (0.02 \times 18.29) = 3.96$.

When prepayment is constant, this statement is straightforward and perhaps even obvious.[7] What is also useful is to think about, especially for swap providers, is a

---

[7] As noted previously, WAL can be interpreted as the (normalised) area under the principal amortisation curve. This conservation-of-cash-through-time statement is equivalent to conservation of area.

dynamic version of Eq. (3.6) when prepayment is not constant. Specifically, differencing two versions of Eq. (3.6) computed with different CPRs, we must have:

$$\Delta WAL_{pool} = \sum_{j=1}^{m} \frac{P_j}{P} \Delta WAL_j \qquad (3.7)$$

where ΔWAL is the change in WAL generated by a change in prepayment rate. Eq. (3.7) can be interpreted as *conservation of WAL sensitivity to prepayment*. In other words, the weighted average WAL sensitivity of the tranches equals the WAL sensitivity of the entire loan pool.

EXAMPLE 3.5:

Consider a very simple two-tranche structure where one tranche is a two-year bullet and the other equal-sized tranche is pass-through. Eq. (3.7) quantifies how much more volatile the WAL of the pass-through tranche will be than the overall pool. Using the same parameters in Example 3.1, if the CPR is 21%, the pool WAL is 3.96 years, hence Eq. (3.7) implies that the pass-through tranche has a WAL of 5.92 years. If the CPR is reduced to 20%, then the pool WAL increases to 4.15 years and Eq. (3.7) implies that the pass-through tranche has a WAL of 6.3 years. So while the pool WAL only increased by 0.19 years (from 3.96 to 4.15 years), the WAL of the pass-through tranche increased by 0.38 years (from 5.92 to 6.3 years). In other words, the pass-through tranche will have twice the WAL sensitivity than that of the overall pool.

Swap providers (and indeed investors) should endeavour to develop an intuitive understanding of how each tranche will behave through time and how it will react to changes in prepayment. Eqs. (3.6) and (3.7) provide the simple quantitative basis of that intuition.

Master Trust RMBS Structures

In this section we cover the typical elements of RMBS master trust structures – specifically the much more prevalent socialist de-linked structures that were introduced in Chapter 2. As per previous sections, we focus solely on the elements that are required knowledge for swap providers.

The Seller Share The most important feature of an RMBS master trust from the swap providers' perspective is the *seller share*. It is the seller share that significantly reduces both swap prepayment risk and swap extension risk. Legally, the seller share represents the sponsor's beneficial interest in the trust, whereas the funding share represents all the outstanding RMBS notes. From a credit perspective, the seller share ranks *pari passu* with the funding share, that is, any credit losses are allocated across both shares in proportion to their relative size. However, the financial impact of the seller share is that it provides over-collateralisation to the structure. This over-collateralisation provides additional principal cash flows to support controlled amortisation and soft bullet tranches without the need for a CAF as per standalone SPVs. So, although the seller share ranks *pari passu* with the funding share from a credit perspective, it is time-subordinated from a cash flow perspective.

Figure 3.4 illustrates two other key points about socialist de-linked master trusts:

- The class B and lower notes provide credit enhancement to all the class A notes, irrespective of which series they belong to.
- The seller share does not provide any credit enhancement to any funding share tranches whatsoever. Conversely, the class B and/or lower notes do not provide any credit enhancement to the seller share whatsoever.

The rating agencies impose a *minimum seller share* condition on master trusts in order to mitigate several non-credit risks, including set-off risk.[8] This means that the sponsor must ensure that the size of the seller share is above this minimum level at

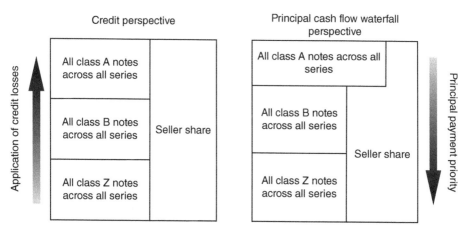

FIGURE 3.4 Credit and cash flow perspectives on RMBS master trusts. The A notes may receive more than their pro-rata cash flows if required to support controlled amortisations and/or bullet maturities. These additional cash flows are diverted from the seller share. However, credit losses are applied *pari passu*.

---

[8]Set-off risk is the risk that (i) an originator becomes insolvent and (ii) a borrower of an underlying loan in the underlying master trust mortgage pool offsets the amount of their mortgage liabilities, which have been securitised against any deposits it may hold with the defaulting originator. This can reduce the amount of interest receipts and amount of security available to the RMBS master trust.

all times. This is achieved by the sponsor adding new mortgages into the revolving pool. In reality, for well-functioning programmes, the seller share is usually well in excess of this minimum level. For a swap provider, the minimum seller share provides a floor of cash flow support for controlled amortisation and soft bullet tranches, at least in the absence of an issuer credit event.

Triggers Another complexity of master trusts are the various *triggers* that modify the cash flow waterfall. There are two types of triggers: non-asset triggers and asset triggers. Non-asset triggers are specific events, which are not related to the credit quality of the underlying assets. Such events usually include some or all of the following:

- breach of the minimum seller share requirement;
- insolvency of the seller;
- breach of the minimum trust size condition;
- the seller's role as servicer is terminated and a new servicer is not appointed with a specified time period, for example, 60 days; and
- seller failure to make certain payments to the trustee.

In the event of a non-asset trigger, all principal is diverted to the funding share, all notes convert to pass-through and all notes are paid down sequentially in order of seniority and final maturity date (also known as the legal final maturity date). The purpose of this modified cash flow waterfall is principally to protect the AAA note holders by accelerating their repayment to the maximum extent possible. One consequence of this is that some noteholders may have their repayments delayed, for instance B noteholders with short maturities. A swap provider swapping such a B note would be exposed to swap extension risk upon a non-asset trigger event (Figure 3.5).

One further consequence of a non-asset trigger event is that no further loans can be added to the pool.

By prioritising payments to the funding share over the seller share, non-asset triggers cause the funding share to more rapidly decrease as a proportion of the overall pool. Given that credit losses are allocated *pari passu*, the growing seller share proportion will absorb a greater percentage of future credit losses.

On the other hand, asset triggers are specific events that *are* related to the credit quality of the underlying assets. Such events can include one or both of the following:

- Notes of a specified credit rating suffer a loss due to underlying mortgage defaults not compensated for by excess spread.[9]
- 90+ day mortgage arrears exceeding a given limit of the mortgage pool.

---

[9]This will result in a debit to the *principal deficiency (sub-)ledger* (PDL) for the relevant class of notes.

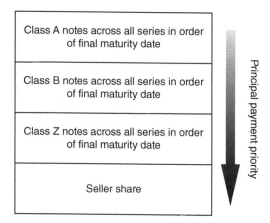

FIGURE 3.5 Cash flow waterfall following a non-asset trigger event.

Asset triggers have different consequences to non-asset triggers, for the simple reason that investors are seeking returns by deliberately exposing themselves to the credit risk of the underlying mortgages, whereas they do not wish to have credit exposure to the sponsor. The consequences of breaching an asset trigger are that all notes convert to pass-through and are paid down sequentially in order of seniority and final maturity date and no further mortgages may be added to the pool. The key difference to non-asset triggers is that the seller share is not time-subordinated (Figure 3.6).

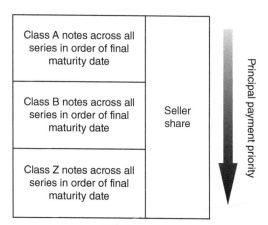

FIGURE 3.6 Cash flow waterfall following an asset trigger event.

It is important to note that terms vary across master trust programmes. Swap providers are well-advised to check the base prospectus in each case to ensure that all terms are well understood and correctly modelled.

New Note Issuance and the Addition of New Mortgage Collateral Modelling a revolving pool can be significantly more challenging than modelling a standalone pool, because of the uncertainty in the quantum of both mortgages and tranches, which can be issued at future times. Unlike standalone pools, the sponsor has wide discretion to add mortgage collateral, and issue new notes at any time so long as certain requirements are met, called issuance tests. These tests contain two key terms and other technical terms. The two key terms are:

1. Confirmation from the relevant rating agencies that the new issuance won't result in an any ratings impacts[10] on any outstanding notes.
2. There has been no credit loss suffered by any rated note.

This sponsor's discretion to issue new notes is unmodellable. One may make assumptions of course, but these assumptions are merely guesses. As a result, a more straightforward modelling approach for the swap provider is the *run-off assumption*. The run-off assumption treats a revolving pool as if it were a standalone pool, with the exception that the minimum seller share is respected at all times. In particular, no new tranches are issued, and no new collateral is added except in order to respect the minimum seller share (or perhaps a higher seller share if the swap provider is sufficiently confident in the sponsor). This scenario provides a firm base case for modelling and is valid in the sense that the issuance tests ensure preservation of (minimum) credit enhancement requirements.

Additional modelling scenarios beyond this base case may be considered by the swap provider, such as assuming the issuance of new tranches, without new loans being added to the pool, while respecting the minimum seller share and issuance test requirements. One might choose to augment these scenarios with a steady state scenario where new loans are added periodically in order to collateralise new issuance. No single scenario is 'right' because the sponsor's future RMBS funding requirements are unknown. However, a small number of scenarios can map out the spectrum of possibilities and their consequences and also inform discussions between the swap provider and the sponsor.

Other Components of Master Trust Structures In UK RMBS master trusts there are typically up to three SPVs for various tax and regulatory reasons. The trust that issues the bonds may be distinct from the trust that purchases the receivables from

---

[10]A rating impact is a rating downgrade, a rating qualification or a withdrawal of the rating.

the seller. Another feature of many RMBS master trusts is the presence of *reserve funds*, which provide additional credit enhancement. So master trusts are exceptionally complicated even before considering the associated securitisation swaps.

Model parsimony is an important guiding philosophy. A parsimonious model is a model that achieves the necessary level of accuracy with as few components and variables as possible. When pricing and modelling the swaps, it is important to focus on the key drivers impacting the swap and resist the temptation to over-engineer a solution. Further discussion of RMBS master trusts in this book is therefore limited other than to mention that there are several additional structural features, but on a case-by-case basis the swap provider will need to consider what is necessary to model, and what is best left out.

Credit Card ABS Structures

Credit card securitisation is fundamentally different from RMBS securitisation in at least three key respects. Firstly, the tenor of the debt is very short – typically monthly. This means that the securitisation process must extend the duration of the underlying debt, which is the opposite of what securitisation achieves for the higher-rated RMBS notes. This is achieved via the continual topping-up of the loan pool. Secondly, this continual topping-up means that the securitisation structure has continuing reliance on the originator to keep issuing credit card debt. This weakens the bankruptcy remoteness of the process. Thirdly, the underlying credit card debt is unsecured, whereas RMBS is backed by the mortgage collateral (i.e. a bricks and mortar dwelling). The second and third points are arguably less relevant for a swap provider than the first, but essential for context nonetheless.

Duration extension is achieved by structuring two distinct periods in to the securitisation: a revolving period and a non-revolving period. During the revolving period, the ABS note principal doesn't amortise. New credit card receivables are added as required in order to keep the pool balance at least equal to the aggregate balance of the outstanding ABS notes. During the non-revolving period, the pool balance amortises. There are two ways this can be dealt with. Firstly, the ABS notes could be structured to amortise along with the pool, in which case the second period is called a *controlled amortisation period*. Secondly, the ABS notes could be structured to be bullets by accumulating the cash receipts and investing them to the note maturity date, at which point the entire note principal is repaid. In this case the second period is called an *accumulation period*.

The tenor of the second non-revolving period depends critically on a metric called the *monthly payment rate* (MPR). This metric determines how quickly the credit card debt is repaid. It is defined as the amount repaid as a percentage of the outstanding card balance at the start of any given month. MPRs can vary widely depending on factors such as the country, the issuer type (retailer, bank, other), whether reward points are earned and borrower profile. For a given issuer, MPRs are best understood via analysis of historical time series data.

Credit card ABS structures can be standalone or master trust in format. The master trust formats can be either capitalist or socialist.

Credit card ABS structures also contain triggers that are akin to the asset and non-asset triggers for RMBS master trusts discussed in the sub-section Master Trust RMBS Structures.

In particular, the asset trigger conditions can be:

- insufficient spread to pay note holders; and
- charge-offs exceed a specified threshold;

while non-asset trigger events can be:

- insolvency of the seller; and
- the originator's role as servicer is terminated and a new servicer is not appointed with a specified time period, for example, 60 days.

The consequence of a trigger event is early amortisation, which involves (i) ending the revolving period (if relevant) immediately and (ii) paying down all notes sequentially (Figure 3.7).

There are four key metrics to consider when analysing the performance of credit card ABS structures:

1. MPRs;
2. charge-off rates;
3. yield; and
4. purchase rates.

Credit card pools typically have much higher charge-off rates compared to auto loans and prime residential mortgages, compensated for by significantly higher interest rates (yield). Typical ranges for these parameters are as follows: MPRs are in the order

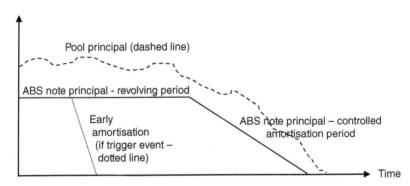

FIGURE 3.7   A credit card ABS pool with a revolving period and a controlled amortisation period.

of 10–15%; charge-off rates are 5–10%; the yield is 15–20% (which is why no sane individual should pay interest on their credit card) and purchase rates are dependent on the originator and are 100% during the revolving period of a well-performing deal.

The key risks for a swap provider are (i) that an early amortisation event will occur and (ii) that the controlled amortisation period will proceed at a slower rate than forecast. In case (i), the swap provider will need to unwind the remaining term of its hedging swap, which, due to mark-to-market (MTM) movements, could result in a financial loss. In case (ii), the swap provider will need to rebalance and extend its hedge. Both these cases can be modelled under the extension risk framework discussed in detail in Chapter 6. A critical pricing decision for a swap provider is to determine an acceptable probability of (i) and (ii) occurring.

COVERED BOND STRUCTURES

Hard Bullets

A hard bullet bond is one where all the principal is repaid at the maturity date, with no possibility of extending the timeline for repaying bond holders. Hard bullets are the simplest structure from the point of view of a swap provider as they have no extension risk. Thus the only non-standard risk for a swap provider is downgrade risk. However, from the issuer's perspective, hard bullets cause two key problems:

1. tight credit rating linkage; and
2. shortening the effective funding tenor.

The first problem begins with the cap imposed by all rating agencies on the number of notches of credit rating uplift for a covered bond relative to the issuer's own senior unsecured rating. This uplift is earned via the additional security provided by the cover pool. One of the key risks that rating agencies examine when rating covered bonds is the repayment risk at maturity. While the cover pool mitigates this risk, in reality it takes time to sell a pool of mortgages. If it needs to be done quickly, then the price impact could be severe. This fire sale risk could be especially acute if the issuer's default occurs concurrently with a general economic downturn. Because of this, the number of notches of rating uplift that a rating agency will give in the case of a hard bullet maturity is quite constrained. This reduces the ratings stability of the covered bonds and, for lower-rated banks especially, makes the issuance of AAA-rated covered bonds difficult or impossible.

The second problem is that rating agencies also require issuers of hard bullet covered bonds to pre-fund the principal redemption to reduce the repayment risk at maturity. Typically this pre-funding needs to occur one year prior to maturity. The consequence of this is that a bank that has issued a five-year covered bond will only receive four years of funding.

These two problems can be reduced with extendible maturity structures, which are becoming increasingly common. There are two types of extendible maturity structures: soft bullet and conditional pass-through (CPT).

Extendible Maturity Structures

Soft bullet covered bonds have become the dominant structure over the last half decade (Rudolf and Rühlmann 2017). This is due to an increasing amount of new issuance in soft bullet format as well as the conversion of existing hard bullet programmes to soft bullets in order to address the credit rating linkage and effective funding tenor problems discussed above.

Soft bullets typically allow an extension in maturity of up to one year in the event of issuer default.[11] This allows the trustee more time to sell down the cover pool and obtain a fair market price for the assets in a default scenario, increasing the probability that bond holders will be fully repaid. As a result, the rating agencies can waive the pre-funding requirement and allow a higher cap on the credit rating uplift.

Note that it is conceivable that soft bullet bond holders may vote to allow the trustee more than one year to sell down the assets if they believe it is in their interests. However, a liability swap provider's legal obligations cease at the one-year extended maturity date, so extension beyond this date is not its concern. Any investors holding covered bonds in foreign currency will be unhedged beyond the swap maturity date and will need to organise their own hedge or accept the FX risk.

Given the extension risk assumed by soft bullet covered bond investors, one might reasonably expect soft bullets to trade wider than equivalent hard bullet bonds. In fact, there is no discernible spread differential at all in the market.

An even greater rating de-linkage can be achieved via the CPT structure, which perfectly aligns the underlying cover pool cash flows with the bond cash flows. Upon an issuer event of default, the bond maturity date extends far into the future, to the final maturity date of the last asset in the cover pool (Figure 3.8). The bond converts to pass-through amortisation, although the cover pool trustee may sell some or all of the pool if they judge it to be in the best interests of the bond holders. Thus there is a modellable element of the amortisation (the pass-through component) and an unmodellable element (the trustee's discretion to sell when conditions are right).

CPT bonds were first issued in 2013 and, while still a very small part of the market, they are rapidly increasing in volume. CPT issuers can take advantage of the increased cap on ratings uplift in order to issue AAA-rated bonds that they otherwise might not be able to issue in soft bullet format. Recent issuers now span multiple jurisdictions, including NIBC (Netherlands), UniCredit (Italy), Anadi Bank (Austria) and the Bank of Queensland (Australia), which required an AUD/EUR CPT covered bond liability swap.

---

[11] For Spanish covered bonds the typical period is two to three years.

Outstanding bond principal

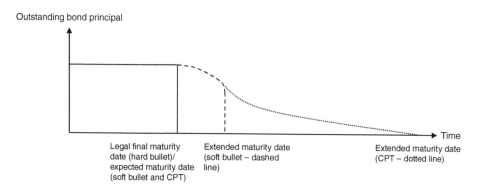

	Legal final maturity	Extended maturity date	Extended maturity date
	date (hard bullet)/	(soft bullet – dashed	(CPT – dotted line)
	expected maturity date	line)	
	(soft bullet and CPT)		

FIGURE 3.8   The three covered bond structures: hard bullet, soft bullet and CPT.

COMPARISON OF STRUCTURES

After presenting a wide variety of structures available to be utilised across securitisation and covered bonds, a high-level comparison of the features of securitisation standalone SPVs, securitisation master trusts and covered bonds is set out below.

	Standalone SPVs	Master trusts	Covered bonds
Recourse	Single – collateral only	Single – collateral only	Dual – sponsor and collateral
Over-collateralised	No	Yes	Yes
Credit enhancement via tranching	Yes	Yes	No
Revolving	RMBS – no; ABS – possibly	Yes	Yes
Structural complexity	Low	High	Medium
New issuance speed-to-market	Low	High	High
Set-up costs	Medium	High	High
Ability to de-link assets and liabilities	No	Yes	Yes
Most common RMBS bond format	Pass-through	Controlled amortisation or bullet	Bullet
Extension risk	Depends on structure, but can be high	Depends on structure, but mitigated by the seller share	Hard bullets – zero Soft bullets – small CPT – high

CHAPTER 4

Swaps in Structured Funding

Chance fights ever on the side of the prudent.

– Euripides

Swaps are essential components of almost all securitisation and covered bond structures, though they play their role very much behind the scenes. In this chapter we explain the different purposes and functions that swaps have in structured funding deals and the different types of risk this brings home to the swap provider.

AN OVERVIEW OF VANILLA SWAPS

Securitisation swaps are a more complex version of 'vanilla' swaps, which are traded in huge volume daily across the globe. Before proceeding to explain the more complex instruments, in this section we present the foundational aspects of plain vanilla swaps for readers from a non-derivatives background. Readers with a derivatives background may wish to skip this section.

Interest Rate Swaps

An *interest rate swap* is an agreement where one counterparty agrees to pay a specified interest rate on a notional principal schedule at regular intervals. In return that party will receive another, different specified rate of interest on the same principal schedule at regular intervals. It is possible for the payment intervals to be different between the parties.

The swap is said to consist of two *legs*. From one counterparty's perspective there is a *pay leg* and a *receive leg*. The interest rates applicable can be fixed rate or floating rate. Fixed-rate legs have a pre-defined interest rate, which may be constant or might change through the life of the swap, but, in any case, it is known in advance. Alternatively, floating-rate legs reference an interest rate index, such as London interbank offer rate (LIBOR) or bank bill swap rate (BBSW). Floating-rate legs usually also have a fixed spread, which is paid over and above the floating index; for example, LIBOR + 20 basis points.

Each leg of an interest rate swap consists of a series of regularly spaced dates that define:

1. interest accrual periods;
2. rate reset dates; and
3. payment dates.

The *interest accrual period* defines the time span over which interest payments accrue. The accrual calculation requires a *day count basis* to be specified, with the most common being ACT/365, ACT/360 or 30/360. This day count basis, together with the start and end dates of the interest accrual period, define the *year fraction* of the interest accrual period. A *rate reset date* defines the date on which the rate index such as GBP LIBOR is fixed for the next interest accrual period. A *payment date* defines the date at which the recently accrued interest is paid and usually coincides with the end of the accrual period.

EXAMPLE 4.1:

Suppose a fixed swap leg pays 3% on a notional principal of GBP 100 million on the 14th of each month with ACT/365 as the day count basis, commencing from 14 January 2018. Then the year fraction of the first interest accrual period from 14 January to 14 February 2018 is equal to 31/365, which equals 0.08493 years (since there are 31 days in the accrual period). The interest accrued during the period will be calculated as $3\% \times £100,000,000 \times 0.08493 = £254,794.52$, which is paid at the next payment date on 14 February.

There are two common types of interest rate swaps:

1. A *fixed/floating swap* is where one counterparty pays a fixed rate of interest and receives a floating rate of interest in return. For example, one counterparty pays a fixed rate of 3% quarterly and in return receives 1 month BBSW on a monthly basis plus a spread.
2. A *single currency basis swap* is where one counterparty pays a floating rate of interest and receives a different floating rate of interest in return. For example, one counterparty pays 1 month EUR IBOR +10 bps monthly and receives 3 month EURIBOR quarterly (Figure 4.1).

The principal schedule on a vanilla interest rate swap can be:

1. Constant/bullet, for example, fixed at the constant rate of USD 500 million for the entire duration of the swap.

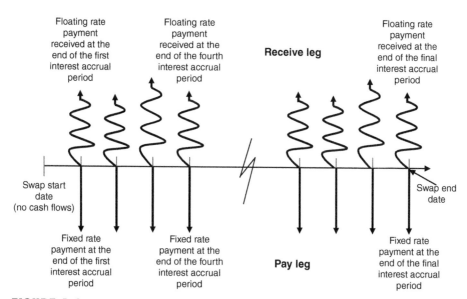

FIGURE 4.1 Cash flows in a fixed/floating interest rate swap with constant notional principal from the perspective of the counterparty paying the fixed rate leg ("the payer"). All the fixed cash flows being paid (straight lines) are known in advance. The floating rate cash flows being received in return (curvy lines) are unknown until their respective reset dates.

2. Amortising, that is, decreasing in a precisely specified manner throughout the life of the swap.

3. Accreting, that is, increasing in a precisely specified manner throughout the life of the swap.

4. Roller-coaster, that is, varying both up and down in a precisely specified manner during the life of the swap.

Note that for securitisation swaps the principal can change in a manner that is not precisely specified in advance; for example, due to the existing prepayment risk and/or extension risk. These features are examined later in the book and are one of the features that make securitisation swaps (highly) non-vanilla.

Counterparties may transact interest rate swaps for a multitude of purposes. Some illustrative examples are:

1. When borrowers choose to fix their interest rate instead of paying floating interest on a mortgage loan, the bank originating the mortgage loan may elect to hedge the interest rate risk that arises via a fixed/floating swap. This ensures that if interest rates increase then it will be compensated (or hedged) for receiving a below-market fixed rate of interest on the mortgage loan.

2. A covered bond issuer who sells fixed-rate bonds to investors but receives a floating rate of interest in return from the underlying mortgage pool. In this scenario, the issuer may transact a fixed/floating interest rate swap to ensure that it is hedged against a decrease in the floating interest rate it receives.

3. Other parties, such as hedge funds, use interest rate swaps to gain exposure to fluctuations in rates, thus expressing a view about the future direction that interest rates may take. Interest rates swaps may also be used as an overlay, for example, to modify the duration of a bond portfolio. With a very wide variety of market participants, vanilla interest rate swap markets are usually reasonably liquid across the standard tenors, with the swap rates reflecting the collective information taken from across the market.

Historically, interest rate swaps were over-the-counter (OTC) products, which required clients to manually communicate with a bank swap provider with whom they were on-boarded and had executed the standard International Swaps and Derivatives Association (ISDA) documentation. These swaps were frequently uncollateralised outside of the interbank swap market, meaning that an in-of-the-money swap could generate a large credit exposure that is not backed by any cash or other collateral. In recent years, new regulation has imposed margining and clearing requirements on vanilla interest rate swaps, which has transformed the operation and risks within the interest rate swap market. However, non-vanilla swaps such as securitisation swaps are still completely OTC and will likely remain so indefinitely, although there is some variation across different jurisdictions.

Cross-Currency Swaps

A *cross-currency swap* is analogous to an interest rate swap but differs in two key respects:

1. each swap leg is denominated in a different currency; and
2. principal is exchanged, that is, there are principal cash flows in addition to interest rate cash flows.

The foreign exchange (FX) rate that connects the principal schedule on one leg of the swap to the other is fixed throughout the life of the swap, which enables cross-currency swaps to be an effective tool for hedging any currency risk.[1]

---

[1] In the *interbank* cross-currency swap market, the FX rate resets every quarterly roll in order to constrain counterparty credit risk. The discussion above refers to the *client* cross-currency swap market where the swaps are not principal resetting.

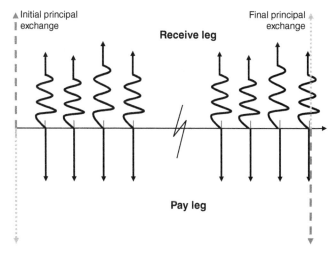

FIGURE 4.2 Cash flows in a fixed/floating cross-currency swap with constant notional principal from the perspective of X-Bank. Principal cash flows are in dashed lines (USD) and dotted lines (AUD). Interest cash flows are in straight lines (USD) and curvy lines (AUD). The size of the arrows is not to scale.

There are three types of principal cash flows that occur during the life of a cross-currency swap:

1. initial principal exchange;
2. intermediate principal exchanges (only if the swap schedule is non-constant); and
3. final principal exchange.

These cash flows operate as if the swap was two simultaneous loans in different currencies (Figure 4.2).

EXAMPLE 4.2:

An Australian company (AusCo) issues USD 100 million of five-year 3% bonds with quarterly coupons to investors in the USA. AusCo transacts a cross-currency swap with X-Bank to swap the funding back into AUD and hedge its currency risk. On day one, AusCo receives USD 100 million from the investors in the bonds. Later that day, AusCo pays USD 100 million to X-Bank and receives AUD 131 million, which is the initial principal exchange of the swap. At the end of every quarter, AusCo pays X-Bank BBSW + a fixed

(Continued)

spread and in return receives 3% USD interest payments, which it uses to pay the noteholders. At maturity of the swap and the bond, AusCo repays the AUD 131 million to X-Bank and receives USD 100 million, which it will then use to repay the bond investors. The cash flows are analogous to AusCo simultaneously lending USD 100 million to X-Bank (with fixed interest) and borrowing AUD 131 million from X-Bank (with floating interest).

If the principal amount of the bonds in Example 4.2 was amortising, then there would also need to be intermediate principal exchanges. In this scenario, suppose that the bond amortised by USD 20 million annually. Then AusCo would receive USD 20 million every year from X-Bank and pay-out AUD 26.2 million to X-Bank as intermediate principal exchanges.

All cross-currency swaps, whether vanilla or non-vanilla, are OTC and likely to remain so indefinitely.

Vanilla Swap Pricing

Vanilla interest rate and cross-currency swaps are priced via a discounted cash flow calculation.[2] The discount factors used in the calculation are derived from a *discount curve*. For a cash collateralised swap, the right discount curve to use is the one built ('bootstrapped') from the overnight index swap (OIS) rates.[3] The forward interest rates, which are used to estimate future floating rates in the swap, are derived from a *forward curve*. Forward curves are calculated from liquid, observable instruments (such as cash, futures, swap rates and single currency basis rates), which are traded in financial markets. Since the Global Financial Crisis (GFC), markets have materially differentiated the credit risk associated with one-month, three-month and six-month reference interest rates such as LIBOR and BBSW, and this is also reflected in different swap rates for swaps that reset off one-month, three-month or six-month interest rates. Forward rates used in swap pricing must therefore be calculated from the right forward curve and built from instruments with the same underlying rate index tenor. We will not delve into yield curve construction any further here; the interested reader is referred to Hull (2018, chapter 4) . Since the price of a swap is computed from market instruments, its (unadjusted) price is also known as its mark-to-market (MTM) value.

---

[2]This can be justified by a no-arbitrage argument – see, for example, Joshi (2003, chapter 13) for details. A *no-arbitrage argument* demonstrates that if the price of an instrument was anything other than its (unique) no-arbitrage price, then a trader could earn a riskless profit (arbitrage) via some trading strategy. Arbitrage is assumed to be impossible in efficient markets.

[3]Swaps which are collateralised differently will require a derivative valuation adjustment (XVA) to be computed, likely via a Monte Carlo calculation in which case the swap is not really 'vanilla'.

The MTM of an interest rate swap to the counterparty paying fixed is given by the following discounted cash flow formula:

$$MTM = \sum_{i=0}^{n-1} P_i.(f_i + m).\tau_i.DF_{i+1} - \sum_{j=0}^{m-1} P_j.s.\tau_j.DF_{j+1} \tag{4.1}$$

The first term represents the sum of n floating interest rate payments received. The second term represents the sum of m fixed interest rate payments paid. Specifically:

P_i is the ith period notional principal
f_i is the ith forward rate
m is the fixed margin paid over the floating rate
s is the fixed swap rate
τ_i is the year fraction for the ith period
DF_i is the discount factor to the time t_i

The MTM of a cross-currency swap includes additional cash flows representing the exchange of principal. One must also convert the cash flows into a common base currency. The MTM in domestic currency D of a floating/floating cross-currency swap is given by the following formula:

$$MTM^D = \sum_{i=0}^{n-1} P_i^D.(f_i^D + m^D).\tau_i^D.DF_{i+1}^D - P_0^D.DF_0^D + \sum_{i=1}^{n} \Delta P_i^D.DF_i^D + P_n^D.DF_n^D$$

$$- fx. \left[\sum_{j=0}^{m-1} P_j^F.(f_j^F + m^F).\tau_j^F.DF_{j+1}^F - P_0^F.DF_0^F + \sum_{j=1}^{m} \Delta P_j^F.DF_j^F + P_m^F.DF_m^F \right] \tag{4.2}$$

where:

fx is the market spot FX rate
P_i^D is the ith period swap principal in domestic currency D
P_j^F is the jth period swap principal in foreign currency F where $P_j^F.fx_{swap} = P_j^D$.
      We assume[4] that $fx_{swap} = fx$ at inception
$f_{i/j}^{D/F}$ is the ith/jth forward rate in domestic/foreign currency respectively
$m_{i/j}^{D/F}$ is the margin over the floating rate in domestic/foreign currency respectively
$\tau_{i/j}^{D/F}$ is the year fraction for the ith/jth period in domestic/foreign currency respectively
$DF_{i/j}^{D/F}$ is the (basis-adjusted) discount factor from time $t_{i/j}$ in domestic/foreign currency respectively

---

[4]In reality the swap FX rate may be slightly different to the prevailing spot FX rate to ensure a rounded face value of the notional principal. Using a slightly off-market FX rate for the swap results in slightly modified swap margins.

The first and fifth terms of formula (4.2) represent the floating interest payments. The second and sixth terms represent the initial principal exchange; the third and seventh terms represent the intermediate principal exchanges; and the fourth and eighth terms represent the final principal exchange.

The discount factors used in cross-currency swap pricing are often different to those used in single currency swap pricing. This is the case whenever there is a non-zero *cross-currency basis* for a particular currency vis-à-vis another currency. Cross-currency basis is a spread added to one or both legs of a cross-currency swap and can be thought of as a cost (or benefit) of swapping cash flows from one currency into another. It is driven by supply and demand factors and is something issuers need to be aware of when determining where to source funding from. Cross-currency basis is a dynamic market variable and can make funding from one currency zone cheaper or more expensive than from another. Modifying the discount factors on a cross-currency swap ensures that a swap with the at-market cross-currency swap spreads on each leg prices to par (i.e. has zero MTM).

An important point with cross-currency swaps is that spreads do not swap from one currency to another without being altered. For example, consider a standard quarterly-rolling AUD/USD cross-currency swap with zero MTM where the USD leg pays 3 month USD LIBOR +100 bps. What is the spread on the floating AUD leg (i.e. the spread over 3 month BBSW)? If AUD interest rates are higher than USD interest rates, then the spread on the AUD leg will need to be higher than +100 bps so that its (more heavily) discounted value is equal to the (less heavily) discounted value of the +100 bps on the USD leg. The multiplier that converts the spread on the one leg to the other is called the *conversion factor*.[5] The value of the conversion factor is an important component in the overall landed cost of funds on any cross-currency funding trade.

ASSET SWAPS

A single pool of loans often contains a variety of different loan types. This is due to product variations that can be offered to borrowers across the market. For instance, residential mortgages may be floating rate or have a fixed-rate period of a specified tenor; they may have an interest-only period or may be principal amortising. If they are floating rate, that rate could be the originator's standard variable rate (SVR), a tracker rate or possibly something else. The securitisation process considers that there are bond investors who will not buy securities with a bespoke and variable mix of non-standard interest rate cash flows. Bond investors wish to receive either a standard floating rate

---

[5] Another way to define the conversion factor is as the ratio of PV01s of each swap leg. The PV01 is the impact of a 1 basis point (0.01%) change in interest rates on the MTM.

of interest, such as LIBOR, or a fixed rate of interest. So how does one convert the disparate loan pool cash flows into a single standardised cash flow? The answer is via an *asset swap*.[6]

An asset swap is constructed by modelling the expected pool principal amortisation and interest rate cash flows on the receive leg, then solving for the margin over the floating rate index on the pay leg, which causes the swap to have a zero MTM value. This margin, called the *breakeven margin*, is effectively the average interest margin on the underlying loan pool. When doing this calculation, one must take care to model various lifecycle events of the loans, such as the end of an interest-only period or a fixed-rate period. In reality, a higher than breakeven margin may be used so that the asset swap can repatriate excess spread to the originator.

Asset swap parameters can be quite dynamic, especially when revolving pools are involved. They generally require periodic amendment to capture changes resulting from unexpected prepayment and defaults, changes to an originator's SVR and the substitution or addition of new loan collateral.

Lending institutions that engage in structured funding transactions typically have Treasury teams that are well-versed in managing asset swaps. The risk management of static pool asset swaps is relatively straightforward. Fixed-rate loans swapped to floating through the asset swap can be hedged with vanilla interest rate swaps to manage the interest rate risk. SVR rate loans swapped to a standard floating index plus a spread 'only' have *basis risk*; that is, the differential risk between two floating indices, which is generally, but not always, more benign than outright interest rate risk. Usually most lenders in a particular loan market segment will have comparable costs of funds and hence roughly similar net interest margins (NIMs) on their loan pools.

Originators who do not have sufficiently high credit ratings will be forced by the rating agencies to post collateral on their asset swaps on rated transactions (see the section on Rating Agency criteria in Chapter 7 for further detail). Some of these originators may find that it is more efficient to pay for a better-rated third party to provide the asset swap than supply it themselves. In such instances, the third-party swap provider will need to think very carefully about how to structure and risk manage the asset swap. Given that some key parameters are beyond the control of the third-party swap provider – for example, the SVR rate can be changed at the discretion of the originator – many third-party swap providers will only *intermediate* an asset swap, rather than provide one on an outright basis. Intermediating the asset swap ensures that all market risk and swap prepayment risk is transferred back to the originator. This puts the originator back in the position they would have been had they had the requisite credit rating and been able to provide the swap themselves (Figure 4.3).

---

[6]Note that asset swaps are sometimes referred to by different names in different contexts. In some covered bond transactions, asset swaps may be called *total return swaps*; and in some RMBS deals, asset swaps may be called *basis swaps*.

FIGURE 4.3   An intermediated asset swap. The swap with the SPV is called the *front swap*. The hedging swap back to the originator is called the *back swap*.

Furthermore, when a third party provides an intermediated asset swap over a revolving pool, the addition of new collateral can substantially change the swap characteristics. Hence swap providers are well advised to ensure they have the latitude to either change the risk-based fee charged for providing the swap, or otherwise constrain the permitted variation in swap characteristics by the originator. See the sub-section on Intermediated Asset Swaps in Chapter 5 for a further discussion on pricing intermediated asset swaps.

LIABILITY SWAPS

Once the asset swap has transformed the interest cash flows from the loan pool into a standard floating rate, those cash flows may need to be further transformed to align with the cash flows on bonds issued to investors. This latter transformation is performed via a *liability swap* (Figure 4.4).

Liability swaps are therefore a very broad class of swaps covering different combinations of fixed/floating cash flows, currencies, prepayment risk types and extension risk (Figure 4.5).

The conventions on whether a bond is fixed or floating depend on the country and the type of bond. Covered bonds in Europe are usually fixed-rate instruments paying interest annually. Residential mortgage-backed securities (RMBS) and asset-backed securities (ABS) in Australia, Europe and the UK are usually floating rate instruments paying interest monthly or quarterly. ABS in the USA can commonly pay either fixed or floating interest. The job of the liability swap is to deliver the cash flows in the right format for the bond.

Another way to classify liability swaps is via their prepayment risk and extension risk characteristics. Once again, there are many possibilities (Figure 4.6).

RMBS and ABS from standalone special purpose vehicles (SPVs) are often pass-through if issued in domestic currency. RMBS and ABS from master trusts are frequently controlled amortisation or soft bullet whether issued in domestic or foreign currency. Covered bonds are always bullets prior to any issuer event of default whether issued in domestic or foreign currency.

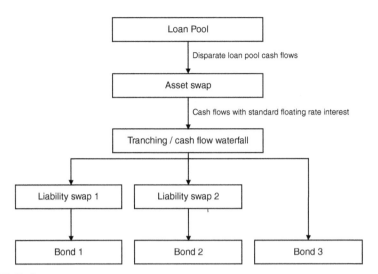

FIGURE 4.4 Cash flow transformation via asset and liability swaps in a securitisation or covered bond structure. Note that not all bonds require a liability swap. In the above example, Bond 3 would be issued in the same currency as the loan pool cash flows, and would pay a coupon with the same standard floating rate index as provided by the asset swap.

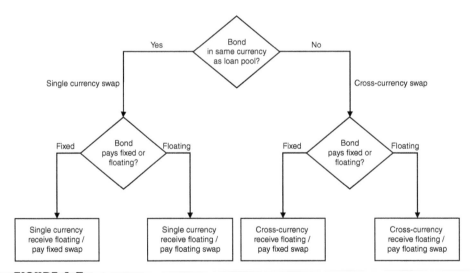

FIGURE 4.5 Four different types of single/cross-currency and fixed/floating liability swaps from the perspective of the swap provider. The receive leg is always floating rate in the currency of the loan pool.

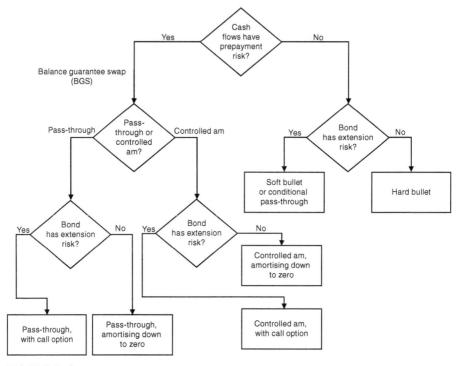

FIGURE 4.6 Liability swaps can have a wide variety of embedded risks.

STANDBY SWAPS

As discussed in the section on Asset Swaps, if an originator is not sufficiently well rated, it will be required to post collateral on any asset swap it provides to an SPV. In such cases, some originators will choose to engage a third-party swap provider to intermediate between themselves and the SPV. However, the rating agencies allow a second possibility: the originator can provide the asset swap without posting collateral so long as it has engaged an appropriately rated *standby swap provider*. A standby swap provider is a party who is willing and able to step into the shoes of the asset swap provider if it defaults and continue to provide the asset swap to the SPV (Figure 4.7).

Standby swap terms and conditions can vary, but typically involve the following:

1. The Standby swap provider will assume all functions and duties of the asset swap provider upon its default.
2. The Standby swap provider will be subject to the same counterparty criteria as if it were the asset swap provider.

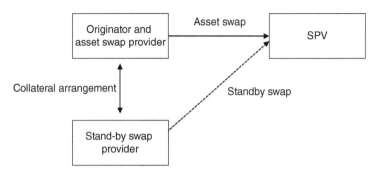

FIGURE 4.7 A standby swap provider.

3. If the asset swap is in-the-money to the SPV, the asset swap provider must post collateral to the standby swap provider.

Point 2 above means that standby swap providers are subject to downgrade risk on their swaps and must charge a fee accordingly (see Chapter 7 for full details). Point 3 is critical for any standby swap provider: without this collateral, it risks having to step in to a large, negative MTM position if it ever becomes the actual asset swap provider, which would make the pricing of standby swaps uncommercial. With the introduction of new margining regulations, collateral may need to be posted on a two-way basis rather than on a one-way basis; that is, the standby swap provider may also need to post collateral to the asset swap provider if the asset swap is out-of-the-money to the SPV.

The main benefits to the originator of having a standby swap are that the original asset swap counterparty will avoid having to post the additional amount component of the collateral and also avoid any replacement risk, which can be significant for less-well rated swap providers. It may also cost less than an intermediated asset swap in some cases.

The valuation of a standby swap depends on two things: (i) the specific terms of the swap and (ii) an assumption on the default correlation of the SPV and the asset swap provider. Assuming that one views default of the SPV and asset swap provider as independent (hence uncorrelated) events, the value V of the standby swap is:

$$V = p.(CVA_{AS} + FVA_{AS} + CFVA_{AS} + other_{AS}) + (1 - p).(CVA_{SS} + FVA_{SS} + CFVA_{AS})$$

$$= CFVA_{AS} + p.(CVA_{AS} + FVA_{AS} + other_{AS}) + (1 - p).(CVA_{SS} + FVA_{SS}) \qquad (4.3)$$

where:

p is the probability of default of the asset swap provider

CVA_{AS} is the credit valuation adjustment (CVA) charge on the asset swap (from the asset swap provider's perspective)

FVA_{AS} is the funding valuation adjustment (FVA) charge on the asset swap (from the asset swap provider's perspective)

$CFVA_{AS}$ is the contingent funding valuation adjustment (CFVA) charge on the asset swap (from the asset swap provider's perspective)

$other_{AS}$ are any other risk charges, such as prepayment risk, which may be required to correctly price the asset swap (depends on the specific terms of each standby swap)

CVA_{SS} is the CVA charge on the standby swap (from the standby swap provider's perspective)

FVA_{SS} is the FVA charge on the standby swap (from the standby swap provider's perspective)

CVA_{SS} should be very small. Given that collateral is posted to the standby swap provider, this CVA charge only covers the residual risk that the asset swap provider defaults before they can post any required increase in collateral caused by market movements. In contrast, CVA_{AS} is typically not small, as the SPV never posts collateral.

One may legitimately ask whether default of the SPV is really independent from default of the asset swap provider. If one assumes that the two default events are 100% correlated, then $\mathbf{E}[p.\ CVA_{AS}] = CVA_{AS}$ hence

$$V = CFVA_{AS} + CVA_{AS} + p.(FVA_{AS} + other_{AS}) + (1 - p).(CVA_{SS} + FVA_{SS}) \qquad (4.4)$$

which is clearly a higher cost than assuming that the two default events are independent. Ultimately the truth probably lies somewhere between 0% and 100% default correlation – but deciding on the 'right' number comes down to risk appetite, how aggressive one wishes to be on pricing, historical analysis on default correlation and deal specific factors.

SWAP PRIORITY AND FLIP CLAUSES

The mechanics for the distribution of payments within a structured funding transaction are set out within the transaction documentation, normally in the trust deed or the cash management agreement. Also known as cash flow waterfalls these cascading payments are an important element of the structure, which specifies how income and principal are to be distributed between the various classes of noteholders and the other transaction parties. The waterfalls are generally split between two differing scenarios: what happens before an event of default (pre-enforcement) and after (post-enforcement).

The order of priorities, or who should be higher up the waterfall and last to suffer any losses, depends on a multitude of factors. These include the level of risk being assumed by the investor or transaction party and whether a transaction party is performing an administrative level task (such as a trustee or servicer) so should be paid out its fees and expenses in priority to any noteholder. As a service provider, the swap provider will typically sit senior to the noteholders in both the pre-enforcement and post-enforcement waterfalls. That is, when it comes to receiving any payments (including any termination amounts) in relation to the swap it is in a relatively well protected position. However, it is possible for the position of the parties in the waterfalls to change depending on whether the loss arises from its own default and this is particularly relevant for the swap provider as rating agencies will often require these *flip clauses* to be written into waterfalls.

A *flip clause* allows one party to terminate or modify the operation of a contract upon the occurrence of an insolvency event.[7] In a securitisation context, the flip clause operates to change, or flip, the ranking of a swap counterparty relative to the noteholders if that swap counterparty is declared to be insolvent or is otherwise in default of its obligations. Flip clauses are a common feature employed in securitisation swaps to subordinate payments to the swap provider upon their own default. The purpose behind the operation of a flip clause is to de-link the credit risk of the swap provider from the transaction. Thus they provide important protections for noteholders.

In structured funding transactions, a swap counterparty will generally rank above the noteholders in the priorities of payments,[8] which means that even if the swap counterparty were to default on its obligations it may become entitled to receive a termination payment under the swap before any distribution is made to the noteholders. In other words, the defaulting party will have caused the issuer to terminate the swap and unwind the structure but may technically be entitled to a pay-out before the noteholders. By moving a defaulting swap counterparty down the payment waterfall, the noteholders are better protected and more likely to receive a greater proportion of the termination payment, which de-links the structure from the credit risk of the swap counterparty.

However, since the onset of the financial crisis and more particularly the insolvency of Lehman Brothers, the validity of the flip clause has been the subject of increased judicial scrutiny with a number of cases coming before the courts. Two cases in particular that have had implications for the continuing use of the flip clause are the decision of the UK Court of Appeal in *Perpetual Trustee Company Limited v BNY Corporate Trustee Services Limited and Lehman Brothers Special Financing Inc.* (**Perpetual**) and the decision of the US Bankruptcy court in a parallel proceeding heard in the USA.

The facts of the *Perpetual* case involved the establishment of a credit-linked note programme by Lehman Brothers International (Europe) in 2002, where notes were

---

[7] A flip clause is a particular type of *ipso facto* or bankruptcy clause.

[8] An asset swap will generally sit senior to the noteholders. However, it is not uncommon for a liability swap to sit equal, or *pari passu*, with the noteholders. In the event that the swap counterparty was equal to the noteholders in a cash waterfall by virtue of the operation of a *flip clause* they would then become subordinated.

issued to investors by a number of SPVs. The SPV issuers then entered into a credit default swap with Lehman Brothers Special Financing Inc. (LBSFI) under which LBSFI bought credit protection from the SPV on the underlying reference entities. The premium paid under the credit default swap by LBSFI to the SPV was then paid to noteholders as a coupon of the notes. As we have discussed, generally the swap counterparty will sit senior to the noteholders within any cash waterfall. However, in this case, in order to secure the relevant ratings flip clauses had been written into the documentation that would reverse the priority of payment in the event the swap counterparty defaulted.

When Lehman Brothers entered into insolvency, the MTM value of these swaps was heavily in favour of LBSFI. However, because LBSFI was the defaulting party under the swap (as a result of the insolvency) this meant that the flip clause would reverse that priority position. The parallel legal proceedings in the UK and USA ensued as a result.

In the UK proceeding the scope and application of the 'anti-deprivation rule' was considered, which provides that contractual terms (such as the flip clause) purporting to dispose of property on a bankruptcy would be invalid upon the bankruptcy of that particular party. The principle being that this amounts to an evasion of insolvency laws. However, in the UK case it was successfully demonstrated that the operation of the flip clause did not amount to a forfeiture under the anti-deprivation rule and that the priority of LBSFI to the swap proceeds was conditional upon it continuing to perform under the swap agreement. Alternatively, the parallel proceeding in the USA contradicted the UK decision by finding that the flip clause was unenforceable on the basis of the application of the US Bankruptcy Code. This has subsequently led to confusion on how flip clauses should be treated across different jurisdictions[9] (see The Flip Clause box for a litigation timeline).

Because the operation of the flip clause is an important factor with regard to compliance with rating agency criteria, this has seen rating agencies request legal opinions on the validity of flip clauses within securitisation structures and the inclusion of risk factors into offering documentation to disclose the risks to investors. This has also led to an exploration of alternative solutions, ranging from the removal of

---

[9]The Australian Government introduced new legislation on 1 July 2018, which would render certain contractual provisions allowing a party to terminate or amend a contract by reason of an insolvency event – for example, an *ipso facto* clause – unenforceable. This could have further implications for the validity of flip clauses in Australia. At present, the Australian position on flip clauses follows the UK decisions, which have upheld flip clauses to be valid. However, under the new statutory proposals this position could be reversed so that the Australian position becomes more akin to that of the USA, where flip clauses have been held to be invalid. Importantly, the new legislation excludes close-out netting contracts made under the Payment Systems and Netting Act, which should mean that securitisation swaps in Australia would not be affected by these changes.

swaps from a securitisation altogether[10] to the permanent subordination of swap counterparties. Ultimately, consideration will need to be given at the structuring stage to how important the inclusion of a flip clause is in order to obtain a particular credit rating.

THE FLIP CLAUSE – A LITIGATION TIMELINE

2009 (UK). In *Perpetual Trustee Co. Limited v BNY Corporate Trustee Services Limited & Lehman Brothers Special Financing Inc.* [2009] EWCA Civ 1160 the High Court of England and Wales and the UK Court of Appeal found, as a matter of English law, that the flip clause was effective and did not contravene the anti-deprivation rule.

January 2010 (US). Parallel proceedings were then commenced by Lehman Brothers Special Financing Inc. in the USA covering the same factual circumstances. The US Bankruptcy Court contradicted the previous UK ruling with the presiding Judge Peck noting that the flip clause in question was an impermissible *ipso facto* clause and did not fall within the safe harbour under the US Bankruptcy Code and was therefore unenforceable. This decision was then appealed to a higher court; however the parties settled the matter before it was heard.

July 2011 (UK). The UK Supreme Court upheld the previous rulings of the lower UK courts in 2009. This reaffirmed the UK view that flip clauses were valid and paved the way for their future use in structured finance transaction.

2011 (US). – In a new US case, *Lehman Brothers Special Financing Inc. v Ballyrock ABS CDO 2007-1 Ltd*, Judge Peck upheld the US position on flip clauses ruling that subordinated swap termination payments that occurred upon the occurrence of certain insolvency events were invalidated.

2013 (US). A further US case before the US Bankruptcy Court, *Michigan State Housing Development Authority v Lehman Brothers Derivatives Products Inc. and Lehman Brothers Holdings Inc.*, distinguished itself from the previous US decisions and found that the safe harbour provisions of the US Bankruptcy Code applied.

2016 (US). In September 2016, the US Bankruptcy Court issued a judgement in *Lehman Brothers Special Financing Inc. v Bank of America National Association* that departed from the previous position established in the *BNY Trustee (2009)* and *Ballyrock (2011)* decisions rejecting the rationale that certain flip clauses were unenforceable *ipso facto* clauses as a matter of US law. An appeal

(*Continued*)

---

[10]In this scenario, any cash flow risk could be addressed through increasing credit enhancement.

to this decision has been lodged and at the time of writing a decision is pending from the District Court in New York

What Comes Next?

These conflicting decisions have generated considerable uncertainty in the market over the enforceability of flip clauses. It is generally considered that the involvement of a US counterparty increases the risk that the flip clause will be deemed invalid. The latest US decision goes some way to dispelling the legal uncertainty and is a welcome development; however it is reasonable to assume that the validity of flip clauses remains a risk that needs to be factored in when structuring a securitisation swap.

CHAPTER 5

Swap Prepayment Risk

Don't cross a river if it is four feet deep on average.

– Nasim Taleb

WHAT IS SWAP PREPAYMENT RISK?

Prepayment is the unscheduled early repayment of principal on a loan, either in part or in full. Most prepayment is characterised by repayment in full when borrowers refinance their loan with another lender at a more favourable rate or sell the underlying asset that is the subject of the loan. *Prepayment risk* is the associated risk for the lender generated by that unscheduled early payment. The associated risks are twofold, namely that (i) a lower-than-expected profit was made on the loan due to the truncated stream of interest payments; and (ii) when the returned principal is re-invested in new loans, there is a risk that loan pricing has tightened and margins have fallen. Most lenders attempt to manage prepayment risk via retention strategies, which can include a range of reactive and proactive activities from targeted rate reductions to predictive analytics. In some jurisdictions and asset classes, prepayment penalties may exist and these can have a significant impact on prepayment behaviour.

Prepayment behaviour depends very significantly on the available incentives and disincentives borrowers have available to them. These can vary widely across countries, asset classes and even lenders. In this book, as far as prepayment risk is concerned, we focus solely on loan markets that are predominantly floating rate. This includes residential mortgage and auto loan markets in the UK, Australia and New Zealand. The residential mortgage market in the USA is predominantly fixed rate and therefore works very differently – in particular due to the correlation between prepayment rates and interest rates. In floating-rate markets, this correlation is much weaker and, for the purposes of modelling *swap* prepayment risk, can be ignored, which simplifies the modelling process.

When loans are securitised, the prepayment risk is transferred into the loan pool and averaged out across the entire pool, before being transformed in the cash flow waterfall and then passed on to investors in the asset-backed debt that is issued. Therefore, depending on the nature of the cash flow transformation, the end investor may also be subject to prepayment risk. Investors, rating agencies, arrangers and originators all seek to understand the expected future prepayment rate for a particular asset class and loan pool. The most common approach is to look at a time series of historically realised prepayment rates from the same asset class and lender. If the historical prepayment rates are sufficiently stable and if the lender's origination strategy is consistent, one may infer that the future prepayment rates will be the same as in the past. Although very simple, this approach often works well and is standard across the industry.

It is important to note that prepayment risk is unhedgeable because there are no instruments that can be used to hedge it. There are no prepayment futures – nor will there ever be – since there would need to be a separate futures contract for every loan pool or lender to ensure a proper hedge. It's hard to see the incentives for other participants to assume offsetting risk positions in such a futures market. This means the only plausible hedge is the same physical securitised notes that the swap provider is swapping. Yet those notes are either all issued to investors (or they wouldn't need to be swapped) or, if they are in an equivalent domestic currency tranche, also illiquid, as they are generally held to term by investors and hence unsuitable for hedging. The upshot is that there are no instruments available to hedge prepayment risk with.

Swap prepayment risk is a significantly more complicated form of prepayment risk. When a swap provider swaps securitisation cash flows from one currency to another or from floating to fixed interest payments, it is additionally exposed to changes in market rates. Changes in interest rates, single- and cross-currency basis and foreign exchange (FX) rates can greatly magnify the impact of prepayment and careful modelling to quantify and manage this risk is required. The good news is that the significant effort required to model swap prepayment risk yields up valuable insights and can provide a solid foundation for pricing swaps with prepayment risk. Swaps with prepayment risk are generally known as *balance guarantee swaps* (BGSs).

Because prepayment risk is unhedgeable, BGS modelling must be performed under a combined real-world/risk-neutral approach. The prepayment process is calibrated to historical data, while the other market variables can be calibrated in the usual risk-neutral way to market instruments. This is discussed in the sub-section on Working with a Mixed Measure. Modelling BGSs involves stepping through time and calculating how much swap re-hedging may be required at each step. As a result, prepayment volatility is just as important as the level of prepayment due to its impact on the quantum of swap re-hedging. In a similar way that higher equity volatility increases the price of a stock option, so too does higher prepayment volatility increase the price of a BGS.

The Expected Swap Schedule

When modelling swap prepayment risk, it is critical to obtain the *pool cut*, that is, the loan-level data for the securitised pool. This is a spreadsheet where each row describes every relevant parameter of a loan: the interest rate, the maturity date, the asset being financed and so on. These are always made available to investors and rating agencies and, in some jurisdictions, *must* be periodically reported to a regulator and investors in a standardised format after issuance. The pool cut is critical for swap providers too, for the following reasons:

1. *Constructing the expected amortisation.* This is the initial data from which the expected pool amortisation profile is built. One starts by applying the formula in Eq. (3.1) in Chapter 3 to each individual loan, then, for each loan period, summing all loans to obtain the overall pool schedule. Care must be taken for variant cases; for example, for interest only (IO) loans there will be no amortisation during the IO period. Cohorts may also be defined; for example, fixed-rate loans may have a different (lower) prepayment assumption than floating-rate loans if there is a prepayment penalty applicable. If one wishes, one can set $p = 0$ in Eq. (3.1) in Chapter 3 when computing each loan amortisation. In that case, a non-zero prepayment rate will need to be applied to the aggregated, contracted pool schedule. This is computed as follows:

$$\widehat{P}_i = \widehat{P}_{i-1} \frac{P_i}{P_{i-1}} .(1 - p)^{\tau_i} \tag{5.1}$$

where P_i is the ith scheduled principal with zero prepayment and $\widehat{P}_i$ is the ith principal with non-zero prepayment.

2. *Insight.* The pool cut provides visibility over any loan concentrations or about risks, which the swap provider will want to know. It is also key data for the pre-deal due diligence process. For example, if there is a significant cohort of loans with teaser rates and those teaser rates expire at clustered points in time, then one can expect spikes in prepayment rates around such times.

Once the expected pool amortisation profile is built, the expected *tranche* amortisation profile can be built by overlaying the cash flow waterfall. This anticipated tranche amortisation profile is the initial expected principal schedule for a BGS over that tranche.

Where possible, it is always a good idea for the swap provider and the arranger to work closely when modelling and structuring a BGS. In particular, both parties should agree with precision on fundamentals such as the zero prepayment tranche amortisation profile and weighted average life (WAL). The arranger and originator are always on the front-line of awareness of real-world issues that may impact the expected amortisation schedule and the swap provider really needs to ensure it is in the loop. If the expected swap amortisation profile is not quite right, it will undoubtedly result in a re-hedge, which may be costly. A simple example is as follows. Pools are usually cut weeks, and sometimes months, prior to issuance from standalone structures. This allows the rating agencies time to rate the issuance and investors time to conduct due diligence. During this time, the loans will generate principal receipts, which are held on deposit for the benefit of the special purpose vehicle (SPV), rather than repatriated to the originator. When the SPV issues notes, those accumulated principal receipts are usually paid to investors at the end of the first coupon period. This shortens the WAL of the notes. A naïve swap provider might simply take the loan-level data and generate a forward amortisation profile from the date of issuance. This would result in over-hedging the BGS with a longer-dated swap.

Computing Historical Prepayment It is crucial to be able to compute historical prepayment rates on loan pools, especially loan pools from the same issuer as a proposed transaction. This is useful for several purposes, namely:

1. To understand qualitative behaviour:
   - Does prepayment ramp-up as the pool age increases?
   - Are there any interesting patterns or trends?
   - How volatile is prepayment?
   - How does one track recent prepayment trends in a live deal?
2. To understand quantitative behaviour:
   - The prepayment time series can be used to calibrate a stochastic prepayment model (see the section on Monte Carlo Modelling of Swap Prepayment Risk) and in particular compute an average prepayment rate and prepayment volatility.
   - Regression analysis or other techniques can be used to model prepayment trends identified in the qualitative analysis, for example, prepayment ramp-up as a function of pool age.
3. For prospective originators:
   - Originators using warehouse funding who have not previously securitised should carefully collate a prepayment history for future use by swap providers and other interested parties. Often such originators, who are typically smaller, are much more diligent about collecting credit data (defaults and arrears) than prepayment data.

To compute historical prepayment for a particular payment period i, one needs the scheduled principal amount P_i and the actual principal amount $\hat{P}_i$, which includes any prepayments. From this basic information, one computes the *single period mortality rate* (SPM):

$$SPM_i = \frac{P_i - \hat{P}_i}{P_i}$$

In the case where the pool amortisation is monthly, this quantity is often referred to in books and articles as the *single monthly mortality rate* (SMM). However, in general, amortisation is not always monthly, but can be quarterly, include irregular 'stub' periods, or of some other tenor. So, it's essential to take a general approach. The annualised equivalent of SPM_i is the constant prepayment rate p, which we will now denote as p_i since this will be the prepayment rate for the ith period. There's nothing constant about prepayment rates in reality, but we refer to p_i as a 'constant prepayment rate' (CPR) since it's the annual equivalent of SPM_i assuming that rate of prepayment was held constant for one year. To annualise SPM_i we use the standard formula:

$$p_i = 1 - (1 - SPM_i)^{1/\tau_i} \qquad (5.2)$$

From here it is straightforward to construct historical time series, so long as the contracted zero prepayment schedule is available.

Balance Guarantee Swaps

A BGS is a particular type of securitisation swap that is subject to swap prepayment risk. A swap over asset-backed securities (ABS) or residential mortgage-backed securities (RMBS) tranche that is either pass-through or controlled amortisation is a BGS. Covered bond swaps, which are always issued as bullets, and soft bullet swaps from ABS or RMBS, are *not* BGS as they have guaranteed zero-amortisation bullet schedules unless and until they extend, at which point they may then become a BGS.

It is worth being very explicit about how a BGS works and what the swap provider's legal obligations are. There are two cases here: a cross-currency BGS and a single-currency BGS. For liability swaps, the former is more common than the latter.

A cross-currency BGS obliges the swap provider to swap the cash flows it receives in one currency (the loan currency) to another currency (the currency of the note issued to investors) at a fixed exchange rate until the final cash flow. In particular, if the swap provider receives more or less cash than expected in a given period, it must convert the amount of cash it receives into investor currency at that fixed exchange rate. The swap provider neither tops up shortfalls nor has the right to take possession of 'overs'. It simply swaps whatever it receives. Most cross-currency BGSs swap floating cash flows in one currency to floating cash flows in another, but some also involve swapping to fixed cash flows if that's what investors want.

A single-currency BGS obliges the swap provider to swap the floating (fixed) cash flows it receives into fixed (floating) cash flows in the same currency. There is no exposure to FX or cross-currency basis, but rather an interest rate risk exposure and, possibly, a single-currency basis exposure.

A swap provider will typically hedge a BGS with a vanilla amortising swap whose principal schedule initially matches the expected amortisation profile of the tranche being swapped (see Figure 5.1). As time unfolds, if the BGS amortisation differs significantly from the hedge, the swap provider's BGS trader will adjust the hedge. A small misalignment can be tolerated, but larger misalignments will generate

FIGURE 5.1   Typical hedging arrangement of a BGS.

material Value-at-Risk (VaR) and market risk capital costs, and potentially tilt trading book risk positions in unwanted directions. Modelling the whole-of-life expected re-hedging cost is key to the correct pricing of BGSs.

Re-Hedging

The fundamental principle for pricing derivatives is that *the cost of replicating the derivative is the fair value price of the derivative*. This principle is founded on a no-arbitrage assumption: if the price of a derivative was different to the cost of replication then one could lock in a riskless profit by going long (short) the derivative and going short (long) the replicating portfolio. Assuming that a riskless profit (arbitrage) is impossible enforces the equality of the fair value derivative price with the cost of replication.

Because prepayment risk is unhedgeable, the hard-and-fast rule described above needs some modification to be applicable. But the basic idea is still relevant to the pricing of swap prepayment risk. In particular, we can 'replicate' a BGS by assuming a dynamic re-hedging strategy with vanilla swaps, which can be modelled via a Monte Carlo simulation. The cost of this re-hedging strategy is the prepayment risk charge.[1]

Note that the previous sentence used the term 'cost' and not 'expected cost'. The reason is that since prepayment risk is unhedgeable, the expected cost may be insufficient in certain prepayment scenarios. Therefore the 'cost' should include some form of risk buffer to cover such eventualities, up to some statistical tolerance. (Try telling a BGS trader who has just lost money on a series of re-hedges that the modelling based on *expected* value is correct!) The sizing of this risk buffer depends on the risk appetite of each swap provider and the competitive pressures in the BGS market. Hence it is very much a real-world price, but computed using familiar risk-neutral techniques.

Before covering the detail of Monte Carlo simulations in the section on Monte Carlo Modelling of Swap Prepayment Risk, it is highly instructive to examine a single re-hedging event in isolation. In particular we will compute the mark-to-market (MTM) of a *portfolio* of two swaps: a cross-currency BGS and its hedge (a vanilla amortising cross-currency swap) at the beginning and end of a single swap period. At

---

[1]The full price of a BGS will also include other charges such as execution costs and XVAs. See the section on Pricing in Chapter 8 for further details on how all-in swap prices are put together.

this stage, we will compute the MTM of the BGS assuming it is a vanilla swap. The cumulative re-hedge costs exposed in this calculation will be included in the full-blown BGS valuation derived in the section on Monte Carlo Modelling of Swap Prepayment Risk. At the end of this sub-section we will repeat the calculation for a single-currency BGS.

Cross-Currency Float/Float BGS   At time t_0 the MTM to the swap provider of the BGS in the loan currency L is:

$$MTM^L_{BGS}(t_0) = \sum_{i=0}^{n-1} P^L_i.(f^L_i + m^L + b^L + s).\tau^L_i.DF^L_{i+1} - P^L_0.DF^L_0 + \sum_{i=1}^{n} \Delta P^L_i.DF^L_i$$

$$+ P^L_n.DF^L_n - fx.\left[\sum_{i=0}^{n-1} P^B_i.(f^B_i + m^B + b^B).\tau^B_i.DF^B_{i+1} - P^B_0.DF^B_0 \right.$$

$$\left. + \sum_{i=1}^{n} \Delta P^B_i.DF^B_i + P^B_n.DF^B_n \right] \tag{5.3}$$

which is a slightly modified form of Eq. (4.2) in Chapter 4, and where we assume both swap legs have the same payment frequency and where:

fx	is the market spot FX rate
P^L_i	is the ith period swap principal in loan currency L
P^B_i	is the ith period swap principal in bond currency B where $P^B_i.fx_{swap} = P^L_i$. We assume[2] that $fx_{swap} = fx(t_0)$
$f^{L/B}_i$	is the ith forward rate in loan/bond currency respectively
$m^{L/B}$	is the inception cross-currency basis margin in loan/bond currency respectively
b^B	is the bond coupon (in bond currency)
b^L	is the *swapped* bond coupon (in loan currency), i.e. the fair value margin that solves:[3]

$$\sum_{i=0}^{n-1} P^L_i.b^L.\tau^L_i.DF^L_{i+1} = fx.\sum_{i=0}^{n-1} P^B_i.b^B.\tau^B_i.DF^B_{i+1}$$

s	is additional fixed swap costs (including XVA and profit spread) charged by the swap provider
$\tau^{L/B}_i$	is the year fraction for the ith period in loan/bond currency[4] respectively
$DF^{L/B}_i$	is the (basis-adjusted) discount factor from time t_i in loan/bond currency respectively

---

[2]In reality the swap fx rate may be slightly different to the prevailing spot fx rate to ensure a rounded face value of the notional principal. Using a moderately off-market fx rate for the swap results in slightly modified swap margins.

[3]Re-arranging this equation gives the value for b^L as the ratio of PV01s of each swap leg.

[4]Although we assume that both swap legs have the same payment frequency, the day count may be different.

The first term in the MTM Eq. (5.3) is the stream of received interest payments. The second and sixth terms are the initial principal exchange; the third and seventh terms are the intermediate principal exchanges; and the fourth and eighth terms are the final principal exchange. The fifth term is the stream of paid interest payments, hence it doesn't include the fixed swap cost term s, which is only received, not paid, by the swap provider.

The MTM of the hedging swap is very similar except that (i) it is reverse-polarity, that is, the loan (bond) currency is now paid (received) instead of received (paid); and (ii) for simplicity we assume $s = 0$.[5] Consequemtly, the portfolio MTM will result in cancellation of all terms except the swap cost s term, that is:

$$MTM^L_{Portfolio}(t_0) = MTM^L_{BGS}(t_0) + MTM^L_{Hedge}(t_0) = \sum_{i=0}^{n-1} P^L_i.s.\tau^L_i.DF^L_{i+1} = s.P^L_0.\overline{WAL}$$
(5.4)

where $\overline{WAL}$ is very similar to the WAL defined in Eq. (3.4) in Chapter 3, except that the outstanding principal is *discounted* to the valuation date and the year fractions τ^L_i may be in a different day count to actual/actual.

In the absence of re-hedging costs, a slower prepayment rate that increases $\overline{WAL}$ would be good for the swap provider as it increases the portfolio MTM (the profit component of s is received for a longer period of time). However, in reality, the re-hedging costs can be very significant.

The MTM of the portfolio at the end of the first payment period (time t_1) is the sum of the MTMs of the BGS, the initial hedge transacted at time t_0 and the new hedge transacted at time t_1.

$$MTM^L_{Portfolio}(t_1) = MTM^L_{BGS}(t_1) + MTM^L_{Old\ Hedge}(t_1) + MTM^L_{New\ Hedge}$$

The principal schedule of the BGS at time t_1 will be different from Eq. (5.4) because prepayment will have changed the expected future principal schedule. We denote the new, updated principal schedules with an overbar $\overline{P}$ and leave the original principal schedules denoted as before without the overbar. Likewise, the new time t_1 spot FX rate and cross-currency basis margin m will have an overbar whereas the original quantities from time t_0 will not. The new hedge is only required to hedge the *difference* in the old and the new principal schedules and has an initial MTM of zero (ignoring transaction costs). We assume that the new hedge uses the initial BGS FX rate, rather than the prevailing market FX rate at t_1. This can be achieved by modifying the new basis margin $\overline{m}^L$ such that the new hedge still values to par at inception.

---

[5] A fully collateralised interbank vanilla swap will have low XVA charges.

We define $\delta P_i = \overline{P}_i - P_i$ to be the principal schedule for the new hedge. We therefore have:

$$MTM^L_{Portfolio}(t_1)$$

$$= \sum_{i=1}^{n-1} \overline{P^L_i}.(f^L_i + m^L + b^L + s).\tau^L_i.DF^L_{i+1} + \sum_{i=1}^{n} \overline{\Delta P^L_i}.DF^L_i + \overline{P^L_n}.DF^L_n$$

$$- \overline{fx}.\left[\sum_{i=1}^{n-1} \overline{P^B_i}.(f^B_i + m^B + b^B).\tau^B_i.DF^B_{i+1} + \sum_{i=1}^{n} \overline{\Delta P^B_i}.DF^B_i + \overline{P^B_n}.DF^B_n \right]$$

$$- \sum_{i=1}^{n-1} P^L_i.(f^L_i + m^L + b^L).\tau^L_i.DF^L_{i+1} - \sum_{i=1}^{n} \Delta P^L_i.DF^L_i - P^L_n.DF^L_n$$

$$+ \overline{fx}.\left[\sum_{i=1}^{n-1} P^B_i.(f^B_i + m^B + b^B).\tau^B_i.DF^B_{i+1} + \sum_{i=1}^{n} \Delta P^B_i.DF^B_i + P^B_n.DF^B_n \right]$$

$$- \sum_{i=1}^{n-1} \delta P^L_i.(f^L_i + \overline{m^L} + b^L).\tau^L_i.DF^L_{i+1} - \sum_{i=1}^{n} \Delta \delta P^L_i.DF^L_i - \delta P^L_n.DF^L_n$$

$$+ \overline{fx}.\left[\sum_{i=1}^{n-1} \delta P^B_i.(f^B_i + \overline{m^B} + b^B).\tau^B_i.DF^B_{i+1} + \sum_{i=1}^{n} \Delta \delta P^B_i.DF^B_i + \delta P^B_n.DF^B_n \right]$$

Fortunately this rather voluminous equation condenses down to just four terms via cancellation, re-arrangement and use of the terms $\delta m = \overline{m} - m$ and $\delta fx = \overline{fx} - fx$:

$$MTM^L_{Portfolio}(t_1) = s.\sum_{i=1}^{n-1} \overline{P^L_i}.\tau^L_i.DF^L_{i+1} - \delta m^L.\sum_{i=1}^{n-1} \delta P^L_i.\tau^L_i.DF^L_{i+1}$$

$$- \frac{\delta fx}{fx}.\sum_{i=1}^{n-1} \delta P^L_i.(f^B_i + b^B).\tau^B_i.DF^B_{i+1} + \left(\overline{m^B} - \frac{\overline{fx}}{fx}m^B \right).\sum_{i=1}^{n-1} \delta P^L_i.\tau^B_i.DF^B_{i+1} \qquad (5.5)$$

The first term is equivalent to $s.\overline{P^L_0}.\overline{WAL}$ as per Eq. (5.4) and is the only term that doesn't include a δP^L_i term. It is the gross swap revenue in the absence of any changes in the principal schedule (caused by prepayment risk). If the principal schedule didn't change between time t_0 and t_1 – that is, if $\delta P^L_i = 0$ – then all the remaining terms in Eq. (5.5) would disappear.

The δP_i^L terms are all multiplied by $\overline{\delta fx}$ and δm terms. We therefore see that prepayment 'switches on' the portfolio sensitivity to market movements. If the principal schedule didn't change, the swap provider would be immune to market movements since the inception hedge would continue to provide a perfect offset.

In the section on Monte Carlo Modelling of Swap Prepayment Risk we will model prepayment, basis, FX and interest rates as (correlated) stochastic variables. In this setting, the expected value of Eq. (5.5) over time is the *prepayment risk charge*, that is, the total expected cost of re-hedging due to prepayment risk. Equation (5.5) is thus the elemental foundation for the Monte Carlo calculation of prepayment. This expectation must be calculated via a Monte Carlo simulation as no tractable closed-form approach exists in general.

Using the definition of $\overline{WAL}$ and defining $\delta \overline{WAL} := \frac{1}{P_1^L} \sum_{i=1}^{n-1} \delta P_i^L . \tau_i^L . DF_{i+1}^L$, one may re-write Eq. (5.5) more transparently as:

$$MTM_{Portfolio}^L(t_1) = s.\overline{P_1^L}.\overline{WAL} - \overline{P_1^L}.\delta \overline{WAL}. \left[\overline{\delta m^L} - \overline{m^B} + \frac{\delta fx}{fx}.(\overbrace{f^B} + b^B + m^B) \right]$$

(5.6)

Equation (5.6) is extremely useful for three different purposes.

Firstly, Eq. (5.6) can be used to roughly size the prepayment risk charge. Ignoring all other swap costs (execution, XVA etc) and solving $MTM = 0$ for s results in:

$$s = \frac{\delta \overline{WAL}}{\overline{WAL}}. \left[\overline{\delta m^L} - \overline{m^B} + \frac{\delta fx}{fx}.(\overbrace{f^B} + b^B + m^B) \right]$$

EXAMPLE 5.1:

Consider a BGS on an RMBS tranche with an expected WAL of 3.0 years and a prepayment history that could change that WAL by 0.3 years to some (high) statistical degree of confidence. Suppose further that *jointly* to that same degree of confidence $\delta m^L \approx 0.10\%$, $\delta fx/fx \approx 0.2$, $\overbrace{f^B} + b^B \approx 4.0\%$ and $m^B \equiv 0$ (e.g. the bond currency is USD). Then the prepayment risk charge $s \approx 0.09\%$ or 9 basis points in markets parlance. Note that it is the *joint probability* of all these WAL and market moves happening *simultaneously* to that same required statistical degree of confidence.

Secondly, Eq. (5.6) can also be used to roughly value the benefit of different structuring options. Suppose that a different RMBS cash flow waterfall can reduce the prepayment risk such that the change in WAL to a given statistical degree of confidence is only 0.1 years, rather than 0.3 years. In that case the prepayment risk charge will be reduced to 3 basis points. If it costs less than 6 basis points to make the structural change to the RMBS cash flow waterfall, then it is worth doing to lower the overall landed cost of funds for the originator. Of course, this is all ballpark and a full-blown Monte Carlo engine is required for accurate pricing. But the art of structuring is greatly improved by useful 'rules of thumb', which can provide efficient guidance towards more promising structures and away from costly ones.

Thirdly, Eq. (5.6) provides simple risk management guidance on which combination of simultaneous changes of risk factors cause gains and losses. For example, if prepayment is slower than expected (so that $\delta \overline{WAL} > 0$) then $\delta m^L > 0$ will generate a loss whilst $\delta m^L < 0$ will generate a profit, all other things being equal. This is essential knowledge for BGS traders and their market risk overseers. Equation (5.6) also allows one to think about wrong-way risk. For example, if a currency pair is a risk currency pair, such as AUD/USD, then one might expect a large fall in prepayment to occur concurrently with a large fall in AUD/USD. Given that prepayment risk is unhedgeable, these considerations are well worth deliberating before executing a BGS. In a similar vein, Eq. (5.6) can give insight into the potential diversification benefits of running a multi-currency BGS book.

Single-Currency Fixed/Float BGS Here we derive the equivalent of Eq. (5.6) for a swap that receives floating and pays fixed in the same currency. This models the case of a liability swap where the SPV's floating cash flows need to be converted for a fixed-rate bond issuance in the same currency. One might also consider a receive fixed/pay floating BGS, which is often the case for an asset swap where fixed-rate loans are converted to floating rate. In this case one can simply switch the signs of all the terms in the equation except the first term.

Instead of repeating the entire calculation for the cross-currency BGS, we simply observe that one can set $fx = 1$; $\delta fx = 0$; $f_i^B = 0$; $b^B = 0$; and set $m^B \equiv F$ where F is the fixed rate paid by the swap provider on the fixed leg of the swap. With these settings made and dropping the superscript L (since it's a single-currency swap with both legs expressed in loan currency) we have:

$$MTM_{Portfolio}(t_1) = s.\overline{P_1}.\overline{WAL} - \overline{P_1}.\delta\overline{WAL}.(\delta m + \delta F) \tag{5.7}$$

where $\delta F = \overline{F} - F$. The δF term represents interest rate risk. Unlike the cross-currency case, where no cross-currency swaption market exists, single-currency BGS may be hedged, albeit imperfectly, with swaptions. This will be discussed further in the section on Greeks, Hedging and VaR.

As per the cross-currency case, one can compute the breakeven value of s to roughly size the prepayment risk change.

EXAMPLE 5.2:

Consider the same case as above where an RMBS tranche with an expected WAL of 3.0 years and a prepayment history that could change that WAL by 0.3 years to some (high) statistical degree of confidence. Suppose further that *jointly* to that same degree of confidence $\delta m \approx 0.10\%$ and $\delta F \approx 0.30\%$. Then the prepayment risk charge $s \approx 0.04\%$ or 4 basis points. It is unsurprising that the prepayment charge on an 'equivalent' single-currency BGS is considerably less than for the cross-currency case due to the absence of FX risk.

There are numerous highly-rated banks globally that do not seem to have developed the capability to price swap prepayment risk. One occasionally hears comments that certain traders or desk heads are very uncomfortable with any type of swap principal dynamics (although those same desks may trade other 'standard' products with a great deal of optionality, such as Bermudan swaptions, without any comparable angst). This is a curious view as some relatively straightforward calculations can size the price for the risk, to a chosen level of statistical confidence.

What Factors Drive Prepayment Rates?

Since prepayment risk is a key driver of securitisation swap pricing, it is important to understand which exogenous factors impact its level and volatility. Prepayment dynamics vary enormously across different asset classes and also across countries within the same asset class. Despite these differences, there are often common factors at play, although the manner in which these factors influence prepayment, and the amount of influence, varies considerably. These factors are worth knowing for qualitative risk management, modelling the expected trajectory around which the probabilistic model will be built and for (re)calibrating model parameters at inception and through the life of a deal. The list is as follows:

1. *Seasoning*. This is the length of time since a loan was originated. For an entire loan pool, the weighted average seasoning (and its distribution) is the relevant factor. Prepayment rates are usually low for a new loan: no-one enters into a loan with the intention of prepaying immediately. The incidence of prepayment increases as loans become more seasoned. For residential mortgages, this can be because the borrowers may need to relocate as their circumstances change over time, or they may decide to refinance loans as market conditions change. These changes can take time to materialise. After longer periods of time, prepayment rates may fall somewhat as everyone who was predisposed to prepaying has done so, leaving more static borrowers in the pool. This phenomenon is known as *burnout*.

2. *Interest rates*. Interest rates can impact prepayment rates in a variety of ways. In fixed-rate markets without prepayment penalties, such as the USA, there is a substantial negative correlation between interest rates and prepayment rates, as there is strong incentive to refinance as rates fall. But even in predominantly floating-rate markets interest rates can be relevant. For example, it has been observed that *partial* prepayments can rise as interest rates fall, as some borrowers keep their monthly repayments constant (see Daniel (2008)), either by choice or default. The slope of the yield curve, or borrower's expectations of future interest rates, can cause borrowers to enter into fixed-rate loans, which can have lower prepayment rates when accompanied by a prepayment penalty (swap break cost).

3. *Alternative investment yields*. It has been observed in floating-rate markets that partial prepayments are less likely when alternative investment opportunities, such as equity markets, are performing strongly (see Daniel (2008)).

4. *Seasonality*. Relocation has been observed to be more likely during summer months than winter months.

5. *Interest rate volatility*. A more uncertain outlook for interest rates, especially with an increased potential for rate rises, can influence borrowers to pay down debt earlier.

Although these factors can be readily identified, their use in models does not guarantee an anywhere near accurate prediction of future prepayment rates. Furthermore, as we will see in the sub-section on Reducing Prepayment Volatility via Diversification, larger loan pools have lower prepayment volatility due to the impact of diversification. Whilst this is unsurprising, it does mean that smaller loan pools will have more 'noise', making accurate modelling of future monthly prepayment rates even less likely.

For *swap* prepayment risk, one needs to be very wary of incorporating too much model risk from complex underlying prepayment models. If a complex and possibly over-fitted prepayment model doesn't work in practice, the re-hedging costs may be considerable. Therefore, the approach we will take in the section on Monte Carlo Modelling of Swap Prepayment Risk is to develop a simple model, based on an expected trajectory of prepayment surrounded by a reasonable distribution of possible prepayment outcomes. This is arguably more robust and useful given that prepayment risk cannot be hedged.

MONTE CARLO MODELLING OF SWAP PREPAYMENT RISK

In this section we will develop a Monte Carlo model to price the expected value of Eq. (5.6) and hence compute the prepayment risk charge. In the sub-section on Working with a Mixed Measure we show that we can work under a so-called *mixed measure*, which is simultaneously real world for unhedgeable risk factors and risk-neutral for tradable ones. In the sub-sections on Modelling Prepayment and Modelling the Market Risk Factors we propose particular stochastic models for each risk factor and discuss calibration. The overall simulation methodology is described in the sub-section on Simulation Methodology.

Working with a Mixed Measure

As mentioned at the outset, swap prepayment risk is unhedgeable. On the other hand, the market factors that are just as important in BGS valuation – FX, basis and interest rates – are indeed hedgeable. As a result, one is compelled to consider a modelling approach that mixes both real-world and risk-neutral measures.

As a practical matter this is straightforward to implement. One uses historically estimated parameters for modelling prepayment risk and market observable parameters for modelling the hedgeable risk factors. However, it is more than an interesting theoretical aside to know that this approach can be justified with rigour, as we will build the entire prepayment model on this premise. The following argument justifying this approach is attributed to Alan Brace (2015)[6] and is included for readers with a sufficiently high level of familiarity with stochastic calculus:

Step 1. Recap of the standard risk-neutral argument for pricing. Consider a risky asset S_t and bond B_t which are both freely tradable. Suppose their dynamics under the real-world measure $\mathbb{P}$ are given by $dS_t = S_t(\lambda dt + \alpha dW_t^1)$ and $dB_t = rB_t dt$. Let the self-financing process $V_t = \varphi_t^1 S_t + \varphi_t^2 B_t$ replicate the present value of an attainable claim C_t with payoff $C_T = C(T, S_T)$ at time T. Defining the discounted processes $S_t^* = S_t/B_t$ and $V_t^* = V_t/B_t$ and applying Itô's lemma to dV_t gives $dV_t^* = \varphi_t^1 S_t^*$. Therefore if S_t^* is a martingale under an equivalent measure $\mathbb{Q}$, then V_t^* must also be a $\mathbb{Q}$-martingale and hence so is the present value of the claim, that is, $C_t = B_t \mathbf{E}_\mathbf{Q}\left[\frac{C_T}{B_T}|F\right]$. By Girsanov's theorem the change of measure from $\mathbb{P}$ to $\mathbb{Q}$ is given by $dW_t^1 = dW_t^1 - \frac{r-\lambda}{\alpha}dt$.

Step 2. Extension to unhedgeable risk factors. Now consider pricing $C_T = C(T, S_T, X_T)$ where the risky factor X_t is not traded and has the dynamics under the real-world measure $\mathbb{P}$ given by

$$dS_t = S_t(\lambda dt + \alpha dW_t^1)$$

$$dX_t = X_t(\mu dt + \beta[\rho dW_t^1 + \sqrt{1 - \rho^2}dW_t^2])$$

$$dB_t = rB_t dt \tag{$*$}$$

---

[6]*Mixing real and arbitrage free measures*, private correspondence (2015). The authors are grateful to Alan Brace for permitting its reproduction in this book.

where $W_t = (W_t^1, W_t^2)$ is a 2-dimensional Brownian motion and the returns have correlation ρ i.e. $\frac{d\langle S,X\rangle_t}{S_t X_t} = \alpha\beta\rho dt$. It can be shown (full details in Brace (2015)) that by discretising the processes, replicating C_T with a *non-self-financing* process V_t and using least squares to minimise the future risk exposure over each time step yields two equations that, by backward recursion, results in $V_t^* = C(t, S_t, X_t)/B_t$. Furthermore, if S_t^* is a $\mathbb{Q}$ – martingale then the least squares equations imply that V_t^* is also a $\mathbb{Q}$ – martingale. Hence $C_t = B_t\mathbf{E_Q}\left[\frac{C(T,S_T,X_T)}{B_T}|F\right]$ just as in step 1. A change to the measure $\mathbb{Q}$ equivalent to $\mathbb{P}$ defined by $d\widehat{W}_t = dW_t - \frac{r-\lambda}{\alpha}\left[1, \frac{-\rho}{\sqrt{1-\rho^2}}\right]^T dt$ converts the Eq. (*) under the real-world measure $\mathbb{P}$ to

$$dS_t = S_t(rdt + \alpha d\widehat{W}_t^1)$$

$$dX_t = X_t(\mu dt + \beta[\rho d\widehat{W}_t^1 + \sqrt{1-\rho^2}d\widehat{W}_t^2])$$

under $\mathbb{Q}$ and maintains the drift, volatility and correlation (μ, β, ρ) parameters of the untraded risk factor X_t. So, although $\mathbb{Q}$ is a martingale measure for S_t^*, it uses statistically calibrated parameters estimated under the real-world measure $\mathbb{P}$ for X_t. We can regard $C_t = B_t\mathbf{E_Q}\left[\frac{C(T,S_T,X_T)}{B_T}|F\right]$ as *the price* since it gives a unique number, returns the statistics of non-traded variables and correctly prices claims on tradable assets.

Note that there are other useful references related to this topic, including Takehashi (2005) and Staum (2008).

Modelling Prepayment

There are actually *two* types of prepayment that need to be modelled. The first prepayment process models the *realised prepayment* rates, which are periodically reported by the ABS or RMBS trust (typically monthly or quarterly). These prepayment rates are backward-looking and report the actual level of prepayment realised in the pool over the previous reporting period. This realised prepayment rate process is used in the Monte Carlo simulation to model the principal amortisation at the very next swap payment date. Realised prepayment rates are historically observable and historical time series can be used to calibrate an appropriately chosen stochastic process to model prepayment.

The second type of prepayment process that needs to be modelled is the *expected average prepayment* rate. This is used to generate the entirety of expected future amortisation schedule beyond the next swap payment date, all the way out to legal final maturity (LFM). This prepayment process is completely unobservable in the real world. However, it is a critical component of the model since changes in the expected future schedule are precisely what drive the re-hedging costs, which generate the prepayment risk charge.

Each type of prepayment process requires different analysis and choices.

Realised Prepayment Because it is readily observed, modelling realised prepayment is an exercise in finding a stochastic process that mimics reality. The best choice is the simplest one that fully captures the salient behaviour. A standard stochastic process in finance is *geometric Brownian motion* (GBM), which is used to model, amongst many other things, stock prices and other risky assets in the Black-Scholes framework. GBM does not qualitatively mimic realised prepayment very well, as it can drift off to unrealistically high or low values, which is not observed behaviour. This is easily corrected by including *mean reversion* into the model. Mean reversion pulls paths back to an expected value if they drift too far away. The simplest mean-reverting stochastic process is the Ornstein-Uhlenbeck (OU) process, which has the stochastic differential equation (SDE):

$$dx_t = -k(x_t - \mu)dt + \sigma dW_t \tag{5.8}$$

with solution:

$$x_t = \mu + e^{-kt}\left[x_0 - \mu + \sigma\sqrt{\frac{e^{2kt} - 1}{2k}}N(0, 1)\right] \tag{5.9}$$

The parameter μ is the long-term mean, σ is the volatility, k is the rate of mean reversion and $N(0,1)$ is a standard normal deviate. Figure 5.2 shows what an OU process looks like and why it is a good model for prepayment risk. Each Monte Carlo path in Figure 5.2 uses the same random number sequence, the same long-term mean and the same volatility – the only difference between the various paths is their rate of mean reversion k.

Rates of mean reversion in the range of 1–10 qualitatively mimic observed realised prepayment across a range of asset classes as their values don't drift off to unrealistic levels. It is also possible – and simple – to slightly generalise Eq. (5.8) to include a non-constant μ so that a ramp-up in prepayment can be modelled.

In the case of GBM, increasing the volatility will increase the width of the envelope of Monte Carlo paths. In the case of OU, if *both* the volatility and rate of mean reversion are increased in the right way, the width of the envelope of Monte Carlo paths will not increase. Instead, the paths will oscillate more vigorously within the given envelope. This is useful intuition when interpreting the parameters.

Expected Average Prepayment Deciding how to model expected average prepayment is as much art as science, since there is no observable benchmark. There are two extreme cases that illuminate the range of modelling choices. The first case is one of

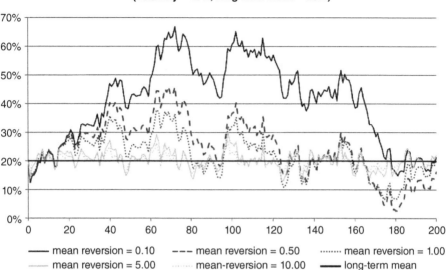

FIGURE 5.2 Using an OU process to model realised prepayment.

invariant prepayment expectations. In this case, the expected average prepayment is set at trade inception and never updated. The only re-hedging costs will be from updating the current principal amount, and the consequential flow-on effects of that update through the rest of the principal schedule. One problem with this approach is that if prepayment relentlessly drifts lower or higher over time, it could be unrealistic not to incorporate that trend. That could always be done by human override – but at that point the BGS valuation may jump dramatically.

The second case is where the expected average prepayment always changes equally with realised prepayment. So, if realised prepayment oscillated between 15% and 25% every period, the expected future prepayment would also oscillate between 15% and 25% every period. The rather obvious problem with this approach is that the WAL of the BGS would oscillate dramatically, with very high re-hedging costs every period, whereas in fact an invariant long-term mean of 20% is spot-on.

A third case, which is in between these two extremes, is to use an exponentially-weighted moving average. This approach gradually incorporates trending realised prepayment, but averages out oscillating realised prepayment. One implementation of this is via the formula

$$p_i^{EA} = \left(1 - \frac{1}{n}\right) p_{i-1}^{EA} + \frac{1}{n} p_i^{R}$$

where p_i^{R} is realised prepayment and p_i^{EA} is expected average prepayment.

The prepayment risk charges generated by these different approaches will be very different. The first case will create the lowest risk charge as it generates the least re-hedging. The second case will generate the highest risk charge as it generates the most re-hedging. The third case is intermediate. Ultimately the choice is a judgement call informed by historical observations, expectations of future behaviour and, for third-party swap providers, how competitive the market BGS pricing is. In theory one could choose another stochastic model entirely, including one which is completely detached from the realised prepayment process. As with any model choice, there need to be good reasons to go with any particular method: *all models are wrong, some models are useful* . . .

Calibration   There are numerous methods for calibrating the three OU parameters μ, σ and k to historical data. Common methods include ordinary least squares (OLS) regression, maximum likelihood estimation (MLE) and moment matching. All methods are imperfect.[7] Good estimation of the rate of mean reversion is the most prone to difficulty as it needs a longer period of time to reduce the estimation error. Nevertheless, one can only use the data that is available, and ensure that it has been *cleaned* (i.e. free of spurious spikes or other data errors). The topic of calibration is extensively covered in the mathematical finance literature. A good source for MLE is Brigo et al. (2007).[8]

OLS is particularly straightforward. The idea is to turn the OU SDE (5.8) into a difference equation

$$x_t - x_{t-1} = -k(x_t - \mu)\Delta t + \sigma\sqrt{\Delta t}W_{t-1} \tag{5.10}$$

which can be compared with a standard linear regression $y = a + bx + \epsilon$. Regressing x_t on $x_t - x_{t-1}$ equating terms and re-arranging gives

$$\mu = \frac{-a}{b} \quad \text{and} \quad k = \frac{-b}{\Delta t}$$

To solve for σ, note that the residuals ϵ are normally distributed with mean zero, hence $\sigma_\epsilon = \sigma\sqrt{\Delta t}\sigma_W = \sigma\sqrt{\Delta t}$ since $\sigma_W = 1$. Hence

$$\sigma = \frac{\sigma_\epsilon}{\sqrt{\Delta t}}.$$

Modelling the Market Risk Factors

With the exception of cross-currency basis risk, there are very standard approaches to modelling the market risk factors of a BGS, hence they only require a short mention.

---

[7] Whichever calibration method is used, it is never a bad idea to optically sanity-check the output parameters by overlying the distributional envelopes of the calibrated process on top of the real data and subjectively assessing the fit.

[8] See [BDNT].

Spot FX Spot FX can be modelled as a lognormal process as is market standard for vanilla FX options. Using this model allows for calibration to both the forward FX curve and the implied volatilities of market-quoted FX options. Of course one has to still decide *which* FX options to choose. One good choice would be to try and match the WAL of the BGS with the time-to-expiry of the (at-the-money) FX option, at least if there is decent liquidity in FX options at that tenor.

Interest Rates There are many interest rate models available, from older short-rate models such as Hull–White, to the more complex LIBOR market model, also known as the BGM model.[9] Using BGM is arguably overkill for BGS (and indeed most cross-asset models where parsimony goes a long way). A well-calibrated Hull–White model is sufficient and keeps the implementation as simple as possible. Calibrating to (liquid) swaption expiries close to the expected maturity date of the balance guarantee swap (BGS) is a sensible choice. There are myriad books on modelling interest rate derivatives using Hull–White, for example, Pelsser (2000) is a good reference.

Cross-Currency Basis Unlike interest rates, there is no options market on cross-currency basis, so historical calibration is required. The lack of options market also explains the lack of a market-standard model for stochastic basis. So starting from first principles, and guided once again by parsimony, a simple parallel-shift model rather than a full-term structure model is sufficient.[10] Using an OU process for the basis shifts seems to fit the historical behaviour rather well. When calibrating the shift process, one needs to choose which tenor of cross-currency basis to calibrate to. Choosing a tenor, or weighted average of tenors, close to the WAL of the BGS being priced in a sensible choice as it incorporates the basis volatility such a swap would have experienced historically.

Correlation Correlations between the various market risk factors can be estimated from historical data to be used in the Monte Carlo simulation. The historical correlations between prepayment and each market factor can also be included – although this is usually zero on average (in floating-rate mortgage markets). However, for conservatism, and since both prepayment and correlation cannot be hedged, one may choose to use a non-zero prepayment correlation with one or more market factors to 'bias' the simulation and provide a risk buffer to absorb realised re-hedging costs.

Simulation Methodology

The high-level architecture for the Monte Carlo simulation involves two loops: a loop over simulation paths and, for each path, a time evolution loop. The loop over

---

[9]Brace-Gatarek-Musiela model.
[10]To rigorously justify this for each currency pair, one could conduct a PCA analysis on historical basis curve moves and see that the largest proportion of the variance is explained by parallel shifts.

simulation paths is the *outer loop* and the loop over time is the *inner loop*. If 2,000 paths are run in the simulation, the inner loop will be called 2,000 times.

Time Grid Before the simulation is run, one needs to determine the grid of time steps to be used. This will be the shortest of the BGS swap payment periods across both swap legs, allowing for differing roll frequencies on each BGS swap leg.

Discounting The discounting of cash flows will vary between paths depending on how the yield curves evolve through time along each particular path. It is convenient to use the spot measure, which is a series of 'rolled-up' forward measures. The numeraire associated with the spot measure is a discretely compounding money market account (inclusive of any single- or cross-currency basis adjustments). Put in the simplest terms, this means the realised discount factors are compounded up from the previous step to the next step, that is,

$$DF_{i+1}^{compound} = DF_i^{compound} \times DF_i^{forward\ 1\ step}$$

Future-dated realised cash flows at the simulation date are discounted to the revaluation date by multiplication with this compounded discount factor. Future-dated unrealised cash flows beyond the simulation date are first discounted to the simulation date using the current instance of the yield curve, before being further discounted back to the revaluation date using the compounded discount factor (see Figure 5.3).

Loops When coding the Monte Carlo simulation, one needs the following objects:

- A *market object*. This is a collection of all rates and curves needed to value a swap.
- A *BGS object*. This represents the balance guarantee swap.
- A *hedge object*. This represents the vanilla hedging swap.
- A *results object*. This stores the re-hedging costs and realised cash flows for each time step for each path, which is post-processed after the simulation has run.

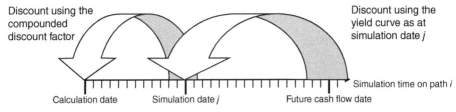

Discount using the compounded discount factor

Discount using the yield curve as at simulation date *j*

Simulation time on path *i*

Calculation date   Simulation date *j*   Future cash flow date

FIGURE 5.3 Discounting cash flows under the spot measure in a Monte Carlo simulation.

Using these objects, the algorithm for the inner loop is as follows:

1. Reset all objects except the results object.
   - Reset the market object to initial market rates and curves (as at the revaluation date).
   - Reset the BGS object to its initial state.
   - Create a new hedge swap that is an at-market (zero MTM), reverse-polarity instance of the BGS with identical principal amortisation.
2. Evolve the market object forward in time to the next time step.
   - Evolve the spot FX rate, interest rates and basis curves.
   - Evolve the realised prepayment process and compute the expected average prepayment.
   - Compute the compounded discount factor.
3. Apply any triggers, step-ups, termination conditions and so on.
   - Check if any trigger conditions are met and change parameters accordingly.
   - If a BGS deal has ended, record the final date in the results object. A deal can end if the principal has amortised to zero, if a call date or call/clean-up condition has been met (and is assumed to be exercised by the issuer) or if LFM has been reached.
4. Generate a new BGS amortisation schedule.
   - Using the updated realised prepayment rate and expected average prepayment rate, compute the new pool amortisation schedule.
   - Apply the cash flow waterfall and generate the tranche amortisation schedule.
5. Rebalance the hedging swap to match the BGS amortisation schedule.
   - Record the MTM of the hedging swap.
   - Change the amortisation schedule of the hedging swap to match the BGS.
6. Record relevant quantities in the results objects.
   - Record the discounted change in MTM of the hedging swap in the results object (re-hedge cost). The bid/offer spread paid to rebalance the hedge can also be recorded as this is an important additional component of the re-hedging cost.
   - Record the discounted realised pay and receive cash flows from both the hedge and the BGS in the results object.
   - Recording the expected WAL, prepayment rate, spot FX rate and other market quantities is also very useful for de-bugging and visualisation (discussed below).
7. Repeat, unless a termination condition was met.

This inner loop is repeated many times when the outer loop is run. The outer loop can run either a pre-defined number of simulations, or can run until a desired level of convergence has been achieved – that is, the standard error of a chosen quantity is less than a specified threshold. This can involve performing some of the post-processing within the outer loop (as opposed to after the outer loop has completed).

Post-Processing After the simulation has concluded, the results object will need to be processed to compute key quantities such as the *prepayment risk charge*, which is the average total discounted re-hedging cost across all paths in the simulation. This can be computed as a dollar charge, or in basis points by averaging the quotient of the total discounted re-hedging cost divided by the value of 1 basis point across all paths.

Re-Hedging Strategy In reality, a trader won't necessarily re-hedge the BGS every swap roll date. There will be some tolerance for misalignment between the hedge and the expected BGS amortisation profile. Such a tolerance could easily be coded into the Monte Carlo simulation. However, re-hedging at every date usually results in the lowest prepayment risk charge (minimum variance hedging). Another difference between reality and the Monte Carlo algorithm above is that a trader will usually transact a new incremental hedge rather than rebalance the old one. The new incremental hedge will have a principal schedule, which is the *difference* between the old and new BGS schedules, and will use the prevailing spot FX rate as the swap FX rate (if the BGS is cross-currency). Modelling an increasing number of incremental hedges in the Monte Carlo simulation would substantially slow down the run time because each swap needs to be revalued at every roll date.

Revolving Pools The simulation methodology above models a closed pool of loans. However, there are good reasons to use this identical methodology for pricing prepayment risk on revolving pools. The addition of both new loan collateral and new tranches is unmodellable and indeed not guaranteed to even occur. So pricing the prepayment risk as if the pool was in 'run-off' is prudent. While master trusts are performing normally, additional loans and tranches are always added in a manner that maintains the risk profile of the existing issuance. (Note that this is not a legal requirement, but rather a commercial one for originators to ensure that rating agencies don't downgrade previous issuance.)

Convergence Usually the prepayment risk charge will converge to an adequate level (i.e. standard error less than 0.25 bps) within 1,000–3,000 paths. Generally, the smaller the prepayment risk charge, the faster the convergence.

Monte Carlo Optimisation As any experienced quant developer will know, there is a well-worn tool-kit of techniques for improving the efficiency of Monte Carlo simulations, and this is essential knowledge for building a robust, production-quality pricer. These techniques include antithetic sampling, using low discrepancy quasi-random numbers and parallelisation of the code. These techniques are comprehensively covered in existing literature – for example, in Jäckel (2002), to which we refer the reader.

Visualisation Tools Cross-asset Monte Carlo models are complex beasts. There is a lot going on under the hood: scalar quantities (spot FX and basis shifts) and vector quantities (interest rates curves and swap principal schedules) are all being evolved. When taking risk, being able to *trust* a model is critical – so how does one know whether everything is behaving as it should?

A simple and powerful way to gain deep insight into the Monte Carlo model is by plotting *time-sliced percentiles* of key metrics. For a given metric, at each simulation time one orders the output across all Monte Carlo paths and measures chosen percentiles, say the 1st, 5th, 25th, 50th, 75th, 95th and 99th. Plotting these percentiles over time untangles the mess of Monte Carlo randomness and shows the trajectory and dispersion of the chosen metric (see Figure 5.4).

Good quantities for visualisation include the realised prepayment rate, the expected WAL of the BGS, the size of the loan pool, the principal of the BGS, spot FX, basis shifts and re-hedging costs. Visual validation that these quantities are evolving as expected – without unexpected bias, error or non-intuitive behaviour – is extremely useful. Sometimes what appears to be a model bias or error turns out to have a simple explanation. For example, plotting the time-sliced percentiles of prepayment rates results in a chart where the 50th percentile drifts down below the OU long-term mean parameter towards the end of a deal. The reason is very simple: paths with higher rates of prepayment pay down faster and have already terminated. Only the longer paths with lower prepayment rates survive towards the end.

Validation In additional to visualisation tools, there are some basic tests one should conduct to validate the Monte Carlo model. The (non-exhaustive) list of simple checks below is hopefully obvious – but worth enumerating to illustrate the validation process:

- Set prepayment volatility to zero. Then the prepayment risk charge should be zero. This is because no re-hedging needs to occur. The swap is a vanilla swap with a deterministic principal schedule.
- Set all market rates and curves to have zero volatility and all curves to be flat. Then the prepayment risk charge should be zero. This is because re-hedging costs are zero (not including bid/offer spread).
- As prepayment volatility increases, the prepayment risk charge should increase. Likewise, as prepayment mean reversion decreases, the prepayment risk charge should increase.
- For a controlled amortisation structure, lowering the long-term mean of the prepayment rate should increase the prepayment risk charge (since it is more likely to go below the breakeven prepayment rate).

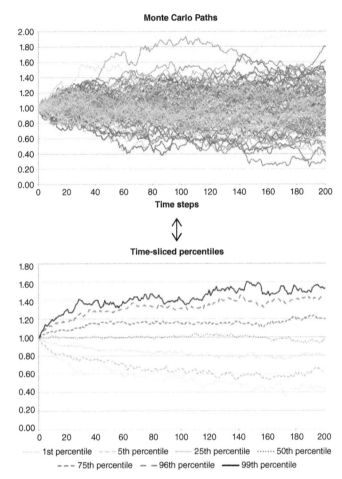

FIGURE 5.4   100 Monte Carlo paths for an arbitrary metric transformed into seven time-sliced percentiles. The metric was evolved as an OU process with a long-term mean of 1.0 a volatility of 10.0% and a rate of mean reversion of 0.05.

- Consider two RMBS tranches with the same WAL and expected amortisation profile. Suppose tranche A begins amortising immediately, whilst tranche B only starts amortising later, once a higher tranche has amortised to zero. The prepayment risk charge of the BGS on tranche B should be higher than for tranche A as the principal schedule has more uncertainty. The extra uncertainty is the variation in the start date, which triggers additional re-hedging costs.

GREEKS, HEDGING AND VAR

Computing Greeks

The greeks are essential hedge statistics and risk management metrics – so knowing how to compute them is an important component of the BGS product build. In general, the computation of greeks via Monte Carlo has been covered extensively in the literature – for example, Jäckel (2002) – and is also the subject of ongoing research in challenging cases (e.g. certain exotic derivatives and derivatives with discontinuous payoffs). We therefore confine this section to a recipe-based summary, which will allow readers to implement BGS greeks in their Monte Carlo pricers.

A very naïve approach to computing the greeks is to simply re-run the Monte Carlo simulation with perturbed market parameters and compute the difference of the perturbed MTM with the unperturbed MTM. This requires a separate Monte Carlo simulation for every greek being computed. The problems with this resimulation approach are that (i) it is computationally intensive and (ii) one is actually differencing the expected value of two distributions – both of which are subject to standard errors – and in fact the result is generally *biased*.

The *pathwise approach* to computing Monte Carlo greeks avoids these two problems, although it only works on continuous payoffs. Introduced by Broadie and Glasserman (1996), the pathwise approach computes greeks as expected values by differencing each path with a perturbed version of itself. The simulation output is a distribution of these pathwise differences, and the average of these is the greek corresponding to the relevant market factor that was perturbed.

Computing pathwise greeks involves modifying the simulation loop outlined in the section on Simulation Methodology. Instead of pricing the BGS with one market object M, one prices the BGS with *multiple* market objects M_i and loops over these in an intermediate loop between inner and outer loops. The index i increments the various different market factors, which are perturbed one at a time (see Table 5.1).

Pathwise differentiation involves pricing the BGS at each time step on each path with respect to each market object M_i. This means the random number sequence is identical for all market objects.

One subtlety is that the prepayment greeks involve pathwise differentiation along paths of potentially different WALs, unlike the other greeks. This can potentially introduce discontinuities. Nevertheless, in the practical implementation of pathwise greeks it is the authors' experience that the prepayment greeks appear validly calculated, without any blow-up problems or excessively large standard errors. It is conceivable that some triggers or waterfall structures could create problems with the pathwise calculation of prepayment greeks due to discontinuities, in which case a more sophisticated, approach to computing Monte Carlo greeks may need to be implemented; see, for example, Chan and Joshi (2013).

TABLE 5.1   An array of market objects used to compute pathwise greeks.

Market object	Description	Greek
M_0	Unperturbed market object	n/a
M_1	FX perturbation: spot rate + 0.01	FX delta
M_2	Loan currency interest rate perturbation: yield curve shift +1 basis point	IR delta
M_3	Bond currency interest rate perturbation: yield curve shift +1 basis point	IR delta
M_4	Loan currency basis perturbation: shift +1 basis point	Basis delta
M_5	Bond currency basis perturbation: shift +1 basis point	Basis delta
M_6	Prepayment long-term mean perturbation: CPR +1%	Prepayment delta
M_7	FX volatility perturbation: vol +1%	FX vega
M_8	Loan currency interest rate volatility perturbation: vol +1%	IR vega
M_9	Bond currency interest rate volatility perturbation: vol +1%	IR vega
M_{10}	Prepayment volatility perturbation: vol +1%	Prepayment vega

Hedging

The greeks give important information about the direction and size of the various risk factors that *could* be used to design a partial hedging strategy. Although prepayment risk is not itself hedgeable, one could choose to hedge the downside risk arising from some or all of the market risk factors such as interest rates or FX. However, this will *always* result in an over-hedge since the upside risk is retained. A simple example illustrates why. Consider a single-currency asset swap where the swap provider receives fixed/pays floating. Table 5.2 shows how the MTM changes as interest rates and prepayment rates move simultaneously (ignoring any profit spread on the asset swap). The last column (hedged BGS MTM) assumes that the BGS is hedged with a receive floating/pay fixed vanilla swap with the initial expected amortisation schedule of the BGS.

Scenarios 3 and 4 generate downside risk. The downside risk in scenario 3 can be mitigated by buying one or more payer swaptions[11] and the downside risk in scenario 4 can be mitigated by buying one or more receiver swaptions. These swaptions will

---

[11] A *payer swaption* gives the holder the right, but not the obligation, to enter into a pay fixed/receive floating swap. Conversely, a *receiver swaption* gives the holder the right, but not the obligation, to enter into a pay floating/receive fixed swap.

TABLE 5.2 Direction and indicative magnitude of MTM movements of an unhedged and a hedged BGS under simultaneous movements of interest rates and prepayment rate.

Scenario	Interest rate move	Prepayment move	Unhedged BGS MTM	Hedged BGS MTM
1	↑	↑	↓	↑
2	↑	↔	↓↓	↔
3	↑	↓	↓↓↓	↓
4	↓	↑	↑	↓
5	↓	↔	↑↑	↔
6	↓	↓	↑↑↑	↑

ideally have amortising swap principals, which may add to their cost. One could buy (i) a strip of co-terminal European swaptions with expiry dates corresponding to BGS roll dates; or (ii) one or more Bermudan swaptions with exercise dates corresponding to BGS roll dates. The size of the swaption principal depends on one's view of how far the prepayment rate can move from the expected level. Scenarios 1 and 6 generate upside risk. However, this upside risk can't be converted into an offsetting received option premium (by selling payer and receiver swaptions) without undoing the risk mitigation for scenarios 3 and 4. As a result, one can really only be unhedged or over-hedged, but never fully hedged. An equivalent argument using FX options applies to cross-currency BGS (although note that there is no options market for cross-currency basis).

Executing a hedging strategy can be expensive. Conversely, not hedging can also be expensive in very adverse prepayment scenarios! However, for prepayment scenarios that don't exceed the extreme end of expectations, the prepayment risk charge provides a statistical hedge to cover expected re-hedging charges. If it is priced conservatively, in most situations there will be excess reserved prepayment risk charge remaining at the end of a deal, which can be taken to profit and loss (PnL). Ultimately the decision to hedge or not comes down to risk appetite and the types of structures and loan pools underlying the BGSs. Prior to hedging, everything else that can be done to reduce swap prepayment risk should be considered. For third-party swap providers, diversification across numerous loan pools, originators and asset classes is a good way to reduce swap prepayment risk. (This may not be possible for originators who provide their own swaps.) In a sufficiently large BGS book, it is only the *undiversifiable* (systemic) swap prepayment risk that should be of material concern. The prepayment risk charge on individual BGS transactions should include a risk buffer[12] to pay for the *incremental* cost of hedging adverse systemic prepayment risk scenarios across

---

[12]For the interested reader, a (quasi) risk-neutral approach to valuing prepayment risk is considered in Davidson and Levin (2005), albeit in the context of MBS rather than BGS.

the whole book. The hedging strategy can be made cheaper by (i) using swaptions that are further out-of-the-money and/or (ii) reducing the principal of the swaptions; both of which allow for losses up to some given threshold before the option protection kicks in. In this way, the hedging strategy could be tailored to a loss statistic, which is a function of an organisation's risk appetite. A multi-layered approach may also be considered, consisting of a portfolio of hedging swaptions with different principal amortisation profiles and strikes designed to hit a target loss statistic.

Another way to further diversify away some of the swap prepayment risk is to seek offsetting positions. For example, to offset the single-currency asset swap in the above example, one could look for a single-currency liability swap where the swap provider receives floating/pays fixed. Whilst the pay down structure will likely be different, there could still be some value in this approach. Of course, the timing and availability of offsetting deals will never be perfect, so it will likely be more of a tactical, opportunistic approach.

In the case of cross-currency BGS, finding such an offset is harder – but potentially possible by seeking a BGS where the pay and receive currencies are reversed. This is much more complicated than the single-currency case since (i) systemic prepayment risk may be quite different in different countries (e.g. if their economies are completely unsynchronised); and (ii) typically credit risk departments are only comfortable taking structured loan risk in certain countries where they judge themselves to have sufficient expertise, so being a receiver in certain currencies may not be feasible. Nevertheless, if these problems can be understood and addressed, there might be some value in diversifying across currencies.

Value-at-Risk

The VaR of a portfolio of derivatives is the worst decrease in MTM that is expected to be suffered over a given period of time (holding period) with a specified probability (confidence interval). For bank trading books, a common holding period assumption is one day and a typical confidence interval is 99%, although these vary across institutions. The expected loss is usually calculated using recent historical market data in the form of daily movements in all the key risk factors such as interest rates, FX, basis and volatilities. These daily movements are applied to the portfolio to construct a distribution of MTM movements.

Since historical realised prepayment data for new loan pools will not be available, one must take a proxy data approach such as using historical data from the same issuer. As we will see in the section on reducing Prepayment Volatility via Diversification, the size of the loan pool does make a big difference to the prepayment volatility, so an adjustment to the data to account for any size difference may need to be considered.

When computing VaR, the historical realised prepayment movements should be used to drive the movements in expected future prepayment. The relationship between these two prepayment rates was discussed in the sub-section on Expected Average Prepayment. Whichever form of model is chosen to link these quantities in the pricing model should also be used when computing VaR.

Since realised prepayment data is generally monthly or quarterly, whereas VaR is (usually) a daily loss statistic, computing VaR for BGS involves putting square pegs in round holes. This issue will persist when the industry transitions from VaR to expected shortfall over the next few years. While a more tailored risk measure other than daily VaR would be preferable for BGS, the regulatory status of VaR makes a practical solution of this problem imperative. Furthermore, integrating BGS risk with the risk from a wider portfolio of derivatives in a Markets or Treasury business unit means that a standard 'one size fits all' risk measure does still have its merits.

There are several approaches one could take, none of which are perfect. The options include:

1. Compute a monthly or quarterly VaR number (as the case may be) and time-scale the result back to a daily VaR number.
2. Use a Brownian Bridge stochastic process to interpolate daily prepayment rate moves between historical monthly/quarterly prepayment rate moves.
3. Compute a daily 99% (or whatever the appropriate VaR percentile is) move in the prepayment rate using a historically calibrated stochastic process, such as OU.

The pros and cons of each of these methods is given in Table 5.3.

TABLE 5.3 Advantages and disadvantages of three different methods for computing the VaR of a BGS.

Method	Advantages	Disadvantages
1	▪ No interpolation or artificial data construction ▪ Faithful to actual historical data at all points	▪ Doesn't allow for daily VaR vector integration into a wider portfolio of derivatives
2	▪ Daily prepayment data integrates easily with VaR over a wider portfolio of derivatives	▪ Interpolation means non-monthly/quarterly points are not actual historical data ▪ Since the Brownian Bridge is stochastic, interpolation can result in capricious data points, which can greatly increase VaR volatility for a given BGS
3	▪ Daily prepayment data integrates easily with VaR over a wider portfolio of derivatives ▪ Relatively stable VaR for a constant amount of BGS risk (unlike the Brownian Bridge)	▪ Interpolation means non-monthly/quarterly points are not actual historical data ▪ The actual monthly/quarterly prepayment movements cannot be recovered from the daily interpolated prepayment movements

So, as long as some level of imperfection is tolerable, a daily VaR number can be computed for BGS.

All of the above discussion applies equally to the *expected shortfall* metric, which like VaR is computed from a vector of daily PnLs. Expected shortfall is likely to replace VaR in the new market risk regulatory framework under Basel III, known as Fundamental Review of the Trading Book (FRTB). See the sub-section on Future Regulation in Chapter 8 for a further discussion of regulatory changes.

XVA

Since the global financial crisis (GFC), many *derivative valuation adjustments* have become market standard. Valuation adjustments are required to modify the risk-neutral price of a derivative – given by the MTM – to a more complete valuation, which is inclusive of key risks. The MTM does *not* include certain real-world costs such as counterparty credit risk and funding risk. The first derivative valuation adjustment to become market standard was the credit valuation adjustment (CVA). A few years later the funding valuation adjustment (FVA) become standard. Collectively we will refer to all valuation adjustments as XVAs. Their number is increasing.

Computing XVA for Swaps with Prepayment Risk

In principle one would like to compute CVA, FVA and other XVAs for BGS in the same centralised XVA engine that most banks now have for computing XVAs on all other derivatives. In practice, such systems – especially if they are vendor systems – don't include prepayment as a stochastic market factor, or BGS as an implemented product. While one might be able to modify a vendor system, such an approach can be surprisingly costly and time-consuming. Justifying that cost can be hard, especially if there are cheaper solutions that, although not perfect, will be adequate for most purposes.

What would an alternative approach be? The simplest method is to assume that the swap schedule is fixed and compute the XVAs as if the swap was vanilla. For soft bullet and controlled amortisation tranches, this approach should be adequate for both price-making at deal inception and revaluation throughout the life of the BGS. Deviation from the expected schedule is generally a very low probability event for these structures. For good order, one can manually scenario test the XVA pricing with a stressed principal schedule when computing the inception XVA price, to cover the case when very low prepayment breaks the schedule on a controlled amortisation tranche. The utility of this scenario test is in potentially adjusting (up) the XVA price charged to the client to account for the prepayment tail risk.

For pass-through tranches one needs to take more care. Instead of using the expected principal schedule, one could price the inception XVA on several different principal schedules (low, expected and high average prepayment) and see what impact this has on the XVA pricing. If the impact is low, then this approach can be justified. If the impact is high then one should consider charging a higher XVA price at inception to account for this potential variance. However, this doesn't solve the problem of the XVA revaluations potentially being quite wrong during the life of the trade – hardly an acceptable outcome. Fortunately this is quite rare.

This problem can be solved in one of three ways. Firstly, the error could be periodically accounted for via a manual adjustment. Secondly, the XVA engine could receive a modified trade feed where the swap schedule has been stressed, for example, using a lower-than-expected prepayment rate. This requires some work in upstream systems to achieve. Thirdly, one could modify the BGS pricer to also include XVA computations. This would be a lot of work, including programming, validation and ensuring consistent data feeds are used as per the centralised XVA engine. This third approach is really only economical if a material number of BGS trades suffer from significant XVA revaluation errors – and fortunately in the authors' experience this is not the case.

Intermediated Asset Swaps

It is not uncommon for originators with credit ratings below single A to engage a third-party swap provider to intermediate the asset swap between themselves and the SPV (see Figure 5.5).

The purpose of this intermediation is to avoid the originator having to post collateral and assume replacement risk, and also for the third-party swap provider to avoid assuming prepayment risk, which the originator is normally comfortable managing, but for its credit rating. This arrangement keeps the swap costs down for the originator, since the prepayment risk charge on longer-dated asset swaps can be significant, even though they are single-currency.

The upshot of this arrangement is that the swap cost is almost a pure XVA cost. There is no execution cost, since the swap provider is hedging with the originator rather than the open market; and there is only prepayment and extension risk to the extent that the originator could default (although those could also be eliminated via suitably structured risk transfer arrangements – see the section on Mitigation Strategies). What remains is pure XVA, composed of the following:

A. CVA to the SPV on the front swap
B. CVA to the originator on the back swap
C. Net FVA
D. CFVA[13] on the front swap

FIGURE 5.5   Asset swap intermediation.

---

[13]CFVA is defined and discussed at length in Chapter 7. It arises due to the cost of the contingent posting of collateral.

The swap cost is simply $A + B + C + D$. Note that A is likely to be large since (i) the SPV doesn't post collateral and (ii) asset swaps are often in-the-money to the originator so that excess spread can be returned to the originator. B is likely to be very small (but not quite zero) because under new margining requirements the credit support annex (CSA) will generally be two-way collateralised with zero threshold. C is likely to be large for the same underlying reason as A. If the swap provider doesn't receive collateral from the SPV but must post collateral to the originator, there is a sizeable funding cost.

All of the four XVA charges above have embedded prepayment risk. As discussed in the sub-section on Computing XVA for Swaps with Prepayment Risk, if variations in prepayment rates materially impact the total XVA cost, then this will need to be reflected in the pricing via an add-on. If the XVA pricer doesn't handle prepayment risk, then manual scenario analysis is required to size the add-on. This process is a little tedious and likely results in pricing, which is more conservative than that from an all-in XVA pricer with prepayment risk. But given the longer-dated nature of asset swaps, such conservatism might not be a bad thing.

MITIGATION STRATEGIES

Risk Transfer

The most effective swap prepayment risk mitigant is to transfer all of the risk to another party. In reality the only party likely to be willing to do this is the originator. The originator has the best understanding of prepayment risk and may also be able to influence prepayment behaviour by, for example, changing standard variable rates (SVRs). Swap providers need to charge a risk premium for swap prepayment risk because it is unhedgeable, so statistically it should usually be cheaper for an originator to assume swap prepayment risk themselves rather than pay a swap provider to take it on.

Swap prepayment risk can potentially be transferred from a swap provider to an originator via a *side letter*. This needs to be structured as a separate legal contract outside the public, rated securitisation so as not to compromise the true sale analysis. The terms of any side letter would need to cover that the originator will pay to the swap provider any re-hedging costs that might be incurred by virtue of an unexpected prepayment, that is, deviations from an expected amortisation schedule. This may be drafted as a one-way or two-way agreement where, in the latter case, any re-hedging benefit would be paid by the swap provider to the originator.

Making such an arrangement work requires careful consideration of the following material issues:

1. *Verification.* How can the originator be confident that any re-hedge cost is fair and reasonable? While sharing calculations is an obvious starting point, the reality is that such calculations involve opaque quantities, such as expected average

prepayment rates and yield curves constructed via proprietary algorithms. So there needs to be either a high level of disclosure between the parties or a certain degree of taking things on faith. A high degree of disclosure can create an operational burden for the swap provider. In the authors' experience, prepayment side letters have only been seen in controlled amortisation BGS where re-hedging events are very unlikely.

2. *Credit risk.* How can the swap provider be sure that the originator will pay future re-hedging costs? If they fail to pay, the swap provider is not permitted to terminate the BGS, since the originator is not a legal party to the swap contract. Even if the expected prepayment cost is collateralised by the originator, the swap provider still has credit risk for unexpectedly high prepayment costs. As a result, the originator needs to consider whether it is worth (i) putting funds aside as collateral and/or (ii) paying a credit risk charge; in preference to simply paying the swap provider a swap prepayment risk change.

3. *Regulation.* Originators are generally prohibited from providing 'implicit support' for a securitisation if they wish to retain the off-balance treatment of any assets being securitised. A prepayment side letter could arguably be viewed as implicit support so any decision to enter into these transactions should be undertaken carefully and reviewed by external legal counsel to ensure it does not result in any inadvertent implicit support. Transactions between the originator and the third-party swap provider should be separate from the underlying securitisation and conducted on an arms-length basis and, most importantly, must be in the best interests of the originator rather than for the benefit of the underlying investors.

Controlled Amortisation Structures

If the potential variation in principal amortisation can be greatly reduced, the prepayment risk charge can also be reduced. We can see this relationship explicitly from Eq. (5.6) in the sub-section on Re-Hedging, which shows that a non-zero $\delta\overline{WAL}$ term is a *multiplier* of market moves in generating re-hedging costs. It is possible to reduce the likely range of $\delta\overline{WAL}$ quite dramatically by structuring a controlled amortisation note, which is the main reason why these structures were developed. Controlled amortisation tranches have a pre-defined amortisation schedule, which can be realised so long as the prepayment rate is above a threshold level – the *breakeven prepayment rate* – so that sufficient principal receipts are generated to fund the scheduled amortisations. The lower the breakeven prepayment rate, the more likely the schedule is to be realised, hence the lower the risk of re-hedging and the lower the swap prepayment risk charge. If the breakeven prepayment rate is quite high, it is more likely that a realised prepayment rate will be less than the breakeven rate, which means there will be insufficient principal receipts to fund the full amount of the next principal amortisation.

As discussed in the section on Securitisation Structures in Chapter 3, there are two ways to structure a controlled amortisation note. The simplest method is when they are issued by a revolving vehicle, that is, a master trust. In this case, the over-collateralisation inherent in master trusts provides prepayment support from additional principal receipts beyond those generated from principal backing the notes one-for-one.

In the case of standalone structures, more elaborate structuring is required. During periods of higher-than-expected prepayment, principal receipts can be captured in a guaranteed investment certificate (GIC) account. During periods of lower-than-expect prepayment, principal can be drawn from the GIC account or, if the GIC has insufficient funds, from a *controlled amortisation facility* (CAF), which must be funded at inception.

Both structures have costs. The over-collateralisation of the master trust has a cost. Funding a CAF has a cost. However, it is often the case that these costs are less than the reduction in prepayment risk charge quoted by swap providers, which is why controlled amortisation structures are widely used.

Controlled amortisation structures are usually configured so that the breakeven prepayment rate needs to be very low before there are insufficient principal receipts to fund scheduled principal amortisations. This breakeven prepayment rate is somewhere in the order of 10% for Australian standalone SPVs and 7% in UK RMBS master trusts. Both of these levels are well below anything in historical experience. As a result, the swap provider is essentially selling *tail risk*, that is very low probability but potentially high impact events. Great care must be taken when selling tail risk as the well-known markets adage of *picking up pennies in front of a steam-roller* makes graphically clear. Taking care involves looking at the inherent wrong-way risk that can be embedded in such swaps if there are major changes in FX rates, basis and interest rates occurring concurrently with a severe slow-down in prepayment rates, which is likely to be caused by a systemic issue. The result of such an analysis usually produces prepayment risk pricing, which, while substantially lower than a pass-through prepayment risk charge, isn't quite as close to zero as many originators would like.

Reducing Prepayment Volatility via Diversification

There's another way to reduce $\overline{\delta WAL}$, which is considerably simpler than structuring a controlled amortisation tranche. Securitising a larger pool of mortgages reduces prepayment volatility by the simple process of *diversification*. One can empirically observe that the system-wide prepayment time series is much less volatile than a prepayment time series from an individual loan pool, and likewise one can see the same effect when comparing large pools to smaller ones. For instance, see Figure 5.6 showing one year long monthly time series for two Australian prime RMBS mortgage pools.

The Torrens pool, with half as many loans as the Medallion pool at their issuance dates, has considerably higher annualised prepayment volatility (13.9% versus 8.9%). Potentially some other differences in specific pool metrics could well influence

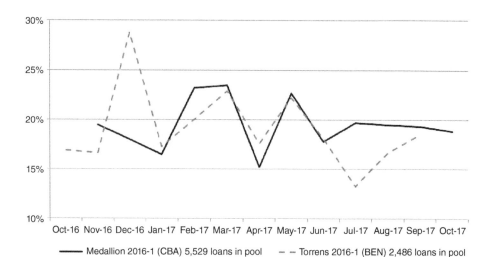

FIGURE 5.6 Monthly prepayment time series for two Australian prime RMBS mortgage pools with very similar average prepayment rates (around 19% per annum).

prepayment volatility, but it is much more likely that they influence the average prepayment rate – and this is comparable between the two pools, averaging 19% per annum for both. (Both pools comprise prime mortgages; 'non-conforming' mortgages have higher prepayment rates.) The likely conclusion is that it is the different number of loans that creates most of the difference in prepayment volatility.

Mathematically, the impact of diversification is well-known from studying portfolios of stocks, and the analysis is identical for prepayment volatility. For single-period prepayment we have that the prepayment variance of a portfolio of n loans with loan weights w_i is

$$\sigma_P^2 = \mathbf{E}[p_P - \mathbf{E}[p_P]]^2 = \mathbf{E}\left[\sum_{i=1}^{n} w_i p_i - \sum_{i=1}^{n} w_i \mathbf{E}[p_i]\right]^2 = \sum_{i=1}^{n} w_i^2 \sigma_i^2 + \sum_{i=1}^{n} \sum_{j=1, i \neq j}^{n} w_i w_j \sigma_{ij}$$

where p_P is the portfolio prepayment rate and σ_{ij} is the covariance between p_i and p_j. For simplicity, taking an equally-weighted portfolio results in

$$\sigma_P^2 = \frac{1}{n}\overline{\sigma}_i^2 + \frac{n-1}{n}\overline{\sigma}_{ij} \tag{5.11}$$

where $\overline{\sigma}_i^2$ is the average of the individual variances and $\overline{\sigma}_{ij}$ is the average of the covariances. In the limit we have

$$\lim_{n \to \infty} \sigma_P^2 = \overline{\sigma}_{ij}$$

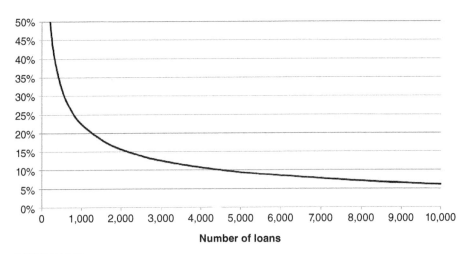

FIGURE 5.7 Prepayment volatility decreases as the number of loans increases (graph calibrated to two prime Australian RMBS pools).

Since the average covariance is low, and average individual variance is high, σ_P^2 is a decreasing function of n. Increasing the number of loans essentially diversifies away the idiosyncratic elements of prepayment volatility (namely $\overline{\sigma}_i^2$), but it is important to note that a systemic element of prepayment volatility (namely $\overline{\sigma}_{ij}$) always remains.

Using the data in Figure 5.6, we can solve Eq. (5.11) for $\overline{\sigma}_i^2$ and $\overline{\sigma}_{ij}$ making the not unreasonable assumption that those two parameters are roughly comparable across both pools – for the purposes of an *indicative* analysis only. This results in $\overline{\sigma}_i^2 = 4.31$ and $\overline{\sigma}_{ij} = -1.22\text{E}{-}04$. These parameters result in the following indicative chart for annualised prepayment volatility as a function of the number of loans n (see Figure 5.7).

This reduction in prepayment volatility can have a significant impact on the pricing of BGS on pass-through RMBS tranches, saving many basis points.

In reality, the timing requirements of an originator's funding programme may dictate that securitisation issuance must proceed before a pool size can be increased. However, if this approach can be used, it is a very simple and efficient approach to saving many basis points off the swap prepayment risk charge on a BGS.

Due Diligence and Surveillance

Before any risk is taken on, it needs to be fully understood. For prepayment risk, this means an analysis of the underlying loan pool, understanding the contractual terms of the loans, understanding how the originator may alter SVRs and comprehending the overall loan market in the relevant asset class. Some key things to look out for include:

1. Are there any concentrations in any relevant metric in the loan pool?
   - For example, are there teaser rates on some of the loans that may expire within a given interval of time? If so, one may expect a spike in prepayment rates at the time when teaser rates expire and interest rates concurrently increase across that cohort of loans. This can be dealt with in several ways: (i) the prepayment spike should be included in the expected amortisation profile to reduce the potential for costly re-hedging later on; (ii) request the originator remove the risk concentration; or (iii) ensure pricing reflects the risk of prepayment spikes.
   - What is the expiry profile of fixed-rate periods on fixed-rate loans in the pool? Does this profile change smoothly or abruptly? Prepayment rates are higher on floating-rate loans that can be prepaid without penalty relative to fixed-rate loans, which may incur break costs.
2. Is the composition of the loan pool broadly similar to previous pools for which prepayment history is available?
   - Prepayment history is only useful insofar as the originator is consistent in their lending behaviour and pool construction/loan selection.
3. Do the underlying loan terms contain any disincentives or incentives to prepay? If so, what are they?
4. Is the originator responsive, relative to competitors, in changing interest rates?
5. Under what circumstances does the originator have to buy back loans or what might constitute refinancing activity?

This initial due diligence should be complemented by ongoing surveillance to ensure the loan pool is behaving as expected. Ideally such surveillance should include updated loan-level data.

The above analysis is mainly qualitative and intersects with some of the credit analysis conducted by other teams who may be working the same transaction (e.g. credit risk department, securitisation arrangers). As such, it is wise for swap providers to tap into other experience available to them, as it can prove invaluable. Swap prepayment risk does not respect departmental boundaries so a collaborative approach is best.

Duty of Continuous Disclosure

If the originator plans to make any changes that may impact prepayment behaviour, it might be helpful for the swap provider to have advance knowledge. For instance, if an originator plans to change (or not change) a SVR in broad alignment with its competitors, one might reasonably expect this to have an impact on prepayment behaviour. It can only be useful for the swap provider to know this in advance, as windows of opportunity for more efficient hedging come and go and markets move. Making the disclosure of such plans a legal obligation of the originator to a swap provider assists the swap provider's trading desk to be in the best position to proactively manage such risk. However, in reality, these agreements can be difficult to obtain and may not be followed. In such circumstances there may be little *legal* recourse for non-compliance.

Step-Ups

One final potential mitigant, very rarely used in the authors' experience, is to allow for a step-up in the margin received by the swap provider if prepayment turns out to be substantially higher/lower or more volatile than initially expected. This is effectively another type of risk transfer, albeit a partial one, but where the taker of the risk is the SPV rather than the originator. Such step-ups are complex to model and may be treated punitively by rating agencies. Nevertheless, in certain transactions, it might be useful to consider this option.

SYSTEM ISSUES AND WHOLE-OF-LIFE DEAL MANAGEMENT

Recording and maintaining a BGS in a bank's trading system takes considerably more effort than a vanilla swap. This is due to the large amount of extra information required and the dynamic nature of that information. If this functionality isn't properly built in an industrialised fashion (e.g. on a spreadsheet), the operational risk consequences could be serious. Having a fit-for-purpose systems solution is just as important as getting the modelling, structuring and legal documentation right.

Trade Capture

In addition to the standard vanilla swap parameters,[14] the following trade data needs to be recorded:

- the tranche structure of the ABS or RMBS (for each tranche: principal, currency, cash flow allocation);
- any triggers (conditions and consequences);
- the zero prepayment (contractual) pool amortisation schedule; and
- downgrade criteria (see Chapter 7).

---

[14]For each swap leg, these parameters are: currency; date schedules for principal exchanges, interest payments and floating rate resets; floating rate index; fixed rates and/or spreads over floating rates; and principal schedule.

Additional market data is also required:

- prepayment parameters (mean, volatility, rate of mean reversion);
- parameters for evolving interest rates, FX and basis (model-dependent, but inclusive of volatility); and
- correlations.

A key challenge here is implementing a method of recording the tranche structure that is sufficiently flexible to account for all the variations in the market. Without this flexibility, either the analytics will need re-coding for each new variant, or deals will be mis-recorded or even declined by the Risk department if the mis-recording is sufficiently bad. Recording the tranche structure can be done in different ways. One method is to interface to an external model library such as Intex, although this may involve additional cost. Another way is to implement *algebraic scripting* of the cash flow waterfall. This means that the cash flow allocation for each tranche is recorded in the trading system as a mathematical formula, in a syntax that the underlying code can comprehend. The downside of this approach is that the formulae and syntax will not be obvious to everyone who looks at the trade capture screen (traders, risk managers, product controllers, operations staff etc.). A more intuitive, graphical approach to representing the tranche structure might also be considered. Whichever approach is taken, it pays to consider the pros and cons at the outset. Once a solution is built, it is usually very difficult to change.

Trade Maintenance

Several trade data and market data parameters are dynamic and require periodic maintenance throughout the life of the trade. In particular:

- The outstanding principal amounts for each tranche need to be updated every time it amortises (and not just for the tranche being swapped – *all* the tranches need to be updated[15]).
- The prepayment parameters may need to be updated on an ad-hoc basis, or according to an internal revaluation policy.

Where processes are not fully automated, changing trade and market data involves consideration of issues such as separation of duties. Ideally, front office staff should not be involved as a matter of good governance. Middle or back office staff will therefore need to be up-skilled to understand the workings of ABS, RMBS and BGS. The cost and operational aspects of this staffing requirement will need to be factored in.

---

[15]Possibly several tranches might be able to be aggregated to simplify the recording of the tranche structure without mis-modelling the BGS, but this is case-by-case judgement call.

Risk Systems

From a systems perspective, pricing and computing greeks in a front office trading system is less than half the work. At least three other systems are usually involved:

- A VaR engine: computing VaR, stress VaR and stress tests.
- A potential credit exposure (PCE) engine: computing potential credit exposure (sometimes also called potential future exposure).
- An XVA engine: computing CVA, FVA and possibly other valuation adjustments.

As discussed in the sub-section on Computing XVA for Swaps with Prepayment Risk in the context of XVA, the simplest approach to PCE and XVA is to assume that the swap schedule is fixed, with zero prepayment volatility, and compute the risk metric as if the swap was vanilla. This cannot be done for VaR as prepayment is an essential risk factor for the loss distribution. However, for XVA and PCE prepayment is much less important. This approximation-by-vanilla approach avoids the need for a costly and time-consuming model integration exercise. For soft bullet and controlled amortisation structures, this approximation will be almost perfect. For pass-through BGS, the acceptability of the approximation will need to be understood on a case-by-case basis. A potential enhancement for PCE would be to compute a stressed, decreased, prepayment to elongate the swap schedule and use that stressed schedule for PCE calculations. If this approximation is not used, then the proprietary BGS analytics will need to be integrated into the XVA and PCE systems. If this approach is taken, consideration must be given to the required compute time as the BGS Monte Carlo model can take up to several minutes for a single pricing run.

Computing VaR for BGS will either require a model integration exercise in a core VaR engine, or else a standalone application will need to be built that can feed VaR vectors into the core engine for aggregation. The pros and cons of each approach will very much depend on the systems and system architecture in each bank where this is done.

CHAPTER 6

Swap Extension Risk

Remember that time is money.

– Benjamin Franklin

WHAT IS SWAP EXTENSION RISK?

Acting as a swap provider to a highly-rated securitisation is a serious long-term commitment. A large number of securitised bonds have a call date some time in the future, and the market expects originators to honour their implied commitment to call their bonds. However, if the originator doesn't call the bonds as expected, both the bonds *and the swap* will extend until either (i) the bonds are eventually called or (ii) the final cash flow has occurred. While non-call events are very rare, they are potentially high impact, necessitating careful consideration of deal structuring, pricing and risk management. For swap providers, accepting this risk is akin to writing a swaption on a complex swap, where the exercise condition is not driven by observable market rates, but rather by the financial position of the originator.

Covered bond swaps can also extend in tenor, but the cause is issuer default rather than the bonds not being called. This is a simpler exercise condition, which is easier to model. For ease of exposition, this chapter will discuss extension risk mainly in the context of swaps over residential mortgage-backed securities (RMBS) and asset-backed securities (ABS). However, almost all of the content is equally applicable to covered bonds swaps, with the term 'non-call' replaced by 'default'. Footnotes will clarify this explicitly where it is helpful.

Since swap providers, like investors, initially expect issuers to call their bonds, it makes sense for traders to only hedge the swap until the call date.[1] This expectation can

---

[1]Even if one wanted to hedge beyond the call it would be very difficult, as the expected average prepayment rate beyond the call date is harder to discern, especially if the non-call was triggered by a systemic market shock.

persist right up until the time at which the issuer is expected to announce the calling of the bonds. However, if the bonds aren't called, the swap provider will suddenly find themselves having an unhedged position in a longer-dated swap. For a variety of reasons discussed in this chapter, the mark-to-market (MTM) value of this swap might well be negative and large, unless robust mitigants were included in the deal terms during the pre-deal structuring phase. In addition to the adverse MTM impact, the valuation adjustments due to counterparty credit risk (CVA) and downgrade risk (especially contingent funding valuation adjustment (CFVA)) from the increased tenor can also be very significant.

> We define *swap extension risk* to be the risk that a swap extends in tenor, unexpectedly generating (i) unhedged market risk and (ii) increased credit risk, prepayment risk and downgrade risk.

A natural question to ask is: can't the swap provider simply agree to swap the cash flows up until the call date, and no further? The answer is no. The rating agencies will not provide a high rating to any ABS, RMBS or covered bond that is not fully hedged until its legal final maturity (LFM). The special purpose vehicle (SPV) would simply be too exposed to market movements, which could easily lead to its default. As a result, no originator who intends to issue a highly-rated note can engage a swap provider who doesn't agree to provide a swap through to LFM.

Another natural question to ask is: why would a Bank agree to provide a swap that could suddenly and unexpectedly extend? The answer here depends on who provides the swap.

Firstly, there is the case of originators who provide swaps for their own structured funding trades. These originators provide the swaps because they can (they are typically reasonably well-rated), because they think they will always call their bonds as expected and providing the securitisation swaps is an unavoidable part of their necessary funding task.

Second, is the case of third-party swap providers who provide swaps as a discretionary line of business to other issuers who are invariably lower rated. These swap providers will want comfort that the probability of non-call is very low and preferably disincentivised; if a non-call event happens, they have some effective mitigants available to protect themselves. Such mitigants are discussed in detail in the section on Mitigation Strategies.

Anecdotally, it appears to be the case that third-party swap providers think much more seriously about mitigating extension risk than originators who provide their own swaps. Originator swap providers would do well to structure their swaps as if they were third-party swap providers. Should an issuer be downgraded, it may have to novate its swaps to a third-party swap provider. Novation will be significantly cheaper when extension risk mitigants, such as step-ups, have been included in the terms of the swap. Such terms are difficult, if not impossible, to incorporate retrospectively after the bonds have been issued. The process of obtaining the consent of a trustee to such a change of terms (and the potential need to obtain directions) from the majority of noteholders can be a time-consuming, costly and reputationally fraught process. As a result, it pays to think ahead and structure the deal as though one was a third-party swap provider.

So, the key message in this chapter is that extension risk should be extremely carefully considered at a very early stage during the deal structuring phase. The good news is that there is a ready tool kit of risk mitigants and a robust framework within which any residual extension risk can be priced and risk-managed.

Examples of Extension Risk

In this section we illustrate the dynamics of extension risk with examples in a simplified framework for ease of calculation. The calculations can be found in full in the Securitisation Swaps – Numerical Examples spreadsheet available at this book's website www.securitisationswaps.com.

Firstly, consider a USD500 million RMBS pool where a single, pass-through, AAA-rated tranche represents the top 92% of the capital structure and the remaining tranches are all subordinated. Further assume that the swap provider is swapping the USD460 million A note from AUD into USD. The amortisation profile of this tranche, assuming 20% CPR, is shown in Figure 6.1. The weighted average life (WAL) with the call exercised is 2.5 years with the final cash flow in four years; the WAL with the call not exercised is 3.4 years with the final cash flow in ten years.

Note that the extension risk inherent in this example is of 'medium' severity. We will see in the sub-section on Dependence on the Capital Structure: Standalone SPVs that different tranche structures can result in extension risk that is worse than, or less severe than, this example.

Secondly, we use a simplified market rates and curves environment where:

- The AUD yield curve is 3.0% flat (monthly compounding, ACT/365).
- The USD yield curve is 1.0% flat (monthly compounding, ACT/360).
- AUD/USD spot foreign exchange (FX) is 0.7500.
- AUD/USD cross-currency basis ('Bills/LIBOR') is 20 basis points flat.
- The A notes pay USD1 month Libor +1.0%.

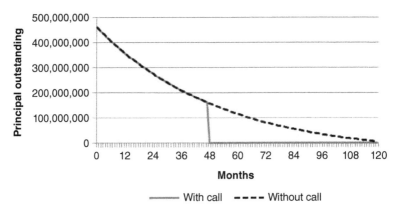

FIGURE 6.1 An example of extension risk – amortisation profiles with the call exercised and unexercised.

EXAMPLE 6.1: EXTENSION RISK ON A SIMPLE PAR SWAP

Consider a monthly/monthly swap with principal amortisation tracking the A tranche, assuming the call is exercised by the originator in month 48. The breakeven margin over 1 month BBSW is 1.237%. In other words, if the swap provider receives 1.237% over 1 month BBSW, and pays 1.0% over 1 month USD LIBOR, then the inception MTM of the swap is zero, ignoring XVAs and all other swap costs (including prepayment risk). Assume the swap provider transacts this swap facing the securitisation SPV and also transacts an equal-but-opposite hedging swap, which is also at par at inception (see Figure 6.2).

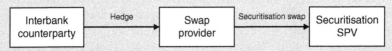

FIGURE 6.2 Typical arrangement where a swap provider has transacted a vanilla hedge for a securitisation swap. The vanilla hedge matures at the call date.

Now suppose that just prior to month 48 the originator announces that it won't call the A notes. At this point the swap schedule changes from the solid line to the dashed line in Figure 6.1. Also assume that the yield curves and cross-currency basis curve in month 48 are exactly the same as at month 0 when the swap was initially priced, but that the AUD/USD spot rate has decreased sharply[2] from 0.7500 to 0.4800. This represents the type of wrong-way risk inherent in extension risk: macro-economic factors may force issuers into distress at the same time as significant adverse market swings are occurring. For simplicity, assume that neither the bond coupon, nor the receive spread on the swap, changes in any way. At this point in time, the MTM of the swap decreases very sharply to AUD −93.1 million, while the MTM of the hedging swap, which matures at the call date, increases to AUD90.91 million, due to the decline in the AUD/USD spot rate. **The net MTM of the swap and the hedge is AUD −2.2 million**.

Immediately before the swap provider announced the non-call of the notes, the net MTM was zero. This is true no matter what the spot FX rate was, or any other market rate for that matter, because the swap was perfectly hedged (continuing to ignore prepayment risk and XVA costs for the moment). But as soon as the schedule extends, the swap is unhedged and the change in MTM is dramatic. This type of event would make for a very bad day on any trading desk carrying this exposure!

Why did the MTM decrease? The primary driver is the decrease in the AUD/USD spot rate. The FX rate used in the swap remains unchanged at 0.7500 upon extension, otherwise the US investors would not be currency-hedged and they wouldn't receive their principal back in full. The swap provider now has to continue to pay expensive USD for a longer period, while receiving AUD that has significantly decreased in value.

Transacting a new hedge for the extended swap at month 48 won't mitigate any loss, because the new hedge will be struck with an at-market spot FX rate of 0.4800, not 0.7500.

EXAMPLE 6.2: EXTENSION RISK ON A NON-PAR SWAP

Consider the same swap, but where the swap provider receives 1.40% over 1 month BBSW. Since this is above the breakeven rate, the swap is in-the-money to the swap provider with an inception MTM of AUD +1.8 million. In month 48, just before the issuer announces the no-call, the net MTM of the swap and the

(Continued)

---

[2]Note that 0.7500 is the approximate long-run average of AUD/USD and 0.4800 is the approximate all-time minimum.

hedge is AUD22,000. Immediately following the no-call announcement, the net MTM is AUD −1.6 million. This represents an almost complete unwind of the day one profit and loss (PnL) (assuming the entire MTM was taken to PnL[3]).

The reduction in MTM upon extension is 600,000 less bad in this example than in Example 6.1. The reason is that the 0.163% additional spread earned by the swap provider is now earned for a longer period of time and this partially offsets the decrease in MTM due to the spot rate decrease.

If the initial receive margin was considerably higher, say 2.8% over 1 month BBSW, then an extension event would be a desirable outcome for a swap provider, as earning the higher spread for longer would *more than offset* the decrease in MTM due to the spot rate decrease. In this case, the net MTM of the swap and the hedge increases from AUD22,000 to AUD +3.9 million. However, earning this type of profit spread on a swap in not achievable in the market for two key reasons: (i) it is not economical for the originator to raise funds at such a high cost; and (ii) even if (i) didn't apply, there is usually sufficient competition in the swap market to ensure more efficient swap pricing.

This example is nevertheless instructive: it illustrates that raising the spread on the receive leg of a swap can have a substantial mitigating effect on the swap provider's level of extension risk.

EXAMPLE 6.3: THE EFFECT OF STEP-UPS

Now consider the same swap as in Example 6.2, but where after the call date (i) the bond coupon to investors steps up by 0.50% and (ii) the receive spread on the swap steps up by 1.25%. This is a much more realistic example, reflecting more typical market features.

In this case, the net MTM of the swap and the hedge at month 48 immediately following the non-call announcement is AUD -15 k. While the 0.50% step-up paid to investors is an added cost for the swap provider, this has been more than offset by the larger 1.25% increase received. The overall result is that the extension event has only caused a minimal impact to the PnL of the swap provider's trading desk.

Had the swap provider been able to negotiate a larger step-up with the issuer and rating agencies of, say, 2.00%, then the MTM immediately following the non-call announcement would be AUD +2.7 million and would represent a

---

[3]See the section on Accounting in Chapter 8 for a more detailed discussion of accounting and revenue reserves.

windfall gain to the swap provider. Of course, had the spot AUD/USD rate fallen to a lower level than 0.4800, then this MTM would be lower, and potentially negative.

A key observation here is that no matter how high the step-up is, there is still residual extension risk. This is because if the spot FX rate falls sufficiently, and/or any other market variable changes sufficiently adversely, the benefit of the step-up can be entirely offset. As a result, there should always be a non-zero price for extension risk. We examine the pricing in more detail in the section on A Simple Pricing Framework for 1-Factor Stochastic FX.

EXAMPLE 6.4: CAPPED MARGIN RESET

A more sophisticated form of step-up is the *capped margin reset*. This mechanism more efficiently allocates risk and available spread between the originator, investors and the swap provider post non-call. It works as follows. At the time of the non-call announcement:

(a) The SPV trustee nominates a future roll date as the potential maturity of the extended swap.
  - While the swap provider is liable to provide a swap to LFM, the nomination of this date accommodates any issuer expectations that they can refinance the tranche prior to LFM.[4] Importantly, it also allows any swap spread increase to be reduced, as less spread will likely be required to be charged for a swap to a near-term roll date than all the way to LFM.
(b) The swap provider computes the expected amortisation profile to the nominated roll date and the new breakeven margin on the receive leg of the swap.
(c) The swap provider charges that new breakeven margin plus a pre-agreed profit spread, so long as it does not exceed a cap. To the extent that the breakeven margin exceeds the cap, those payments are subordinated in the cash flow waterfall.
(d) If the issuer wasn't able to refinance the notes before the nominated roll date, the trustee nominates a new future roll date and steps (b)–(d) are repeated until either all the loans are sold or LFM, whichever occurs first. Note that the cap level is constant throughout, to ensure rating agencies can grant a high rating to the issuance.

(Continued)

---

[4]In the case of a CPT covered bond, this accommodates trustee expectations that it can sell the loan pool to a prospective purchaser.

Now consider the same swap as in Example 6.3, except that the additional receive margin is *capped* at 1.25% rather than automatically stepping-up by 1.25%. Suppose the trustee has nominated a potential maturity date six months in the future, and assume that the spot AUD/USD rate has decreased to 0.60. In this case the breakeven margin on the swap is 2.07%; that is, a spread increase of 0.67% over the initial receive spread of 1.40%. This is substantially less than the 1.25% step-up in Example 6.3. The issuer and investors are much better off in this case.

On the other hand, assume that the spot AUD/USD rate has fallen to 0.40. In this case the new breakeven margin on the six-month extended swap is 3.13%; that is, a spread increase of 1.73%. This would be paid to the swap provider as an extra 1.25% spread from a senior position in the cash flow waterfall plus a further 0.48% spread from a subordinated position in the cash flow waterfall (if there is any cash left at that level of subordination).

If the originator hasn't refinanced the notes prior to the six-month nominated roll date, the swap will be re-extended. If the spot FX rate has recovered to a level closer to the inception level, then the swap costs will come back down. This is another clear advantage of the capped margin reset mechanism for the originator and investors: higher costs, which may prevail at the call date due to severe market-wide stress, need not be locked in to LFM, but only to the next nominated roll date.

Dependence on the Capital Structure: Standalone SPVs

The examples in the previous sub-section on Examples of Extension Risk all considered a swap that had amortised down to 35% of the initial principal at the call date in month 48. An alternative capital structure could have the A tranche of notes as a soft bullet, which doesn't amortise at all. In this case, the length of extension would be significantly longer for two reasons: (i) the amortisation of the A tranche begins at 100% of the initial principal rather than 35%; and (ii) one or more tranches below the A tranche will have amortised significantly prior to the call date, which means they will generate a smaller flow of principal receipts to help pay down the A tranche – that is, there is less *prepayment support* for the A tranche than in the examples set out in previous sub-section.

All things being equal, a longer period of extension will create increased swap extension risk, hence prudent structuring and pricing will need to reflect this.

Another variant in standalone RMBS capital structures that can significantly impact the length of extension are *triggers*. These triggers typically change the allocation of principal receipts from sequential to pro-rata at a certain point in time, or when a given level of credit subordination has been reached. Changing from sequential to pro-rata pay down slows the amortisation of the A tranche since principal receipts must be shared amongst several other tranches. This slowing amortisation has the consequence that the outstanding principal at the call date will be higher than it would have been in the absence of a trigger. This increases swap extension risk.

It is not unknown for some clients and sales people to phone derivatives structurers working at third-party swap provider banks and simply ask 'what's the rough price estimate of a balance guarantee swap (BGS)'? The answer that derivative structurers are obliged to give is 'it depends'. This often frustrates those looking for a quick, simple answer. But the reality is that the range of pricing is very wide depending on many different factors including the capital structure of the securitisation.

The solution is to involve the derivative structurers as early as possible, letting them know what potential clients are being pursued so that they can collect the data and prepare. This not only means faster responses to any client queries, but clients can also be approached proactively with structures that optimise pricing and lower total cost of funds for issuers.

Extension Risk in UK RMBS Master Trusts

Standard UK RMBS master trusts have some particular features that serve to reduce the impact of extension risk in comparison to standalone structures. The key difference is the presence of the seller share. In the event of non-call by the originator, a sequence of triggers is activated as follows:

1. No new loans may be sold into the master trust, triggering pool-level amortisation.
2. At two (generally different) points in time, the pool size will fall below its minimum requirement and the seller share will fall below its minimum requirement. When the first of these two triggers is breached, all principal receipts flow to investors; that is, the seller share receives no principal receipts and hence becomes time-subordinated.

As a result, the seller share provides prepayment support to all of the funding share notes. Depending on a variety of factors, such as the minimum levels specified in the base prospectus of the relevant master trust, the seller share can provide material acceleration of note amortisation and reduce swap extension risk significantly.

Note that in the event of issuer default, step 1 above is bypassed and all principal receipts will flow immediately to investors.

Covered Bond Extension Risk

As discussed in the section on Covered Bond Structures in Chapter 3, covered bonds come in three basic varieties:

1. hard bullets;
2. soft bullets; and
3. conditional pass-through ('CPT').

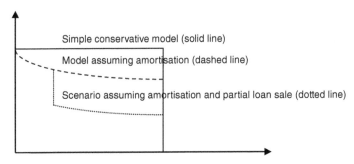

FIGURE 6.3 Possible amortisation schedules following a covered bond issuer default.

Hard bullets do not extend on issuer default and therefore have zero swap extension risk.

Soft bullets may extend for up to a maximum of one year upon issuer default. They therefore generate relatively mild swap extension risk. The exact amortisation profile during this one-year extension period can be quite uncertain because the trustee typically has an obligation to attempt to sell the mortgage pool, in part or in full, to purchasers. As a result, there can be a range of potential amortisation schedules (see Figure 6.3).

CPT bonds can generate very significant swap extension risk as they can *potentially* extend all the way to LFM. Full extension to LFM is only a possibility because, like soft bullets, the trustee typically has an obligation to attempt to sell the mortgage pool to purchasers. However, given that this aspect is neither guaranteed nor modellable, a conservative approach would be to assume full extension to LFM.

Key factors determining the amortisation profile are:

1. the assumed prepayment rate; and
2. the level of over-collateralisation (OC).

The level of OC at the time of issuer default used in modelling requires some thought to be developed on a case-by-case basis. Arguably it should be a stressed version of the current level of OC, or possibly the minimum legal level (or maybe even lower again). The lower the level of OC, the less prepayment support the bonds have, hence the longer the extension period.

A SIMPLE PRICING FRAMEWORK FOR 1-FACTOR STOCHASTIC FX

In this section we analyse swap extension risk on float/float cross-currency swaps with a capped margin reset in the simplified setting where only spot FX is stochastic.

Since spot FX is by far the largest risk factor for float/float cross-currency swaps,[5] this captures a high proportion of the overall risk.

The cap introduces optionality since it keeps extended swaps at-the-money unless the spot FX rate drops to a sufficiently low level which requires extra spread over and above the cap to keep the MTM equal to zero. Assuming any subordinated spread above the cap level is worth zero, we show that the price of swap extension risk with a capped margin reset is similar to a European FX put option, weighted by the probability of non-call. (For single currency fixed/float securitisation swaps there is an analogous argument that pricing is similar to a European swaption weighted by the probability of non-call.)

The starting point for understanding swap extension risk on any swap is to model the amortisation profile to (i) the call date; and (ii) to LFM in the event of non-call. This part of the exercise is entirely dependent on the structure of the structured funding being issued: the derivative aspects are not relevant at this stage of the process. Once these two schedules have been computed, the swap extension risk analysis can begin.

Consider the MTM of the *extended swap*, that is, the swap that exists from the expected call date to LFM. We define the extended swap to have an initial principal exchange that cancels the final principal exchange of the non-extended swap (see Figure 6.4). Prior to the expected maturity (EM) of the bond, the MTM of the extended swap depends heavily on the FX rate. If we assume, for illustrative purposes, that interest rate and cross-currency basis are deterministic and FX is stochastic and any

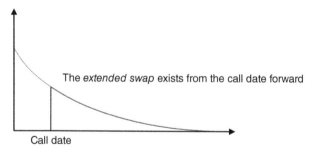

FIGURE 6.4   An extended swap.

---

[5]Strictly speaking, this is true only after the initial principal exchange. Prior to the initial principal exchange, the FX delta of a cross-currency swap is not large, since the initial and final principal exchanges have offsetting FX deltas. The fixed swap spreads generate the residual FX delta.

subordinated cash flows (i.e. spread above the cap level) is worth zero, then the MTM of the extended swap is:

$$MTM_{Extended\ Swap} = \Pr(D|T \leq EM) \cdot \mathbf{E}[MTM_{RL} \cdot fx - MTM_{PL}.]$$

$$\geq -\Pr(D|T \leq EM) \cdot \mathbf{E}[-MTM_{RL(cap)} \cdot fx + MTM_{PL}.]$$

$$= -\Pr(D|T = EM) \cdot MTM_{RL(cap)} \cdot \mathbf{E}\left[-fx + \frac{MTM_{PL}}{MTM_{RL(cap)}}\right]$$

If fx falls below $\frac{MTM_{PL}}{MTM_{RL(cap)}} = k$ then the term inside the square brackets of the expectation becomes positive and the overall right-hand side becomes negative. Hence the value k is the threshold level for fx below which the extended swap has a negative MTM. The risk of fx falling below k is the residual extension risk retained by the swap provider. The larger the cap, the smaller k is, hence the smaller the residual risk. This is exactly analogous to the strike of an FX put option. Indeed, the value of this retained risk is:

$$\Pr(D|T = EM) \cdot MTM_{RL(cap)} \cdot \mathbf{E}[max(k - fx, 0)] = \Pr(D|T = EM) \cdot MTM_{RL(cap)}$$

$$\cdot \mathbf{BS}(fx, k, T, \sigma, r_f, r_q) \tag{6.1}$$

where:

$\Pr(D|T \leq EM)$	is the cumulative probability of non-call up to EM
MTM_{PL}	is the MTM of the pay leg of the swap in pay leg currency
MTM_{RL}	is the MTM of the receive leg of the swap in receive leg currency
$MTM_{RL(cap)}$	is the MTM of the receive leg of the swap with the spread set to the cap
fx	is the spot foreign exchange rate from pay leg to receive leg currency
$\mathbf{BS}(fx, k, T, \sigma, r_f, r_q)$	is the forward Black-Scholes price of a put option with strike k with time-to-expiry T, FX volatility σ and foreign and domestic interest rates r_f, r_q respectively
k	is the strike of the Black-Scholes option given by

$$k = \frac{MTM_{PL}}{MTM_{RL(cap)}} = \frac{\sum_{i=m}^{M} P_i^{PL}(f_i^{PL} + IS)\tau_i^{PL} DF_{i+1}^{PL} - P_m^{PL} DF_m^{PL} + \sum_{i=m+1}^{M} \Delta P_i^{PL} DF_i^{PL}}{\sum_{j=n}^{N} P_j^{RL}(f_j^{RL} + SPS)\tau_j^{RL} DF_{j+1}^{RL} - P_n^{RL} DF_n^{RL} + \sum_{j=n+1}^{N} \Delta P_j^{RL} DF_j^{RL}} \tag{6.2}$$

where:

P_i^{PL}/P_j^{RL}	is the pay/receive leg principal for the ith/jth coupon period respectively
f_i^{PL}/f_j^{RL}	is the pay/receive leg forward interest rate for the ith/jth coupon period respectively

τ_i^{PL}/τ_j^{RL}	is the pay/receive leg year fraction for the ith/jth coupon period respectively
DF_i^{PL}/DF_j^{RL}	is the pay/receive leg discount factor for the ith/jth coupon period respectively
IS	investor spread i.e. the bond coupon over the floating rate
SPS	swap provider spread i.e. what the swap provider receives over the floating rate (i.e. the initial receive spread plus the cap).
m/n	are the first coupon periods of the extended pay/receive legs
M/N	are the last coupon periods of the extended pay/receive legs

Analysing Eq. (6.2) shows that the greater the MTM of the receive leg, the lower the strike of the option – that is, the further out-of-the-money it becomes. This can be achieved by increasing the swap provider spread relative to the other quantities, especially the investor spread.

A natural question arises at this point: why not simply set a very high swap provider spread to apply after EM? The answer lies in the cash flow subordination. The swap provider usually ranks *pari passu* or senior to any notes issued, and thus has the (equal) first claim on any cash generated by the underlying assets. If the spread accruing to the swap provider is too large, the rating agencies will not provide a high rating to the RMBS or ABS – there simply wouldn't be sufficient spread left to pay bond holders under all the rating agencies' stress scenarios. Hence the rating agencies limit the size of the swap provider spread, at least to the extent that it is senior in the RMBS or ABS cash flow waterfall. Additional swap provider spread could still be included without impacting the bond rating if it is sufficiently subordinated – but the swap provider would be well advised to carefully consider how much value can be ascribed to these. Any subordinated cash flows are required in the event of non-call by the issuer – which may well be correlated to wider macro-economic stress where credit risk in the underlying pool is also likely elevated. This is a clear case of wrong-way risk.

All of the parameters in Eq. (6.1) are observable with the exception of $Pr(D|T \leq EM)$. How should this parameter be estimated? A lower bound on this quantity is clearly the originator's probability of default.[6] If the originator has defaulted, they certainly won't be calling the bonds! The probability of default may be market observable if:

(a) the originator also issues senior unsecured bonds; and/or
(b) there is a sufficiently liquid, traded credit default swap (CDS) market on the originator.[7]

---

[6] In the case of a covered bond swap, this is not a lower bound, but the correct quantity.
[7] The probability of default may be solved for mathematically from (i) the bond or CDS spread respectively; and (ii) an assumed recovery rate. Note that the implied probability of default from bonds can be markedly different from that implied from CDS on the same issuer. This can be due to technical factors such as supply/demand differences in the bond and CDS markets and different funding, capital and accounting treatments of the bond and CDS instruments.

In many cases there won't be unsecured bonds or traded CDS and a proxy curve will need to be used as per what a CVA desk would use for pricing.

How much higher is the probability of non-call compared to the lower bound probability of default? This is not an easy question to answer, not least because there are so few historical data points. In many institutions, sizing this quantity will require discussion amongst the Front Office, Product Control and Risk departments, possibly at a formal committee, and might include consideration of issues such as:

- How reliant is the originator on securitisation for funding? If it is wholly or substantially reliant on securitisation as its main source of funding, the difference between the probability of non-call and default *may* be smaller than other originators that have greater diversification of funding sources (e.g. deposits, equity, unsecured debt). Also to be considered in this vein: is the originator's business model/approach to funding likely to change in future? A real-life example is the case of a non-bank lender that relies solely on securitisation but is actively working towards a stock exchange float to raise equity funding.
- How big is the potential differential between the funding cost assuming non-call and the funding cost assuming the originator obtains new funding? If the increase in funding cost is small, perhaps the originator is more likely not to call the bonds.

Ultimately sizing the probability of non-call is more art than science and variation amongst different institutions is to be expected. In the real world, one of the more important considerations can be how badly a third-party swap provider wants the business!

EXAMPLE 6.5: EXTENSION RISK PRICING

Consider the same swap as in Example 6.4, with the receive margin capped at 1.25% above the inception margin. The price of the retained extension risk can be calculated using Eq. (6.1). The strike of the FX put option is 0.53. Using an implied FX volatility of 30% and a 20% probability of non-call, the extension risk is 1.4 basis points on the receive leg of the (unextended) swap. Note that a high FX volatility may be justified due to (i) the volatility skew and (ii) wrong-way risk; that is, the risk of an adverse currency move being positively correlated with non-call risk.

FULL PRICING FRAMEWORK IN A MULTI-FACTOR SETTING

In practice, proper pricing and good risk management requires consideration of stochastic interest rates as well as stochastic FX and, if one wishes, stochastic basis as well. The interest rate component is important because (i) even float/float swaps contain fixed spreads and (ii) many bonds pay fixed rate coupons.

Given the number of stochastic risk factors, Monte Carlo simulation is the only tractable approach to pricing and the computation of risk metrics. We have already covered the necessary Monte Carlo framework for swap prepayment risk in Chapter 5. The adaptation of that framework for pricing extension risk is straightforward.

If the swap has simple step-ups after non-call, the extension risk can simply be priced by running the extended swap through the Monte Carlo pricer. The cost of extension risk can be converted into a basis point charge by dividing it by the PV01 of the (non-extended) swap.

If the swap has a capped margin reset, then the Monte Carlo pricer will need to include functionality to price the breakeven margin at the call date. The most conservative assumption to make is that the swap extends to LFM and the least conservative assumption to make is that the issuer nominates every roll date as the potential maturity date. A simple way to validate this Monte Carlo pricer is to ensure that the pricing with zero interest rate volatility and basis volatility matches the analytic pricing derived in the section on A Simple Pricing Framework for 1-Factor Stochastic FX.

MITIGATION STRATEGIES

Pre-Trade Structuring versus Real-Time Hedging

The most effective way to mitigate swap extension risk is to include appropriate terms and conditions in the deal documentation *a priori*, that is, prior to the swap being transacted. Once the swap has been transacted, the only way to mitigate the impact of swap extension risk is to (i) attempt to put on hedging trade(s) as quickly as possible after a non-call event has occurred, or in anticipation of non-call in the future; or (ii) novate the swap to another institution if one can be found. Given (ii) is both hard and potentially takes too long, one is really left with (i) as the only realistic option. This type of real-time hedging is extremely problematic. The key challenges of this approach include:

1. *Unwind risk.* Suppose a swap provider transacts a hedge because they suspect that the originator will not call their bonds. Contrary to that expectation, suppose that the issuer does indeed call the bonds. In this case the swap provider must close out the hedge. If the market has moved the wrong way, the cost of unwinding the hedge could be significant. Similarly, a cost of a hedge after an unexpected non-call event may just lock in the MTM loss already realised.

2. *Slippage.* Suppose the swap provider is taken by surprise and only transacts a hedge after the originator has unexpectedly announced the non-call of their bonds. If this has occurred during a period of market volatility, the relevant market parameters (interest rates, FX and/or basis) may have moved a considerable way in a

short space of time, resulting in further loss before the hedge can be transacted to halt the damage. Speed is important. To the extent that the necessary speed is even achievable, close and continuous surveillance of the originator and its bonds is crucial. However, it is important to note that even if market rates are stable during a non-call announcement, there can still be very substantial loss due to market moves since deal inception. As already discussed, this slower, drifting type of slippage is completely unhedgable.

3. *Mis-hedging.* Even if unwind risk and slippage have (miraculously) been avoided, there is the problem of transacting the *right* hedge. This is not straightforward either. RMBS and ABS become pass-through after the expected call date. What average prepayment rate will prevail? How volatile will the prepayment rates be? Which hedging instrument(s) should be used? Being prepared in advance, with up-to-date loan-level data and good analytics, will greatly assist in the task of constructing a hedge that is closer to the mark than would otherwise be the case.

Given these challenges, one readily arrives at the conclusion that it is best to do as much as possible to mitigate extension risk prior to transacting the swap. There are three broad strategies for reducing extension risk *a priori*:

1. *Incentives.* In general, the originator's reputation alone should provide a powerful incentive for it to call the bonds at the EM date. However, if the originator is in serious financial difficulty or if the originator believes it has other sources of available funding, they may be tempted to allow some or all of its bonds to extend. In order to reduce the chances of this happening to the greatest possible extent, the deal terms should include a penalty to inflict significant pain on the originator should it choose not to call. This can be achieved via a stepped-up coupon to investors. This raises the cost of funding to the originator and increases the likelihood that it can find cheaper sources of funding, which can be used to repay investors at the call date.

2. *Step-ups and capped margin resets.* If the incentives have failed to prevent a non-call event, the next fall-back position for the swap provider is to receive an increased margin. There are several ways to structure this, but in all cases, an increased margin can partially or completely offset adverse market moves in interest rates, FX and/or basis. Understanding how far market parameters can move before the benefit of the stepped-up margin is completely offset are key matters to understand for both pricing and risk management purposes.

3. *Outright risk transfer.* Extension risk can be transferred back to the issuer via a mechanism known as a *collateralised back swap.* This is a private arrangement between the originator and the swap provider, which is outside of the public rated deal with the SPV. This arrangement requires the issuer to post collateral to the swap provider for the value of the extended swap – *even though the swap hasn't*

extended yet.[8] While this is the gold standard of extension risk mitigation, it has several adverse consequences that must be carefully considered by both the issuer and swap provider alike. This will be discussed in more detail below. In some jurisdictions it may not be compliant with local regulations.

Many of the above strategies are used simultaneously. Incentives and step-ups are commonly used on RMBS and ABS and the associated swaps. Should they fail, real-time hedging will undoubtedly be considered by the swap provider's trading desk, although hopefully the structural pre-hedging will have materially diminished slippage risk.

Likewise, step-ups or capped margin resets are used simultaneously with collateralised back swaps to reduce the amount of collateral posted by the originator. The larger the step-up or cap, the lower the spot FX rate can go before the extended swap is out-of-the-money, requiring the issuer to post collateral.

Pre-Trade Structuring

Step-Ups in the Investor Coupon RMBS and ABS notes often include the payment of an increased coupon or step-up payable to the noteholder if a note is not called on the expected call date. The purpose of this step-up is twofold. Firstly, it (partially) compensates investors for the extended term of the notes and potentially also the decreased creditworthiness of the notes. Secondly, it communicates to the market at the inception of the transaction that there is a strong intention to call the notes at pain of materially increased funding costs (in addition to breach of faith).

Covered bonds do not typically include a step-up upon extension and this is likely because there is no call option to incentivise calling, since extension is only triggered by issuer default for these instruments. However, most covered bonds do change from paying fixed coupons to paying floating coupons following extension and this may mitigate some swap extension risk.[9]

In theory, the higher the step-up to investors, the less likely it is for the originator not to call the notes and the more comfort investors will have that the call will be honoured. In practice, step-ups cannot be too large before they begin to impact the rating agencies' ability to bestow a high rating on the notes. There is only so much

---

[8] In effect, this is the originator (NOT the issuing SPV) selling the swap provider a collateralised cancellable swap that is cancellable in the event of the call (but collateralised fully). As the swap provider in effect sells a (potentially also collateralised!) swaption to the issuer that is exercised only on the call, these two cancel out.

[9] In currencies with very low or negative interest rates, the change to floating interest may increase derivative extension risk if there is an embedded negative strike floor. Such floors are required to ensure that the SPV doesn't need to pay the swap provider on its receive leg of the swap when interest rates are below the floating margin.

excess spread in the underlying loan pool and rating agency stress tests will test for the ability to pay back all principal and (stepped-up) interest to LFM.

In practice, it is likely that step-ups are less of a disincentive not to call bonds than the reputational damage it will cause. From this perspective, the extension of notes beyond the call date really only occurs when originators are faced with no choice but not to call the notes. If that is the case, then step-ups mainly exist to compensate investors for the increased term when extension occurs. Swap providers concerned about swap extension risk should therefore not take much comfort in the presence of step-ups in the investor coupon. Other mitigants are necessary to protect the swap provider's risk position.

Step-Ups and Capped Margin Resets   If a swap provider could receive an arbitrarily high margin upon extension, then any adverse market move in FX, rates or basis could be easily compensated for by that increased margin and the swap provider would be immune to market moves. As mentioned previously, the rating agencies won't permit an arbitrarily high step-up for highly-rated notes, at least not senior in the cash flow waterfall. As a result, the swap provider must make do with a step-up that is only sufficient to cover market moves of a given size. Any market move beyond these threshold levels in rates, FX or basis will require the trader to start hedging to offset the negative MTM of the swap.

The maximum size of the step-up permitted by the rating agencies will depend on various factors such as:

- which rating agencies are rating the deal and the specifics of the stress tests they apply;
- the amount of excess spread in the underlying loan pool;
- the weighted average spread on all the notes issued from the SPV issuing the bonds; and
- potentially any of the key parameters of the underlying loan pool such as the amount of any over-collateralisation and/or credit enhancement, LVR distributions and interest only (IO) percentages.

Fixed step-ups to swap providers have two potential drawbacks:

1. The step-up may not be large enough to compensate for a large market move at the time the non-call announcement is made.
2. If market moves are small, the fixed step-up may be (much) larger than a swap provider needs, thus depriving investors lower down in the capital stack of spread and/or the issuer of the return of excess spread.

As a result, a potential improvement on a fixed step-up is the capped margin reset discussed in detail in Example 6.4 in the section on What is Swap Extension Risk?.

Collateralised Back Swaps A collateralised back swap is an arrangement to totally transfer the risk of extension back to the originator. It works as follows. During the life of the swap, and before any non-call event has even occurred, the swap provider receives collateral equal to the value of the extended swap. Should the issuer not call the RMBS or ABS, the swap provider keeps the collateral and can use it to pay for a hedging swap (which will likely be highly in-the-money given that the swap with the SPV will probably be highly out-of-the-money). This is a private arrangement between the originator/sponsor and the swap provider and does not form part of the public transaction rated by rating agencies or disclosed to investors (see Figure 6.5).

This arrangement has several noteworthy characteristics. Firstly, since it eliminates swap extension risk for the swap provider, it also eliminates the extension risk fee that a third-party swap provider would charge. This reduces the revenue, and also the return on equity (RoE), on a securitisation swap. On the other hand, it can be used to reduce the cost of a securitisation swap to win business that would otherwise be lost,[10] depending on the circumstances. So, the use of a collateralised back swap requires careful consideration from a business perspective, but it is a very useful structuring and pricing lever where it can be used.

Secondly, it cannot always be used. This could be due to (i) originator preference or (ii) regulation.[11] Some originators don't like it because of the operational or liquidity risk aspects of the collateral obligations *vis-à-vis* third-party swap providers (originators providing their own swaps need not care about this point). They are willing to pay an extension risk charge in preference to the burden of potentially posting collateral (or, being a little paranoid, possibly because they think they really might not call the notes!). On the other hand, many originators like the cost reduction and are comfortable

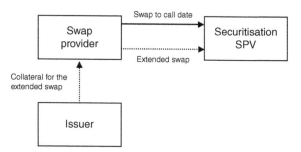

FIGURE 6.5 A collateralised back swap.

---

[10]Business could either (i) be lost to a cheaper swap provider or (ii) if the cost of the swap is too high, an issuer may choose to issue domestically, rather than offshore, even if they have to pay a higher spread to attract the required volume.

[11]This is something to be checked in each jurisdiction on a case-by-case basis.

with the risk transfer because they regard themselves as the natural holder of extension risk as owners of the underlying call option.

Thirdly, with new non-centrally cleared derivative (NCCD)[12] margining regulation, the collateral posting between the issuer and swap provider may need to be two-way, depending on how the regulation has been locally implemented, and the nature and size of the originator. If the collateral posting is two-way, the swap provider may need to charge a funding valuation adjustment (FVA) to cover the cost of collateral posting. Use of a capped margin reset, which keeps the MTM of the extended swap at zero over a wide range of spot FX and general market moves, would greatly assist in keeping such an FVA charge low.

Finally, one last issue for consideration is the systems aspect of implementing a collateral arrangement over an instrument that doesn't yet exist; that is, the extended swap. Systems vary widely across different banks, and so different solutions will be required depending on the architecture and particular software used. Suffice to say that unless a workable solution to implementing collateral posting for a collateralised back swap can be found – whether via manual process or full automation – it shouldn't be contractually included in a live transaction.

Real-Time Hedging

We have previously discussed the difficulty of real-time hedging in the sub-section on Pre-Trade Structuring Versus Real-Time Hedging, and the problems of unwind risk, slippage and mis-hedging. Nevertheless, if a non-call event really does appear imminent, or actually occurs, every third-party swap provider will need to actively hedge its exposure or potentially risk a larger hole in its trading book PnL.

In order for real-time hedging to be most effective it needs to be accurate and fast to reduce mis-hedging and slippage risks.

Accuracy is best achieved by having up-to-date loan-level data that can help provide the best prediction of the future amortisation profile of the swap. Updating the expected future average prepayment rate to include more recent trends is also important. As discussed in Example 6.4 in the sub-section on Examples of Extension Risk, deals that have capped margin resets, and hence allow for shorter extension periods (which can be 'rolled forward'), are a little less risky from a mis-hedging point of view, since every time the swap is rolled forward, the swap provider can re-compute the expected future amortisation schedule.

Speed is greatly assisted by having regular, automated generation of extended swap schedules, as discussed in the sub-section on Real-Time Hedging. While generation of these schedules should be happening anyway as part of the risk monitoring

---

[12]NCCD is a G20 financial markets reform initiative. See http://www.bis.org/bcbs/publ/d317 .htm.

process, having them instantly to hand in case of an unexpected non-call announcement is critical. The continuous and close surveillance of the issuer is also important in order to be able to react quickly. No third-party swap provider wants to be the last one on the street to find out about a non-call announcement!

STRESS TESTING

Because extension risk is such a rare event, Value-at-Risk (VaR) cannot capture the low-probability, high-impact nature of this risk. While VaR can be used on the revaluation of extension risk, this is likely to be very small, and is of no diagnostic value to understanding the true magnitude of extension risk should it ever be realised.

Therefore, arguably, the best risk metric for extension risk is a simple stress test: simply remove the call date, stress the market rates as per an institution's existing market risk stress tests and measure what the PnL impact is. Such an approach has two key benefits:

1. It removes the vagaries of proxy credit spreads used to compute the probability of downgrade.
2. It communicates to senior management a 'no surprises' number, which accurately (if also brutally) reflects the actual PnL damage a no-call event would inflict. No one in senior management can complain they didn't know what extension risk their traders were running with such simple and transparent stress tests in place.

Another useful risk metric to track for each issuer is the likely margin for new issuance versus the funding cost of not calling existing issuance. The bigger the difference, the larger the potential incentive is for issuers not to call their outstanding issuance, in theory at least.

CHAPTER 7

Downgrade Risk

No matter what some agency may say, we've always been and always will be a AAA country.

　　　　　　　　　　　　　　　　– Barack Obama (after S&P downgraded the USA)

I t is possible to structure securitisation notes so that they have a higher credit rating than the banks providing swaps to those transactions. For this to occur, swap providers must assume strict obligations imposed by the rating agencies. Swap providers certainly don't have the luxury that some governments may think they have to ignore the agencies' ratings and criteria!

These obligations typically involve one-way collateralisation and mandatory novation of the swap when the swap provider's credit ratings fall below specific trigger levels. We will refer to these obligations collectively as *downgrade risk* assumed by the swap provider.

Downgrade risk and its consequences differentiate securitisation[1] swaps from most other types of derivatives, even before considering prepayment and extension risk. With the exception of sovereigns, supranationals and agencies (SSAs),[2] derivatives with non-securitisation counterparties rarely involve the imposition of such conditions on the swap provider. The rating downgrade of a financial institution that also acts as a swap counterparty can have a profound impact across the entire market, which is unique to structured finance and securitisation transactions.[3]

We devote this chapter to understanding downgrade risk, pricing it and how to optimise it, and to the considerable risk management consequences for swap providers that continue throughout the entire life of a deal.

---

[1] Including whole-business securitisation, where any derivatives done by the business are subject to these rules.

[2] SSAs who issue AAA-rated bonds also routinely incorporate downgrade language.

[3] A rating downgrade of a key market participant can have far-ranging consequences for other structures. For example, in 2008 after American Insurance Group (AIG) ceased to have the required ratings to act as a swap counterparty across all of its structured finance transactions. Similarly, when the Royal Bank of Scotland (RBS) was downgraded in March 2014 this resulted in approximately 150 ratings trigger events across Europe, the Middle East and Africa.

RATING AGENCY CRITERIA

Each rating agency takes a different approach when assigning a credit rating to structured issuance. One common thread is the *weakest link* method under which the overall rating of a security cannot be any higher than the weakest link in the structure.[4] *Prima facie* this presents a problem whenever swaps are involved. There are, at the time of writing, only four banks rated AAA by each of the three major rating agencies,[5] and none of them are likely swap providers to a securitisation transaction. Nevertheless, a high proportion of structured issuance is AAA rated.

The rating agencies overcome this hurdle by requiring certain terms and conditions to be incorporated into the legal documentation that require swap providers to assume specific obligations depending on their credit rating. The aim of these terms and conditions is to de-link the swap provider's credit rating from that of the structured security as far as practicable. This de-linkage from the risk of counterparty downgrade works when rating downgrades happen prior to a swap provider defaulting, which provides sufficient time for any remedial actions to be taken. However, the de-linkage will fail if there is a jump-to-default, which is assumed to be extremely rare.[6]

While the exact terms vary widely, there are usually two key obligations assumed by swap providers to rated secured issuance:

1. When the swap provider's credit rating falls below a given minimum threshold called the *first downgrade trigger*, the swap provider must post collateral *one-way* to the special purpose vehicle (SPV).
2. When the swap provider's credit rating falls below another, lower, minimum threshold called the *second downgrade trigger*, they must (attempt to) replace themselves by novating the swap to another provider.

In general, we will refer to such terms and conditions as *downgrade language*. The specific terms and conditions are typically included in the Schedule and the Credit Support Annex (CSA) to the International Swaps and Derivatives Association (ISDA) Master Agreement. Whether a swap provider is providing a swap to its own issuance (when it is also the originator of the transaction), or on a third-party basis to a client, such downgrade language must be included in order for the rating agencies to assign a high rating to the issuance in accordance with their own rating criteria, as may be desired by the issuer.

Both downgrade triggers create material risk management issues for swap providers. The first trigger creates rating-contingent funding and liquidity risk. Since the recent introduction of the Basel III regulatory reforms, this risk is specifically

---

[4] See, for example, Fabozzi and Choudhry (2004), p38.
[5] The four banks are: KfW, Zürcher Kantonalbank, Landwirtschaftliche Rentenbank and L-Bank.
[6] Jump-to-default is certainly not without precedent however. Lehman Brothers had investment-grade credit ratings from the three major rating agencies immediately prior to default on 15 September 2008.

captured by the *liquidity coverage ratio* (LCR), discussed in detail in the section on Basel III and the Liquidity Coverage Ratio. The upshot of securitisation swaps having an LCR impact is that swap providers must hold *high-quality liquid assets* (HQLAs) against their contingent collateral outflows, which may be generated by a three-notch rating downgrade. Since holding HQLAs is usually a net cost to a swap provider, this must be carefully priced into any deal. This is discussed in detail in the sections on Liquidity Transfer Pricing and Contingent Funding Valuation Adjustment.

The first downgrade trigger is highly asymmetric. The obligation is for the swap provider to post collateral to the SPV, without the possibility of ever receiving collateral in return if the swap moves in-the-money to the swap provider. The reason for this asymmetry is that securitisation and covered bond SPVs by their nature have no access to spare liquidity and therefore are not in a position to post collateral. In addition, the amount of collateral required to be posted is often more than simply the mark-to-market (MTM) of the swap: there is usually an *additional amount* over-and-above the MTM to ensure that the SPV is covered for market movements in the period between a swap provider default and signing on a new swap provider. The size of these additional amounts can sometimes be very substantial: up to 20% or more of the swap notional amount.

The second downgrade trigger, dealt with in the section on Replacement Risk, creates a different type of risk. A forced novation in adverse circumstances could well mean that a swap provider needs to pay an egregiously large amount to another bank to step into the swap.

In the case that the swap provider fails to uphold its obligations either to post collateral or to novate the swap and also fails to come to an agreement with the rating agency(ies) who are rating the bonds, the rating agency(ies) are very likely to downgrade the issuance. This is likely to have a material impact on both the secondary market price of the impacted bonds and investor confidence for future issuance by that originator. In this regard, originators should choose their swap providers with care as their reputation with bond investors is additionally dependent on their swap providers meeting their commitments.

Each rating agency publishes its own *counterparty criteria*, which defines the terms and conditions under which swap providers can provide swaps to structured finance transactions. For the three main global rating agencies, the most recent criteria at the time of writing are:

Fitch	*Counterparty Criteria for Structured Finance and Covered Bonds* and *Structured Finance and Covered Bonds: Derivative Addendum* dated 1 August 2018
Moody's	*Assessing Swap Counterparties in Structured Finance Cash Flow Transactions* dated 26 July 2017
S&P	*Counterparty Risk Framework Methodology and Assumptions* dated 25 June 2013

These criteria define:

- The minimum credit ratings a swap provider must have in order for a structured finance transaction to receive a given rating.
- How much collateral a swap provider must post, depending on its rating and the type and tenor of swap.
- What type of collateral can be posted, and what haircuts are applicable.
- The timeframe within which collateral posting, or other remedial actions, must be taken.
- The precise obligations in relation to swap provider replacement if ratings breach the second downgrade trigger.

Criteria Specifics

The individual rating agency criteria are subject to a wide range of factors. Depending on the rating agency, these factors can include the following:

- *Note rating*. The higher the note rating, the higher the collateral requirement and the higher the two triggers discussed in the previous section.
- *Bond type*. Covered bonds can result in different downgrade obligations to asset-backed securities (ABS) and residential mortgage-backed securities (RMBS). In the case of covered bonds, some rating agencies make a distinction depending on whether the swap provider is the issuer or a third party.
- *Swap parameters*. As a general rule, the more risk and complexity a swap has, the harder it is to replace and hence the higher collateral requirements it will attract. Specifically:
  - The tenor or weighted average life (WAL) of the swap. Longer tenors require more collateral as their MTMs have greater potential variance.
  - Cross-currency swaps require more collateral than single currency swaps, as their MTMs have greater potential variance due to foreign exchange (FX) sensitivity.
  - Swaps with fixed-rate legs require more collateral than swaps with floating-rate legs as their MTMs have greater potential variance due to interest rate sensitivity.
  - Swaps with prepayment and/or extension risk require more collateral as they are more difficult and costlier to replace than swaps without those complex risk factors.
  - Any swaps with exotic features, or swaps referencing non-standard floating-rate indices, such as a specific bank's standard variable rate, require more collateral than swaps referencing standard floating-rate indices such as London interbank offer rate (LIBOR) or an overnight index swap (OIS) rate.
  - The currency or currencies involved. Emerging market or less liquid currencies require more collateral as they tend to be more volatile.

- *Legal aspects.*
  - Whether the legal documentation has appropriately catered for the de-linkage of credit risk to transaction counterparties – for example, if legal comfort has been provided in the form of a legal opinion regarding the enforceability of *flip clauses*. Where no legal comfort is provided, the second downgrade trigger can be higher. For a more detailed explanation of the operation of a flip clause see the section on Swap Priority and Flip Clauses in Chapter 4.
  - Appropriate legal opinions addressing true sale, any insolvency risk of the SPV and the potential for clawback in an insolvency situation.
  - Which jurisdiction the issuer is regulated in. The impact of bail-in on derivatives has resulted in more favourable treatment by some rating agencies in certain jurisdictions.

As a result of the above, different swaps can impose very different downgrade risks on the swap provider, even when rated by the same rating agency.

A further source of variation of terms is that the three main global rating agencies' counterparty criteria can differ very substantially. In practice, where an issuance is rated by multiple rating agencies the swap provider will be required to meet the most stringent applicable criteria.[7] This means that the same swap can have different pricing depending on which rating agencies are rating the transaction. This is not always widely appreciated by some issuers. Price-sensitive originators who have a choice of which rating agencies to use would be well advised to obtain a price comparison of the different cost consequences across the various rating agencies. It is not unheard of for some originators to select rating agencies for their transaction based purely upon the price of rating the issuance. Ignoring the various consequences of counterparty criteria is at one's own peril as it can create unnecessarily expensive swap costs for the life of a funding programme.

Yet another source of variation of downgrade terms is that historically each rating agency has revised its own criteria every few years. As a result, swap providers must take great care to model the correct criteria for each particular deal. Novations of back-book swaps that were initially transacted many years ago are usually governed by non-current counterparty criteria. It is not routine for such criteria, which are contractually embedded in the swap documentation, to be updated at the time of novation. This can be for a number of reasons, including the potential impact of the criteria changes on the underlying notes, the increased costs and the difficulties with obtaining consent from the trustee to any documentary changes to reflect the new criteria. As a result, any trade capture system must be able to record both current and non-current

---

[7]For example, if the swap provider has to post collateral under two different counterparty criteria, the amount posted must be the higher of the two. If, under one criterion the provider is required to post collateral, but under a different one to novate, the provider is legally obliged to attempt to novate whilst simultaneously posting collateral.

counterparty criteria against all swaps with downgrade risk. Without automation, the operational burden of tracking all the applicable counterparty criteria is not to be underestimated.

Examples

The three examples in this sub-section illustrate the obligations assumed by swap providers for different types of issuance. Note the difference in terms between the three swaps and between the different rating agencies for each swap. The reader is referred to each rating agency's counterparty criteria for the full terms and conditions, which can be complex.

EXAMPLE 7.1:

FinCo is issuing a AAA-rated ABS into a foreign currency, rated by Fitch and S&P. The foreign currency tranche pays floating interest plus 100 bps and is pass-through with a call option in three years. The swap provider is X-Bank, which is rated AA− by Fitch and S&P. X-Bank is providing the cross-currency balance guarantee swap, which has both prepayment risk and extension risk.

Under the Fitch criteria dated 1 August 2018, and assuming the swap is a continuation derivative with a flip clause, X-Bank must:

- Post collateral one-way to the SPV when either its:
  - long-term credit rating falls below A; or
  - short-term credit rating falls below F1.
- Replace itself with another eligible swap provider when either its:
  - long-term credit rating falls below BBB−; or
  - short-term credit rating falls below F3.
- The amount of collateral to be posted, assuming it is cash in the currency of the RMBS tranche, is:
  - $MTM + (1.25 \times 11.75\% \times 60\%) \times$ Swap Notional if X-Bank's rating is A−; or
  - $MTM + (1.25 \times 11.75\% \times 100\%) \times$ Swap Notional if X-Bank's rating is below A−.
- The timeframes for remedial actions are:
  - For posting collateral: 60 calendar days if X-Bank's rating is AA−; 14 calendar days otherwise.
  - For replacing the swap provider: 60 calendar days if X-Bank's rating is AA−; 30 calendar days otherwise.

Under the S&P criteria dated 25 June 2013, and assuming 'replacement option 1' under the criteria,[8] X-Bank must:

- Post collateral one-way to the SPV when its long-term credit rating falls below A.
- Replace itself with another eligible swap provider when its long-term credit rating falls below BBB+.
- The amount of collateral to be posted, assuming it is cash in the currency of the RMBS tranche, is:
  - MTM + 8% × Swap Notional (assuming currency Risk Group 1[9]).
- The timeframes for remedial actions are:
  - For posting collateral: 10 business days;
  - For replacing the swap provider: 60 calendar days.

EXAMPLE 7.2:

Y-Bank is issuing a AAA-rated covered bond in a foreign currency, rated by Fitch and S&P. The foreign currency tranche pays a fixed annual coupon of 0.50% and has an expected maturity of seven years, with a legal final maturity of eight years. Y-Bank, which is rated A− by Fitch and S&P, has engaged X-Bank, which is rated AA− by Fitch and S&P, to provide the cross-currency liability swap.

Under the Fitch criteria dated 1 August 2018, X-Bank must:

- Post collateral one-way to the SPV when either its:
  - long-term credit rating falls below A; or
  - short-term credit rating falls below F1.
- Replace itself with another eligible swap provider when either its:
  - long-term credit rating falls below BBB−; or
  - short-term credit rating falls below F3.

(Continued)

---

[8]There are four replacement options under S&P's 25 June 2013 counterparty criteria.
[9]As per S&P's 25 June 2013 criteria, Risk Group 1 currencies include: AUD, CAD, CHF, DKK, EUR, GBP, JPY, NOK, NZD, SGD, SEK and USD. Risk Group 2, 3 or 4 currencies include: HKD, KRW, MXN, TWD and ZAR.

- The amount of collateral to be posted, assuming it is cash in the currency of the RMBS tranche, is:
  - MTM if X-Bank's rating is A−; or
  - MTM + (1.25 × 11.75% × 60%) × Swap Notional if X-Bank's rating is below A−.
- The timeframes for remedial actions are:
  - For posting collateral: 60 calendar days if X-Bank's rating is AA−; 14 calendar days otherwise.
  - For replacing the swap provider: 60 calendar days if X-Bank's rating is AA−; 30 calendar days otherwise.

Under the S&P criteria dated 25 June 2013, and assuming 'replacement option 1' under the criteria, X-Bank must:

- Post collateral one-way to the SPV when its long-term credit rating falls below A.
- Replace itself with another eligible swap provider when its long-term credit rating falls below BBB+.
- The amount of collateral to be posted, assuming it is cash in the currency of the RMBS tranche, is:
  - MTM + 18% × Swap Notional (assuming currency Risk Group 1).
- The timeframes for remedial actions are:
  - For posting collateral: 10 business days.
  - For replacing the swap provider: 60 calendar days.

EXAMPLE 7.3:

Y-Bank is issuing a AAA-rated RMBS, rated by Fitch and S&P. Y-Bank, which is rated A− by Fitch and S&P, has engaged X-Bank, which is rated AA− by Fitch and S&P, to provide the single currency asset swap to swap the *tracker loans*[10] to LIBOR. This is a *basis swap*[11] with prepayment risk. Under the Fitch criteria dated 23 May 2017, X-Bank must:

---

[10]Tracker loans reference (or 'track') a central bank base rate.
[11]A basis swap is an interest rate swap where both legs reference a (different) floating rate index. When swapping tracker loans to LIBOR, the swap provider receives OIS from the SPV and pays LIBOR.

- Post collateral one-way to the SPV as per Example 7.1.
- Replace itself with another eligible swap provider as per Example 7.1.
- The amount of collateral to be posted, assuming it is cash in the same currency as the swap, is:
  - $MTM + (1.25 \times 0.75\% \times 60\%) \times$ Swap Notional if X-Bank's rating is A−; or
  - $MTM + (1.25 \times 0.75\% \times 100\%) \times$ Swap Notional if X-Bank's rating is below A−.
- The timeframes for remedial actions are as per Example 7.1.

Under the S&P criteria dated 25 June 2013, and assuming 'replacement option 1' under the criteria, X-Bank must:

- Post collateral one-way to the SPV as per Example 7.1.
- Replace itself with another eligible swap provider as per Example 7.1.
- The amount of collateral to be posted, assuming it is cash in the currency of the RMBS tranche, is:
  - $MTM + 7\% \times$ Swap Notional (assuming currency Risk Group 1 and a WAL of 10–15 years).
- The timeframes for remedial actions are as per Example 7.1.

Legal Aspects

Legal Position of the Rating Agencies   Since the establishment of the first bond rating methodology in the early twentieth century[12] the principles underpinning the rating of credit have fundamentally remained the same. Namely, there is a demand for information about credit risk within the market and rating agencies attempt to fill this gap by issuing credit ratings. In this respect, rating agencies act as intermediaries who are able to provide an interface between investor and issuer that reduces the information asymmetry that naturally exists between them.

Credit rating agencies perform an integral role within the structured funding marketplace by acting as specialist purveyors of information to investors, including an

---

[12]In 1909 the first bond rating scheme was published in a book entitled *Analysis of Railroad Investments,* which synthesised a number of reports containing complex data on the financial and operating position of railroad companies and attributed a single rating symbol to the bonds issued by them. The author was a Wall Street analyst named John Moody, who later went on to found Moody's Investor Services in 1914.

opinion about the creditworthiness of the securities, the likelihood of repayment and the potential for recovery in the event of default. As the use of credit ratings has evolved as an investment tool, the rating agencies increasingly hold the key to both capital and liquidity for securitisation issuers.

However, despite performing such an important role, the industry remains largely unregulated. Rating agencies exist in a relative oligopoly, with the landscape being dominated by comparatively few major players.[13] There are also high natural barriers to entry, which begs the question of what protections are available to investors when the rating agencies get things wrong.

In recent memory there have been a number of financial catastrophes that have damaged the credibility of rating agencies and dented the levels of confidence of investors. The business of rating credit based on notions of trust and accuracy and the reputational capital that a rating agency holds within the market is its lifeblood. This provides a strong incentive not to get things wrong, which can explain why the rating agency criteria applicable to securitisation has undergone many iterations since commencement of the financial crisis.

In the end, the rating agencies find themselves in a powerful and unique position. Within the structured funding market ensuring compliance with any rating criteria can make or break the transaction. On the other hand, these gatekeepers are still private institutions and if something goes wrong they are not classified as a transaction party so, in practical terms, there is limited recourse for both investors and issuers.

Role of the Trustee   Up to the time of any securitisation issuance, the underlying transaction documentation will be subject to an extensive period of review and negotiation between all of the relevant transaction parties. However, following the issuance of notes, the ability to make further amendments to the underlying documentation, particularly where any change may impact the interests of the noteholders in a material way, is constrained.

It is standard for any securitisation (whether it be a standalone or master trust) and covered bond documentation to require that any modification, waiver or amendment of the documentation will require the prior consent of the trustee. However, the level of discretion afforded to a trustee to agree to such changes is generally limited and may not be easily forthcoming.

The trust deed (or the terms and conditions of the notes) will set out a procedure that a trustee must follow in order to consent to amendments on behalf of noteholders.

---

[13]The credit rating industry is presently dominated by three rating firms, Moody's, S& and Fitch. To a lesser extent DBRS is also active within the securitisation marketplace. These entities are generally privately held companies and by their nature they are unashamedly commercial entities. This is illustrated by the market capitalisation of Moody's, the only rating agency to be a publicly held and traded company, which is over USD 31 billion (as at April 2018).

These conditions generally require that any significant change must be directed by an extraordinary resolution of the most senior class – or potentially all classes – of noteholder. Depending on the changes required, this can mean that noteholder meetings will need to be convened, which can be a costly and time-consuming process.

There are usually exemptions to this requirement to obtain noteholder consent but these tend to be limited to situations where the trustee is of the opinion that the relevant modification, amendment or waiver is:

- proper to make and not materially prejudicial to the interests of the relevant note-holders;
- to correct a manifest or proven error; or
- where the change is of a formal, minor or technical nature.

It is evident from the above that any trustee discretions available to be exercised are limited. It can be a struggle to implement change that may be favourable to a swap provider – for example, implementing new favourable criteria – if the changes cannot be attributed to one of the above discretions, and even then the trustee can be a counterparty that is difficult to deal with. Because of the nature of the trustee role, the trustee will often need to be indemnified for taking any action, such as amending documentation, which could expose it to liability from the noteholders. These challenges are something that the seasoned securitisation swap practitioner should be aware of and take into consideration before attempting to change any terms of a securitisation swap.

Contractual Protections In order to minimise the need to obtain consent from noteholders in response to rating criteria change, there are a number of contractual provisions available for the savvy swap provider to incorporate into its documentation during the negotiation phase. These can include language that freezes the applicable rating criteria to the criteria that was applied at the time of the rating of the notes. Down the track this can have either a positive or a negative effect, depending on how a counterparty may change in the future. Nevertheless, it does provide a level of certainty for the swap provider throughout the life of the transaction.

The second contractual protection is making consent to criteria changes by the swap provider subject to the proviso that such consent from the trustee 'not be reasonably withheld or delayed'. These can be tactical points that form part of the document negotiation and it pays for the securitisation swap provider to be thinking of these potential future issues at the outset of the transaction.

Updates of Counterparty Criteria

The rating agencies' counterparty criteria are subject to change at their discretion. Over the last decade, each of the three main global rating agencies has amended its counterparty criteria every few years. There have been two distinct phases to these changes. The first phase was in the immediate aftermath of the global financial crisis (GFC), when each rating agency made its criteria significantly more onerous. This, combined with the downgrade of many banks, forced a number of third-party swap providers – especially investment banks – completely out of the business of providing securitisation swaps to third-party issuers. In addition to ceasing new business, many investment banks novated some of their existing trades to higher-rated banks. The second phase, since around 2012, has involved the rating agencies moderating the obligations somewhat, though the obligations are still significantly higher than pre-GFC.

When a rating agency changes its criteria, previously transacted secured issuance can be impacted. If a rating agency tightens its criteria, for example, by increasing the amount of collateral to be posted, the notes are very likely to be downgraded by that rating agency if the documentation isn't amended to incorporate that change.

Issuers are usually very keen to avoid technical[14] downgrades because this will be seen as a serious breach of faith by investors. When the originator acts as the swap provider to its own transaction, ensuring that the notes are not downgraded is a straightforward priority. There will be a strong incentive for the issuer, in its capacities as a swap provider and originator to agree changes to the documentation. In this respect, the trustee should also accept such amendments (upon obtaining independent legal advice) since an investors' rights would be clearly enhanced by the stricter obligations.

It becomes more complicated when the swap transaction involves a third-party swap provider. Firstly, as discussed in the previous section, third-party swap providers who properly manage their risk should always ensure that their obligation to post collateral and any other obligations imposed upon them can't be made stricter without their consent. In this respect, it is not advisable for the swap provider to include language in the legal documentation that automatically incorporates any future changes to the rating criteria. Instead, it is preferable to reference the specific obligations contained within the criteria prevailing at the time of the transaction and upon which the rating agencies will have relied to assign any credit at that time.

If this approach has been adopted then the issuer will need to obtain the consent of the swap provider prior to the amendment of any documentation. It should be noted that a third-party swap provider is under no obligation to agree to any such change and this is a risk that the originator needs to understand very clearly at the outset.

A commercially reasonable third-party swap provider that is eager to maintain a favourable relationship with an originator and its reputation more generally will usually be open to negotiating the incorporation of criteria changes into a deal, subject to any internal risk controls, limits and appetite. Typically this will need to include the repricing of the downgrade risk and the payment of a fee[15] by the originator to the swap provider. In this respect, if the originator declines to pay that fee, and the terms

---

[14] Any downgrade really, but over technical downgrades they have some control.

[15] As discussed in the section on Risk Limits, the revaluation of downgrade risk can be significantly affected by changes in the market curves and rates. So, such a fee will likely incorporate market changes *in addition* to the stricter downgrade terms and conditions.

of the deal are not updated, then the originator faces the very real prospect of its notes being downgraded by the relevant rating agency.

Another possible scenario occurs when rating agencies reduce the burden of their criteria and it is the swap provider, rather than the originator, that is incentivised to amend the terms to reflect the new criteria. In this case, it can become more difficult to amend documentation if the changes do not clearly benefit investors. In any event, the Trustee is likely to require the guidance of the investors to agree to any documentary changes as discussed in the sub-section on Legal Aspects.

One way around this is to specifically pre-empt the scenario prior to the deal being transacted and including appropriate contractual provisions that may protect the swap counterparty in the situation. For example, it is possible to introduce language that acts as an automatic 'down-ratchet', that is, at the outset it is agreed that any favourable downgrade terms may be incorporated automatically without the need for consent at that time, but can't be tightened without the permission of the swap provider. In effect this is the same as the originator selling an option to the swap provider; a smart originator will be able to use this in negotiations.

Trade Capture and System Challenges

As we will see in later sections, it is imperative that banks accurately model their downgrade risk, both for good internal risk management purposes and also for regulatory compliance. In order to do this, the downgrade risk present in each swap must be accurately recorded in the trade capture system in which it is booked, or some supplementary system.[16] The best way to achieve this will vary considerably between banks depending on their internal systems. However, it is clear from the sub-section on Criteria Specifics that a large amount of information needs to be recorded in order to correctly calculate metrics such as contingent collateral obligations and other aspects of downgrade risk. If this information is incomplete or inaccurate, an incorrect understanding of collateral outflows could be very problematic in the event that the swap provider's credit rating is downgraded by one or more rating agencies.

Another systems issue that requires consideration is how to link the collateral obligations captured in a bank's front office trading system to the bank's collateral system. Normally, a trading system only sends MTM numbers to the collateral system for processing of collateral payments. However, securitisation swaps routinely involve the calculation of (contingent) collateral obligations in excess of the MTM. As a result, some kind of systems solution needs to be implemented to handle these additional amounts. Even for highly-rated banks, which are unlikely to be downgraded to the first downgrade trigger anytime soon, it is prudent that a *plan* for a systems solution is specified even if one is not actually built. More immediately, it is still likely that institutions in this category will have to capture the entire amount for LCR exposure

---

[16]Capturing the full parameter space of downgrade terms is well outside the capability of typical vendor trading systems, without proprietary modifications.

TABLE 7.1 Long-term senior credit ratings of 41 major banks in developed countries.

	Country	Bank	Fitch	S&P		Country	Bank	Fitch	S&P
	Australia	ANZ	AA–	AA– (neg)		Netherlands	Rabobank	AA–	A+ (pos)
	Australia	Commonwealth	AA–	AA– (neg)		Singapore	DBS Bank	AA–	AA–
	Australia	National Australia Bank	AA–	AA– (neg)		Singapore	OCBC	AA–	AA–
	Australia	Westpac	AA–	AA– (neg)		Singapore	UOB	AA–	AA–
	Canada	Bank of Montreal	AA–	A+		Spain	BBV	AA–	A–
	Canada	Bank of Nova Scotia	AA–	A+		Spain	Santander	A–	A
	Canada	CIBC	AA–	A+		Switzerland	Credit Suisse AG	A (pos)	A
	Canada	Royal Bank of Canada	AA	AA–		Switzerland	UBS AG	AA–	A+
	Canada	Toronto Dominion	–	AA–		UK	Barclays Bank plc	A (pos)	A
	France	BNP Paribas	A+	A		UK	HSBC Bank plc	AA–	AA–
	France	Natixis	A (pos)	A (pos)		UK	Lloyds Bank plc	A+	A+
	France	Societe General	A+	A		UK	Nationwide	A+	A (pos)
	Germany	Commerz Bank	BBB+	A– (neg)		UK	RBS Int Ltd.	BBB+ (pos)	BBB+ (pos)
	Germany	Deutsche Bank	BBB+ (neg)	BBB+		UK	Santander UK	A (pos)	A
	Italy	Intesa Sanpaolo	BBB	BBB		USA	BAML Int Ltd	A	A+
	Italy	UniCredit	BBB	BBB		USA	Citigroup	A	BBB+
	Japan	MUFG Bank	A	A		USA	Goldman Sachs Int	A	A+
	Japan	SMBC	A	A (pos)		USA	JP Morgan Bank	AA–	A+
	Japan	Mizuho Bank	A–	A		USA	Morgan Stanley Bank	A+	A+
	Netherlands	ABN Amro	A+	A (pos)		USA	Wells Fargo Bank	AA–	A+
	Netherlands	ING Bank	A+	A+					

Source: bank websites 22 June 2018. Note that some banks may use different corporate entities as swap providers.

calculations, as will be discussed later on in the section on Basel III and the Liquidity Coverage Ratio.

These issues are all the more important for lower-rated banks, which may already be in the position of having to post collateral. Having to manage this process manually is a significant operational risk with potential consequences for reputation.

The Competitive Landscape for Third-Party Swap Providers

The counterparty criteria emphasise the importance of a bank credit rating and, in this respect, the credit rating of a bank forms the foundation upon which an institution may decide whether to act as a third-party swap provider to a securitisation SPV or act as a swap counterparty to its own securitisation issuance. Table 7.1 shows major banks around the world ranked by their Fitch and S&P long-term credit ratings as at June 2018.

Even amongst the more highly-rated banks on the above list, many do not provide securitisation swaps to third parties as a current line of business. At the date of writing, third-party swap providers on the above list include: National Australia Bank, ANZ, Royal Bank of Canada, BNP Paribas, HSBC, Natixis, ING and Wells Fargo.

Theoretically, entities other than banks could provide securitisation swaps and, if they had higher credit ratings, could be at a considerable competitive advantage. However, in practice this does not really happen. There have been instances of AAA-rated *derivative product companies* (DPCs) structured by parent banks to specifically provide swaps and/or act as a third-party guarantor of the parent bank's swap liabilities (see Box 7.1), however, these vehicles are subject to their own particular constraints. Fund managers of unleveraged, long-only or even sovereign funds could also potentially achieve a high credit rating if they sought one, but to the best of the authors' knowledge this hasn't occurred – at least not for the purposes of becoming a third-party swap provider. This may be due to a range of factors including lack of knowledge of the opportunity, fund mandates not accommodating such activities and lack of risk appetite.

BOX 7.1: DERIVATIVES PRODUCT COMPANIES

A DPC is created by a sponsor bank or parent as a bankruptcy remote off-balance sheet vehicle that is able to enter into swaps and other derivatives transactions. DPCs can be structured to comply with specific rating methodologies, which enable them to achieve higher credit ratings than their parent. The use of DPCs first emerged in the early 1990s but following the financial crisis their use has fallen out of favour because of the regulatory clamp-down on off-balance sheet vehicles.

(Continued)

DPCs can be used as intermediaries in a derivative transaction or as third-party guarantors. When acting as an intermediary, the DPC will enter into a swap with the counterparty and then hedge the market risk of the swap by entering into a mirror trade with its parent. Because of the ability to optimise credit ratings, a DPC can also act as a highly-rated guarantor of the swap liabilities of a swap provider.

Under Basel III, the LCR requires banks to hold enough liquid assets to have the available liquidity to fund themselves through a 30-day stress period. The liquidity buffer must also cover any collateral posting obligations that would result from a three-notch downgrade, which drives up the liquidity costs for securitisation swaps. In this respect, DPCs could be utilised by a bank to provide securitisation swaps, thus reducing the amount of liquid assets required to be held in reserve by the parent bank. In the event that a bank providing securitisation swaps were to be downgraded to a level where it is required to post collateral (subject to the first downgrade trigger) it would be able to novate the trade to a DPC, thus staunching any outflow of liquidity.

Similarly, if the second downgrade trigger is breached it can be tricky for the swap provider to find a replacement – either due to lack of suitably rated counterparties or the costs of replacement. A DPC can provide a cheaper and less difficult replacement option in these circumstances. These features are all extremely attractive to any financial institutions providing securitisation swaps, which has found DPCs the subject of some renewed interest within the marketplace. For example, in 2014, the Royal Bank of Scotland (RBS) established the first rated DPC in over 14 years to guarantee a single interest rate swap within a whole business securitisation. Later that year RBS set up a second DPC, which was designed to guarantee swaps that RBS may have otherwise been forced out of due to changes to its credit rating.

However, despite the perceived benefits there are still a number of issues that need to be taken into consideration when deciding to set up a DPC. Firstly, the costs associated with establishing a DPC can be prohibitive. Amongst other things these can include the cost of capitalising the DPC, legal costs, rating agency fees and the costs associated with setting up a new corporate infrastructure, which can be intensive compared with retaining these capabilities in-house.

It is also likely that originators and SPVs will need to be persuaded to face a DPC in a securitisation swap transaction rather than an established financial institution. The off-balance sheet nature of a DPC will also naturally make regulators wary. In any event, DPCs are able to serve a useful purpose in certain circumstances. While the prospect of creating a DPC will not be suitable for all financial institutions, it is nonetheless a useful tool of which any institution providing securitisation swaps should be aware.

BASEL III AND THE LIQUIDITY COVERAGE RATIO

Since the GFC there have been very significant changes to the way bank liquidity is regulated in G20 jurisdictions. Because these regulatory reforms have very significant consequences for securitisation swaps, we devote this section to outlining the motivation for, and content of, the new liquidity regulations.

In the decades leading up to the GFC, a general complacency developed that banks and other financial institutions in developed economies would not or could not fail. For a customer, depositing their savings with a bank or making an investment in a financial institution was seen as a relatively risk-free proposition. However, from the onset of the GFC in late 2007 many major financial institutions around the world suffered serious liquidity problems leading to bank runs, emergency financial interventions by governments (including some banks being taken into public ownership) and even bankruptcy.

One of the highest profile examples was the collapse of the Newcastle-based bank Northern Rock, which suffered the UK's first bank run since 1866 in September 2007. Shortly after the GFC it was revealed that other major British banks were within two hours of their ATMs running out of cash.[17] Other major institutions to fail or be bailed-out by national governments included Bear Stearns, Lehman Brothers, Wachovia and Washington Mutual in the USA; ABN AMRO, Dexia, Fortis and UBS in Europe; and HBOS, Lloyds, RBS and Bradford & Bingley in the UK. While excessive leverage, poor credit quality and the rating agencies' practices were contributing factors, lack of liquidity was, arguably, the most important culprit.[18]

Two key sources of these liquidity problems were (i) the increasing reliance by banks and other lenders on short-term wholesale funding, which grew significantly as a proportion of total funding in the five years preceding the GFC before drying-up completely in the second half of 2007; and (ii) banks' large stocks of securitised assets (ABS, collateralised debt obligations (CDOs), RMBS), which became illiquid in stressed market[19] conditions and initially very costly, and later impossible to fund via the repo market.

---

[17]See www.independent.co.uk/news/people/profiles/alistair-darling-we-were-two-hours-from-the-cashpoints-running-dry-2245350.html.

[18]Liquidity can hide many other failings for a very long time. Lack of liquidity, on the other hand, can bring down even otherwise sound institutions.

[19]In an attempt to address the illiquid structured funding market for participants, the Bank of England introduced the Special Liquidity Scheme (SLS) in April 2008. This was a form of government assistance to improve the liquidity position of the UK banking system. It did so by helping banks finance assets that had got stuck on their balance sheets following the closure of some ABS markets from 2007 onwards. The SLS was, from the outset, intended as a temporary measure, to give banks time to strengthen their balance sheets and diversify their funding sources. The last of the SLS transactions expired in January 2012, at which point the Scheme terminated.

In response to these problems, the Basel Committee on Banking Supervision (BCBS) developed a range of high-impact regulatory reforms dealing with bank capital, leverage, market risk, credit risk and liquidity risk, collectively known as Basel III. The liquidity risk reforms include the introduction of two new ratios: the LCR and the net stable funding ratio (NSFR). Broadly speaking, LCR deals with short-term liquidity while NSFR deals with medium-term liquidity.

The LCR aims to ensure that banks have sufficient liquidity to survive a 30-day stress scenario. This is achieved by mandating that banks hold a minimum quantity of HQLAs against potential cash outflows. The LCR is defined as:

$$\frac{\text{Stock of HQLAs}}{\text{Total net cash outflows over the next 30 calendar days}} \geq 100\%$$

This stress scenario is prescribed in paragraph 19 of the official BCBS LCR regulation[20] as follows:

19. The scenario for this standard entails a combined idiosyncratic and market-wide shock that would result in:

(a) the run-off of a proportion of retail deposits;

(b) a partial loss of unsecured wholesale funding capacity;

(c) a partial loss of secured, short-term financing with certain collateral and counterparties;

(d) additional contractual outflows that would arise from a downgrade in the bank's public credit rating by up to and including three notches, including collateral posting requirements;

(e) increases in market volatilities that impact the quality of collateral or potential future exposure of derivative positions and thus require larger collateral haircuts or additional collateral, or lead to other liquidity needs;

(f) unscheduled draws on committed but unused credit and liquidity facilities that the bank has provided to its clients; and

(g) the potential need for the bank to buy back debt or honour non-contractual obligations in the interest of mitigating reputational risk.

Sub-paragraph 19(d) covers the downgrade risk in securitisation swaps to rated transactions. Specifically, if at any given time the contingent collateral outflow on a securitisation swap resulting from a one-, two- or three-notch credit rating downgrade is USD10 million, then the bank providing the swap will need to hold at least USD10 million in HQLAs in its liquidity book in order to be compliant with the LCR regulation. Most banks will hold slightly more as a safety buffer against volatility.

---

[20] Available at http://www.bis.org/publ/bcbs238.pdf.

TABLE 7.2 Local regulation implementing the Basel III liquidity requirements.

Jurisdiction	Local regulation	Regulator
Australia	Prudential Standard APS 210 Liquidity	Australian Prudential Regulatory Authority (APRA)
Canada	Liquidity Adequacy Requirements (LAR)	Office of the Superintendent of Financial Institutions (OSFI)
Europe, UK	Capital Requirements Directive IV (CRD IV)	Financial Conduct Authority/Prudential Regulatory Authority (UK)
Japan	LCR Pillar 1 and 3 Administrative Notices	Financial Services Agency
USA	12 Contingent Funding Risk (CFR) Part 249 Regulation WW	Federal Reserve

The cost of holding HQLAs depends on a variety of factors. Firstly, each country's local regulator defines what constitutes eligible HQLAs for its particular jurisdiction. Some jurisdictions define a wider spectrum of eligible securities than others, creating a further source of competitive differentiation. Secondly, within that universe of locally eligible assets, each bank will decide which particular assets to hold, and also how they are to be funded (including any duration mismatch between asset tenor and funding period, subject to NSFR constraints). Table 7.2 lists the local regulation implementing the Basel III liquidity requirements in some G20 jurisdictions.

Theoretically, non-bank entities which are outside the reach of Basel III could provide swaps to rated securitisation transactions without having to hold HQLAs, although they would still need to manage the contingent funding and liquidity risk arising from any downgrade risk, and this wouldn't be without cost. As discussed in the section on Rating Agency Criteria, to the best of our knowledge, non-bank entities have not been involved in this business to date.

LIQUIDITY TRANSFER PRICING

Liquidity transfer pricing (LTP) is the practice of allocating a uniform cost per unit of liquidity risk to the various businesses within a bank that generate that risk. It is a user-pays process that is typically carried out by a central Treasury unit (Figure 7.1). Generators of liquidity risk in banks include numerous business functions, such as deposit-taking businesses, originators of credit and liquidity facilities to corporate and other clients, other markets businesses, which have both current and contingent collateral obligations, and the Treasury function itself via the refinancing risk on its own funding activity.

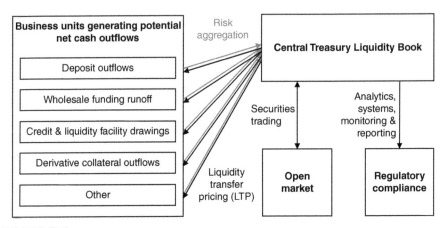

FIGURE 7.1   A typical centralised LTP process in a bank.

Having a well-designed, well-functioning and well-understood LTP process is a key component of good liquidity risk management. A poorly designed or implemented LTP regime may create perverse incentives for different businesses to write a large volume of deals, which could be mispriced or create an unacceptably wide exposure relative to the size of the balance sheet. Indeed, the widespread absence of LTP in banks prior to the GFC and the general treatment of liquidity as a free good was arguably one of the major causes of the GFC. The reader is referred to Grant (2011) for a highly insightful, in-depth discussion of this issue.

We will refer to the contingent outflow of collateral due to a three-notch credit rating downgrade as contingent funding risk (CFR). LTP for CFR will differ from institution to institution depending on its business mix, its level of sophistication and internal policy decisions.

When designing an LTP regime for CFR, the first key decision is defining the 'LTP contract', that is, precisely what each business unit is paying for and what it receives in return. This is important both for (i) third-party swap providers, where a trading desk or central XVA desk within a markets business will pay Treasury the LTP, and (ii) originator swap providers, where the funding units within Treasury that provide the swap *should* pay LTP to the liquidity unit within Treasury.

There are at least two possible options for this decision:

Option 1. Narrow definition: LTP only covers Treasury's cost of holding HQLAs and guarantees that liquidity will be available to cover collateral posting, but at an unknown cost.

Option 2. Broad definition: LTP provides full downgrade insurance, provided by Treasury to the business unit, inclusive of collateral posting costs in the event of downgrade, that is, contingent funding valuation adjustment (CFVA).

These choices entail very different types of risk transfer, incentives, LTP pricing and risk management for the business unit originating the swap with downgrade risk. Option 1 is sufficient to send a liquidity price signal – which should be tenor and currency dependent. However, option 1 does not allow the business unit to transfer CFVA to the liquidity risk unit of Treasury – it must manage that internally itself.

Care should be taken to design what will happen in the event of downgrade with option 1. For example, if a trading desk pays a five-year LTP charge on a CFR exposure, but the bank is downgraded to the first trigger in two years' time, under option 1 the LTP payments stop and the desk must start paying FVA for the collateral posting. However, assuming an upward-sloping LTP curve with tenor dependence, the desk has overpaid Treasury, which has avoided three years of HQLA holding costs.

Whichever option is taken, the decision should be explicit and enshrined in official policy so that (i) everyone knows which business unit is holding the contingent collateral costs and (ii) the business unit holding those costs behaves as the owner of that risk.

Another upfront design point with LTP is that it should only apply to *fixed amounts* of CFR exposure that are pre-agreed at the start of each LTP payment period. Since the MTM of swaps will be variable, there is the risk that there can be simultaneous moves in CFR exposure and funding costs at the same time. This type of *cross-gamma* risk is present in all XVAs and is generally best owned by a central XVA desk or, as a second-best option, the business unit originating the CFR exposure. Liquidity units in Treasury are not usually equipped to deal with cross-gamma risk.

Constructing the LTP Curve

Construction of an LTP curve is the domain of the Treasury liquidity team, which is a specialist function in its own right. Nevertheless, business units originating liquidity risk and paying LTP ought to take a keen interest in how LTP curves are constructed. As a key pricing input, and one that can change, any insight into the drivers of that change is useful both to manage client expectations and also to manage risk – especially retained cross-gamma risk.

A standard way to compute an LTP charge for a given tenor T is to assume a model portfolio of HQLAs, with specific assets identified, and an assumed funding profile, which could be a single fixed tenor T or a spread of tenors with an overall weighted average life of T. This model portfolio will have an average expected future yield Y, while the funding profile will have an average cost C. Given that bank funding costs are generally higher than yields on HQLAs, the LTP charge will be $C - Y$, which should be positive. Note that C should represent a funding tenor that is NSFR compliant.

This model portfolio approach allows payers of LTP a transparent insight into the cost drivers. It even opens up the possibility that some type of LTP hedging could be considered, for example, with a long/short credit default swap (CDS) strategy to proxy hedge credit spread differentials. The model portfolio also provides something akin to a benchmark index for the team responsible for holding and trading HQLAs. Running a liquidity book can be a highly profitable exercise, although not without considerable risk, and so proper attribution of trading skill requires a clear separation of *alpha* (skill) from *beta* (index performance). Good governance requires that the team responsible for designing the benchmark model portfolio should be different from the team holding and trading HQLAs – otherwise there is a potential conflict of interest in gaming the benchmark. Such gaming could potentially result in inflated LTP charges for all business units in the bank including those providing securitisation swaps.

Updating the LTP Curve

When HQLA yields and funding spreads change, as they are liable to do frequently, the model portfolio methodology will produce a different LTP curve. If CFR exposure was static, this wouldn't be a problem. The business unit originating the CFR should have hedged it via a term LTP payment to Treasury. Any future change in LTP couldn't impact a fully liquidity-hedged back-book trade. However, unlike a simple liquidity facility for a fixed amount, CFR exposures from securitisation swaps are far from static. As the MTM changes, so does the CFR exposure. If the LTP curve was static, and only the MTM ever changed, one could conceivably hedge the market risk on the LTP payments – see the sub-section on Revaluation and Hedging for further discussion on this point. However, the cross-gamma risk – the risk of a simultaneous move in LTP and MTM – is completely unhedgeable.

One way to address this problem is to include an additional risk buffer in deal pricing to fund payments caused by realised cross-gamma risk. This is discussed further in the sub-section on Revaluation and Hedging.

A good way to exacerbate this problem is for Treasury to make frequent changes to the LTP curve without prior warning. A transparent process, at fixed, known time intervals, is critical to the viability of managing CFR – and especially the cross-gamma risk – in the business units that generate it. Ideally, the LTP rates would be fixed by Treasury for a long period (say one year), over which averaging can smooth volatility, at least in the absence of extreme market events.

CONTINGENT FUNDING VALUATION ADJUSTMENT

What Is CFVA?

When pricing a securitisation swap, it is essential to know what the expected cost of the CFR will be over the whole life of the swap. This expected cost is a key component of the overall price. In the case of a third-party swap provider, this fair-value cost will need to be charged to the client. In the case of an originator swap provider, this fair-value cost will still need to be factored in to accurately compute the landed cost of funds. This is particularly important for making relative value calls between secured and senior unsecured sources of funding.

> We define the CFVA to be the discounted expected whole-of-life cost of the CFR for a swap or a portfolio of swaps.

In the sub-section on The CFVA Calculation, CFVA will be computed analogously to other market standard derivative valuation adjustments such as credit valuation adjustment (CVA) and FVA; that is, we will integrate an expected exposure over time.

Collectively we will refer to all valuation adjustments as XVAs. XVAs are required to modify the risk-free price of a derivative given by the MTM to a more complete valuation that is inclusive of key risks. The (arbitrage-free) MTM does *not* include certain real-world costs such counterparty credit risk, funding risk, CFR and capital costs, as these are context dependent, specifically on the parties and the legal documentation of the deal. XVA pricing differs from the MTM calculation in one key respect: it depends on the particular bank that is holding the derivative. This dependence can be via portfolio effects[21] or via bank-dependent metrics such as funding curves, or both. In contrast, the MTM of a derivative only depends on external market rates.

For the avoidance of doubt, CFVA only factors in the contingent cost of posting collateral. It does not include pricing for the other component of downgrade risk: replacement risk. Replacement risk is covered in the section on Replacement Risk.

Costs and Probabilities

The fair-value cost of holding a swap with CFR has two components:

1. the expected LTP payments to Treasury over the life of the swap; and
2. (if not included in the LTP contract) the expected cost of posting collateral one-way to the SPV over the life of the swap.

---

[21]Portfolio effects can dramatically impact *incremental* CVA because of the possible existence of offsetting positions in a particular bank's portfolio. One can also compute a *stand-alone* CVA price for a derivative, which only relies on external market rates, including the counterparty's CDS curve (if available). However, such a price may be quite different from the incremental CVA, which is a much better reflection of the fair value of the counterparty credit risk for the particular bank holding the derivative.

Both of the above expected costs depend on the *probability* of the bank being at a given credit rating. There are four cases to consider:

- *Rating band 1.* If a bank is very highly rated – more than three notches above the first downgrade trigger – then the trading desk holding the swap won't have to make any LTP payments at all since there is no LCR impact.
- *Rating band 2.* Within one to three notches of the first downgrade trigger, the trading desk will have to make LTP payments to Treasury to reflect the LCR impact.
- *Rating band 3.* At or below the first downgrade trigger, but above the second downgrade trigger (novation), the trading desk will have to fund actual one-way collateral payments to the SPV (unless that is included in the LTP contract).
- *Rating band 4.* At or below the second downgrade trigger, *assuming that the swap is novated*, there is zero cost. (Alternatively, since novation is not straightforward, one could conservatively assume continued collateral posting.)

As we saw in the section on Rating Agency Criteria, the amount of collateral to be posted can be rating-dependent between the first and second downgrade triggers. Recall that in Example 7.1 in the Examples section, under the Fitch criteria, the amount of collateral to be posted was:

- MTM + (8.8% × Swap Notional) if the swap provider is rated A−; and
- MTM + (14.7% × Swap Notional) if the swap provider is rated BBB+ or BBB.

Such increases in the additional amount within a rating band aren't always the case across all rating agency criteria, but we need a calculation methodology that can handle it when it does occur. So, in general, the CFVA calculation will need to sum over probability-weighted credit rating states in order to incorporate all of the above. These probabilities will need to take credit rating transitions into account, as migration between bands 1–4 and credit ratings is entirely possible over the life of a swap. This aspect of the CFVA calculation is different from all the other XVAs defined to date in the literature.

Note that if the amount of collateral to be posted at a given credit rating is 10 million, then the LTP payments three notches above that rating are also based on a principal amount of 10 million, that is, exactly the same amount as represented by the dashed lines in Figure 7.2.

The probabilities themselves may be obtained from rating agency transition matrices or possibly from internal bank data or other sources. For example, S&P's *2014 Annual Global Corporate Default Study and Rating Transitions*[22] contains historical average one-, three- and ten-year transition matrices for 'All Financials' over the

---

[22] Available at https://www.nact.org/resources/2014_SP_Global_Corporate_Default_Study.pdf. See table 41 on page 79 of this study.

Spot Exposure

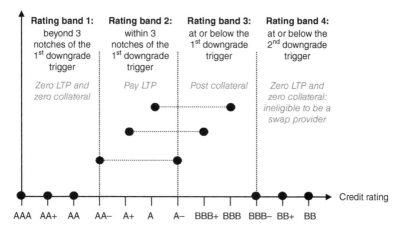

FIGURE 7.2 Example LTP and collateral exposures at different rating levels for a swap provider to a AAA-rated securitisation transaction. There are four ratings bands. This picture illustrates the case when additional amounts increase within a ratings band.

TABLE 7.3 An S&P ratings transition matrix for 'All Financials' that are AA-rated to begin with. The numbers in the table represent percentage probabilities.

	AAA	AA	A	BBB	BB	B	CCC/C	D	NR
1 year	0.52	86.33	8.56	0.41	0.03	0.03	0.04	0.04	4.05
3 years	1.26	64.24	20.11	1.94	0.2	0.18	0.04	0.22	11.81
10 years	1.32	31.54	29.14	4.68	0.38	0.4	0.04	1.19	31.31

period 1981–2014. This data could be used to construct downgrade/upgrade probability curves for different initial ratings. Clearly, the applicability or otherwise of this 'All Financials' data requires careful consideration at each institution (Table 7.3).

The clear downward bias in ratings transitions should focus the minds of all current and prospective swap providers!

The CFVA Calculation

We compute total CFVA for a swap as the sum of individual CFVAs for each notch in the credit rating spectrum:

$$CFVA = \sum_{rating=AAA}^{rating=D} CFVA^{rating} \tag{7.1}$$

In turn, each individual $CFVA^{rating}$ is computed as the time integral of: (i) the discounted expected contingent funding exposure of the swap; multiplied by (ii) the probability of being at that credit rating; multiplied by (iii) the cost of either paying LTP or posting collateral at that rating as the case may be; that is:

$$CFVA^{rating} = \int_0^\infty \mathbf{E}[\max(AM(rating, t) - MTM(t), 0)]$$

$$\cdot DF(0, t) \cdot \Pr(rating, t) \cdot C(rating, t) \cdot dt \qquad (7.2)$$

where

$AM(rating, t)$ is the *additional amount* of (i) collateral required to be posted at a given rating at time t if that rating is within Rating Band 3; or (ii) contingent collateral required to be posted three notches below the given rating at time t if that rating is within Rating Band 2. This must be the maximum additional amount across all rating agencies rating the transaction.

$MTM(t)$ is the MTM of the swap at time t *to the swap provider*.

$DF(0, t)$ is the discount factor from time 0 to time t

$\Pr(rating, t)$ is the probability of the swap provider being at a particular rating for a given rating agency RA at time t

$C(rating, t)$ is the *cost* at time t of (i) paying LTP if the rating is within Rating Band 2; or (ii) posting collateral[23] if the rating is within Rating Band 3.

The term $\mathbf{E}[\max(AM(rating, t) - MTM(t), 0)]$ is the expected contingent funding exposure of the swap at time t and is non-negative. It represents the amount of collateral that (i) would need to be posted upon a three-notch downgrade or (ii) needs to be posted if such a downgrade had occurred at or before time t. If the MTM is positive and larger than the additional amount, then this term is zero. Otherwise it is non-zero and there is a positive CFR exposure.

If $\Pr(rating, t) = 1$, this is consistent with what the FVA calculation would be if collateral were to be posted one-way to the SPV from day one (rather than contingently depending on credit rating).

Monte Carlo Computation of CFVA   As per CVA and FVA, a risk-neutral Monte Carlo simulation is the most efficient method for computing Eq. (7.2) due to the number of stochastic variables typically involved (FX, interest rates in multiple

---

[23]Note that the collateral posting cost would simply equal the LTP charge if the broad definition of LTP is implemented, as discussed in the section on Liquidity Transfer Pricing.

currencies, single- and cross-currency basis). It is now standard market practice for banks' trading units to have a central XVA engine to compute CVA and FVA. Such an engine, or at least the methodology upon which it is built, can be leveraged to compute CFVA in a manner fully consistent with FVA. This consistency is important when considering hedging CFVA, discussed in the sub-section on Revaluation and Hedging. Using the same, central XVA engine for CFVA is clearly the most efficient approach, for at least three reasons:

1. *Code maintenance.* Whenever code changes are required to accommodate a general market change, this only needs to be done once, with no cross-alignment between engines required. Such changes are inevitable and more frequent than one might expect. Examples of things that potentially generate the need for code upgrades to XVA engines are: converting lognormal volatilities to normal volatilities (to accommodate negative interest rates) and changing discounting from LIBOR to OIS.

2. *Plumbing.* Connecting systems to one another is always more expensive and time-consuming than expected. Having one less system to interface with saves time and money.

3. *Guaranteed consistency.* Using one engine means that all XVA metrics can be computed from precisely the same inputs and algorithm.

Despite these clear efficiencies, resource constraints and systems architecture can conspire to ensure sub-optimal tactical approaches are taken in many institutions!

CFVA, FVA and Cross-Gamma   The cost function $C(rating, t)$ can be constructed to be either independent or dependent of the swap provider's credit rating. If it is independent of rating, and assuming (reasonably) that the LTP charge is always lower than the outright collateral posting cost,[24] we have the strict inequality for the one-way posting of collateral:

$$CFVA_{RA} < FVA \qquad (7.3)$$

for each rating agency *RA*. At face value, this intuitively makes sense: it should be cheaper to contingently post collateral than to actually post collateral.

However, if the cost function is rating dependent and the collateral funding cost at lower ratings are assumed to be higher than its current cost, then it is no longer the case that inequality (7.3) will always hold. While higher costs at lower ratings will be offset by the lower probability of being downgraded to those ratings, this offset is not guaranteed to be sufficient to preserve inequality (7.3). In particular, if the assumed

---

[24]This is reasonable since a portfolio of HQLAs should yield more than the OIS rate earned on posted cash collateral. Non-cash collateral could complicate matters, but once haircuts are factored in, the expectation would still be that HQLAs are higher yielding than OIS.

funding cost increases more rapidly with respect to rating level than the decrease in the probability of being at that rating level, inequality (7.3) won't hold.

Arguably it makes sense to ensure that rating-dependent funding costs are chosen to ensure that inequality (7.3) does indeed hold. If not, it would be cheaper to restructure a transaction to have the swap provider post collateral from day one, which would be both perverse and, in the case of third-party swap providers, terminal for business from a competitive swap market perspective.

One might counter-argue that FVA, being non-contingent, can be hedged via fixed-cost funding trades from day one, whereas CFVA cannot. In the case of CFVA the swap provider really is potentially exposed to higher funding costs if it is downgraded, and those future hedge costs could result in inequality (7.3) being violated. However, in reality FVA involves a lot of contingency too. FVA cannot be completely hedged since MTM movements can require additional funding requirements, which could well be at higher cost than originally expected. This is cross-gamma risk once again. Cross-gamma risk *could* be incorporated into the FVA calculation via a correlation assumption where certain scenarios in the Monte Carlo calculation have elevated funding costs. This would be philosophically consistent with a rating-dependent cost function in the CFVA calculation. However, this is far from standard market practice in computing FVA, rightly or not. For consistency, we would argue that cross-gamma should either be incorporated into both CFVA and FVA, or neither.

Potential Net Funding Benefit Prior to Downgrade   Consider a securitisation swap that is market-risk hedged with a vanilla swap under a standard, zero-threshold, two-way CSA with an interbank counterparty. Further suppose that the securitisation swap is expected to go out-of-the-money to the swap provider under standard risk-neutral assumptions. In this case, the vanilla hedge will be expected to go in-the-money to the swap provider and, since it is under a two-way CSA, will deliver an expected funding benefit to the swap provider.

This funding benefit will be lost if the swap provider is downgraded to the first trigger level or below. Equation (7.2) incorporates this potential lost funding benefit, together with the cost of LTP charges and the contingent cost of posting any additional amount.[25]

Multiple Rating Agencies   Many securitisation transactions involve more than one rating agency. Equations (7.1) and (7.2) accommodate this by defining $AM(rating, t)$ to be *maximum* additional amount across all rating agencies rating the transaction. However, it should be noted that there is another assumption operating here, which isn't strictly correct. Equation (7.2) assumes that the probabilities of rating migration are the

---

[25]This can be explicitly shown by decomposing the $E[MTM]$ term into its constituent expected positive exposure (EPE) and expected negative exposure (ENE) terms.

same across all relevant rating agencies and indeed that ratings migrations are perfectly correlated. In reality, this is not the case, although in many instances general trends can be discerned with timing differences amongst the various agencies. However, we would argue that the considerable benefits of model parsimony far outweigh any lower order effects from including de-correlated rating agency actions. Attempting to discern rating agency downgrade correlations would be a fraught exercise in which the model risk would likely outweigh any benefit.

We now provide some numerical examples to provide ballpark CFVA costs. The Example 7.4 is highly simplified for illustrative purposes only. Example 7.5 uses sophisticated Monte Carlo analytics developed by *Quantifi*.

EXAMPLE 7.4:

Consider an n year cross-currency swap where the swap provider is in rating band 2 with 100% probability for the entire life of the transaction i.e. the swap provider pays LTP for the life of the trade. Further suppose that the LTP charge is 50 bps (no tenor dependence), that the swap MTM is zero at all times and the additional amount is 10% of the swap principal (no time-to-maturity dependence). In this case, Eq. (7.2) simplifies to

$$\sum_{i=1}^{n} 10\% \cdot P_i \cdot DF_{i+1} \cdot 0.50\% \cdot \tau_i$$

which is the dollar cost of CFVA. Dividing by the PV01, given by $\sum_{i=1}^{n} 0.01\% \cdot P_i \cdot \tau_i \cdot DF_{i+1}$, results in a CFVA charge of 5 bps.

EXAMPLE 7.5:

Consider a seven-year receive AUD/pay EUR cross-currency swap where both legs are floating rate. Suppose the LTP charge, additional amount, and swap provider rating probabilities are the same as in Example 7.4. Using Monte Carlo paths from *Quantifi* analytics, the CFVA cost is 9.5 bps. The additional 4.5 bps over-and-above Example 7.4 is due to the MTM component, which is, on average, negative. Details are provided in the spreadsheet available at www .securitisationswaps.com. Figure 7.3 shows 20 of the 7,000 Monte Carlo paths used in the calculation.

(Continued)

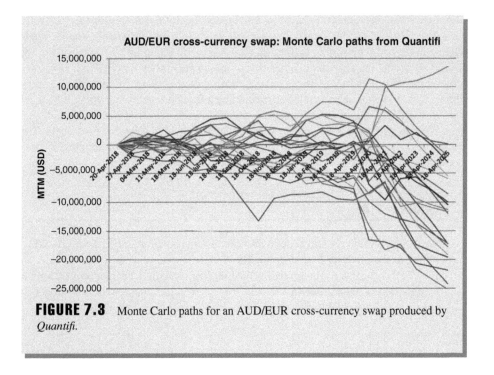

FIGURE 7.3 Monte Carlo paths for an AUD/EUR cross-currency swap produced by *Quantifi*.

Revaluation and Hedging

As per standard derivative valuation adjustments such as CVA and FVA, CFVA should ideally be revalued daily in the same central XVA engine. Anecdotally, most banks have not progressed this far, but it is reasonably clear that this is the correct target state.

The revaluation process can be a source of value. If the bank isn't downgraded during the life of a swap, the component of CFVA relating to downgrade will never be paid and can therefore be released to profit and loss (PnL). Only the HQLA holding costs will be paid away, assuming no rating upgrade. This is analogous to the value release from CVA when a counterparty doesn't default and the credit risk component of CVA (as opposed to the market risk component) isn't hedged. Of course, if MTM and/or funding movements are adverse, then this release value will offset losses rather than providing additional revenue. But if those adverse movements don't eventuate on average, then there will be value to be released as ongoing revenue. We would argue that given the unhedgeability of cross-gamma risk, the release of any positive CFVA accrual should be conservatively managed by the Product Control function.

The revaluation process will show a negative correlation between CVA and CFVA in relation to market risk. If a swap goes in-the-money to the swap provider then CVA will increase and CFVA will decrease. Conversely if the swap goes out-of-the-money, CVA will decrease and CFVA will increase. As a result, if a bank decides to hedge the market risk component of CFVA, there will be efficiencies from aggregating CFVA sensitivities with CVA sensitivities through a reduction in the size of hedge trades and hence also a corresponding reduction in the cost of capital generated from those hedges.

Ultimately the decision to hedge CFVA will be based on several key considerations, which are often driven by underlying accounting standards.

- *Trading book or banking book?* Originators providing their own swaps will generally transact securitisation swaps in their banking book, which is not subject to the same fair-value accounting treatment as trading books.[26] As a result, originator swap providers may not feel compelled to take CFVA to PnL at all, in which case there is no accounting risk to hedge.
- *Materiality.* Trading book positions should be fair-value accounted, which means CFVA should be taken to PnL, at least if it is deemed 'material' in size by either Product Control or auditors. If the position is deemed immaterial, it may not be taken to PnL, in which case there is no accounting risk to hedge. Conversely, banking book positions – which although strictly don't require fair-value accounting – should arguably have CFVA taken to PnL if they are highly material.
- *Relative volatility.* A large CFVA position that isn't particularly volatile (e.g. driven by short-tenor single-currency swaps as opposed to long-dated cross-currency swaps) could arguably be left unhedged, whether or not it's taken to PnL.
- *Systems and analytics.* Once a decision to hedge has been made, it needs to be supported by robust and reliable systems and analytics to deliver aggregate sensitivities for hedge execution. This requires investment and planning, which can be scarce resources in cost-constrained environments.

RISK LIMITS

While market risk management is covered in the section on Market Risk Management in Chapter 8, there are some specific points unique to CFR, which will be covered here.

A bank's total CFR exposure should be governed by a risk limit set at a senior asset and liability risk committee. Beyond this basic starting point, individual institutions

---

[26]Future Basel reforms, such as Fundamental Review of the Trading Book (FRTB) may change this state of affairs.

may wish to impose sub-limits to control the tenor of CFR exposures, the currency of CFR exposures, the purpose of CFR exposures and possibly other parameters. These sub-limits can be useful levers to target specific outcomes when risk appetites change.

Tenor

The tenor profile of CFR exposures should be informed by a bank's view of its own downgrade risk and funding costs. A highly-rated bank will be more comfortable taking-on long-term CFR exposures generated from long-dated swaps than a lower-rated bank on negative watch. The expected timing and number of notches of downgrade in given scenarios is a key factor in sizing CFR sub-limits across time buckets. Reducing the CFR sub-limit of longer-dated time buckets is a more targeted way to manage elevated downgrade risk than solely reducing the overall limit. If a downgrade does occur, but the CFR exposure is entirely short-dated, the roll-off time will be correspondingly short and the likely costs correspondingly modest.

Currency

Banks have differing access to funding, and costs of funding, across the different jurisdictions in which they operate. As a result, a currency-based sub-limit is a useful tool to reflect those realities. Unlike tenor-based sub-limits, a currency-based sub-limit may be relatively easily complied with by inserting currency optionality into the CSA. If collateral can be posted in multiple currencies at the discretion of the swap provider, then currency-based sub-limits really serve to influence deal structuring rather than acting as an impediment to doing deals. Note that different currencies may be subject to different haircuts and market volatilities, which will need to be factored in to exposure calculations and pricing.

Purpose

Some banks may wish to allocate their CFR risk limits to different classes of counterparty preferentially depending on strategic considerations. Preferential considerations amongst different counterparties may include the degree of cross-sell and the country of domicile of the counterparty. Sub-limits facilitate a hard implementation of this strategy, as opposed to a purely discretionary one. It is also useful for a bank to plan how much CFR exposure it will need for its own structured issuance versus availability (if any) for third-party business.

MITIGATION STRATEGIES

There are many things that a swap provider can do to limit the damage from downgrade risk, should it come to pass. As discussed in previous chapters, the key to effective mitigation is incorporating appropriate terms to deal with potential scenarios into the deal during the structuring phase. After the swap has been dealt, there's a lot less room to move.

Choice of Rating Agencies

Given the wide variation in counterparty criteria amongst the rating agencies, there is an opportunity available at the commencement of the programme or standalone transaction to appoint the rating agency to rate the notes that has the most favourable terms, to the extent that investors don't demand a particular agency rate a deal. The impact of such choices can be quite profound as highlighted by some of the following examples.

EXAMPLE 7.6:

A bank rated AA−/AA−/Aa3 by Fitch/S&P/Moody's wishes to transact a fixed/float interest rate swap with a WAL of six years to support a AAA-rated transaction. Investors require any two of the main global rating agencies to rate the deal. Moody's first downgrade trigger level is more than three notches below Aa3, so that is the most favourable terms assuming that the current rating will be maintained. Both Fitch and S&P require collateral posting at A−. However, Fitch requires an additional amount of 4.5% whereas S&P requires 15.0%. Fitch and Moody's are therefore the optimum choices.

Given that it is practically impossible to change rating agencies after issuance has occurred, this analysis needs to be done upfront.

EXAMPLE 7.7:

The same bank as in Example 7.6 wishes to transact a float/float cross-currency swap with a WAL of three years to support a AAA-rated transaction. Investors require any two of the main global rating agencies to rate the deal. Moody's first downgrade trigger level is more than three notches below Aa3, so that is the most favourable terms assuming that the current rating will be maintained. Both Fitch and S&P require collateral posting at A−. However, Fitch requires an additional amount of 11.75% whereas S&P requires 5.0%. S&P and Moody's are therefore the optimum choices.

(Continued)

It is also worth considering rating agencies beyond the big three if the investor base is amenable. A case in point is Toronto Dominion (TD) bank, which has chosen DBRS and Moody's to rate its covered bond programme, to which it provides its own swaps. As at April 2017, TD was rated Aa1 (neg) by Moody's and AA (neg) by DBRS. The collateral triggers are at Baa1 for Moody's and BBB for DBRS. As a result, there is no LCR impact to TD at those levels; that is, it can hold zero HQLAs against its covered bond swaps. In contrast, the other four big Canadian banks all have Fitch rating their covered bond programmes in addition to DBRS and Moody's. As a result, they have an LCR impact from their covered bond swaps.

In Australia, all the covered bond programmes of the big four banks are rated by Fitch and Moody's. Had DBRS been chosen instead of Fitch, there would be zero LCR impact from any of their covered bond swaps.[27]

Contractual Protections

If rating agencies change their counterparty criteria in a favourable way for swap providers, the deal terms should allow for those new terms to automatically become the prevailing terms of the deal. It is critical that this is automatic, otherwise the SPV trustee will not allow any changes to the deal. It is also critical for swap providers that this mechanism does *not* operate if the terms become less favourable for swap providers. Obviously, this will be a point for negotiation and it is not unreasonable to assume that originators will have precisely the opposite perspective!

As a liquidity risk mitigant for swap providers, the inclusion of such 'down-ratchets' in the contractual documentation does two things: (i) they make sure that the most favourable possible terms become part of a deal; and (ii) they ensure things can't get any worse than originally contemplated.

In reality, such a mechanism will not be a game-changer in terms of the amount of risk reduced, but every little bit helps and there's no reason why this shouldn't be a standard condition for all swap providers.

Optimum Implementation of Counterparty Criteria

All the counterparty criteria from the different rating agencies allow some choices to be made. Some choices will be better than others and, in aggregate over an entire swap book, the impact can be substantial. Careful reading of the criteria is important.

---

[27]Given the shortage of HQLAs in Australia (necessitating a *committed liquidity facility* from the Reserve Bank of Australia), such a change of rating agencies would be systemically beneficial.

In addition, for ease of system implementation, some potential CFR exposure reductions may appear to be too complex to model. It is at least worth keeping track of such 'corner cutting' so that future optimisation can be considered if funding and liquidity risk become problematic.

EXAMPLE 7.8: OPTIMISED CALCULATIONS

Both Fitch and S&P stipulate the use of stressed prepayment rates in their counterparty criteria. This lengthens the WAL and can potentially increase the additional amount of collateral. From Fitch's counterparty criteria:

> Fitch's analysis relies on the prepayment assumption being capped at the lowest of: 5% a year; the portfolio-specific prepayment rate reported over the previous six months; and the counterparty's internal prepayment rate assumption. Alternatively, a zero prepayment assumption can be applied for simplicity.

And from S&P's:

> The calculation of the remaining WAL of a derivative agreement should be based on a prepayment speed of 0.0%, or such other stressed low prepayment rate as indicated in the relevant criteria for the hedged asset or liability. The stresses used will depend on the relevant maximum potential rating

A simple, expedient choice in both instances is to simply use a prepayment rate of 0%. However, for a modest amount of additional modelling work, using the highest allowable prepayment rate will reduce the WAL and hence the modelled CFR exposure by a potentially material amount – at least in conjunction with other optimisation choices.

EXAMPLE 7.9: USE OF RATING

Incorporating any advantage that a bank's current credit rating confers can yield material reductions in modelled CFR exposures. S&P has four 'replacement options', which have different additional amounts specified. It is possible for a bank rated A+ or higher to elect replacement option 2, which provides for

(Continued)

substantially lower additional amounts than replacement option 1. However, should that bank be downgraded to A−, it will need to change its election to replacement option 1 or else replace itself as swap provider. Modelling this (allowable) change of election, rather than simply choosing a more punitive replacement option 1 for modelling CFR, can yield substantial reductions.

If in doubt as to what choices or elections are allowable, it is highly advisable to consult with the relevant rating agency to clarify one's interpretation.

Risk Transfer

It may be commercially possible in some circumstances to negotiate a step-up in a swap that is contingent upon the rating downgrade of a swap provider. Such a mechanism would provide for increased swap payments when collateral needs to be posted. Those increased payments may partially or completely offset the increased funding costs borne by the swap provider. Rating agencies would assume such step-ups would be triggered in their stress testing as part of their credit rating process and, as a result, such step-ups need to be reasonable in size (i.e. not hundreds of basis points) so as to not adversely impact the rating of the transaction. Such step-ups transfer the risk of any swap provider downgrade to the SPV in the first instance, although effectively it is transferred to the originator as any step-up on the swap would likely be paid from excess spread, which would normally be returned to the originator via the asset swap and/or equity tranche.

Another way that funding and liquidity risk can be transferred back to the originator is via an at-risk deposit. This mechanism requires the issuer to deposit an agreed sum of money into a bank account. If the swap provider is downgraded, it can take ownership of the deposit to pay for increased funding and liquidity costs. If the swap provider is not downgraded over a given period, the sum on deposit can amortise according to a pre-agreed schedule.

Both the step-up and at-risk deposit may or may not be commercially acceptable to different originators at different times. However, the incremental impact from even a partial risk transfer, when combined with the cumulative effect of the other risk mitigants discussed above, can be substantial.

Collateralisation from Day One

Many originators now require third-party swap providers to post the MTM as collateral from day one of certain rated transactions, particularly covered bonds. This is a commercial requirement in order to reduce the sponsor's aggregated counterparty credit risk and credit risk capital attributable to the swap provider. Such a requirement is clearly in excess of what the rating agencies require, assuming that the swap provider's rating is above the first downgrade trigger.

However, when a swap provider posts collateral from day one, the CFR exposure is greatly reduced. After all, if the swap provider is downgraded to the first trigger level, it doesn't need to post the MTM twice! Only the additional amount is required to be posted upon downgrade. Three notches above first trigger, the CFR exposure from the additional amount is obviously less than the CFR exposure from both the MTM and the additional amount.

For third-party swap providers at least, discussing this collateralisation option with their originator clients during the structuring phase of a transaction is worthwhile. Some clients may not have considered the potential counterparty credit capital savings, which can compensate for the higher swap costs due to the FVA charge.

REPLACEMENT RISK

So far, this chapter has focused on the first downgrade trigger, requiring a swap counterparty to post one-way collateral in the event of a rating downgrade. However, it is essential to also consider that the rating agency criteria have a two-step trigger process.

The aim of this second downgrade trigger is to protect the rating of the notes and ensure enhanced protection for the SPV so that it is not left facing an insolvent swap counterparty. If a swap counterparty were to breach the second rating threshold then it will be forced to take remedial action, which generally involves the replacement of the swap counterparty before the end of a cure period. The various remedial actions available to a swap counterparty downgraded to the second trigger level include:

- The replacement of the swap counterparty with another appropriately rated swap counterparty.
- The appointment of a third-party guarantor (provided that the guarantor holds the requisite rating) to guarantee the downgraded swap counterparty's obligations under the swap.
- Restructuring the swap documentation to adjust the rating trigger levels downward.

We will look at each of these options in turn, however, it is important to note that each of them can be problematic, impractical and expensive. Indeed, as the credit ratings of financial institutions deteriorate and funding costs increase, replacement risk represents a very real issue that needs to be considered by both issuers and swap providers. In an environment of declining credit ratings this has even led some financial institutions to consider removing these types of swaps from their structured funding transactions altogether.[28]

---

[28]In 2016, the Dutch bank ABN Amro removed all of the interest rate swaps from its EUR 24 billion covered bond programme over concerns around the high swap replacement costs

Replacement of the Swap Provider

The replacement of a swap counterparty in a structured funding transaction creates a number of issues that require careful consideration. Firstly, the replacement swap provider will need to hold the requisite rating in accordance with the relevant rating agency criteria in order to act in the role. This means that there is a natural restriction on the number of participants who are actually able to provide replacement swaps and raises questions whether the market for replacement swap providers is deep and liquid enough to absorb any kind of systemic shock. In a market where the number of highly-rated financial institutions is small it could be difficult to find a replacement that not only holds the requisite rating but also the expertise required to be able to participate in such a bespoke market.

In the UK market, utilities companies that have entered into inflation swaps relating to whole business securitisations are a good example of the risks that arise when there is a shortage of eligible replacement swap providers. The inflation swap market is generally considered to be illiquid, with only a handful of financial institutions willing to take on the swap provider role. This creates a concentration risk that could lead issuers to reconsider their funding strategies in the case of any systemic downgrade of the banks that provide those swaps, which could, in a worst case scenario, lead to those utilities issuers losing their operating licences.

The novation of a swap to a suitably rated counterparty also creates significant and uncertain costs for the original swap provider. Any replacement swap provider will be seeking a premium to take on the risk over-and-above all of the risk charges that will need to be included in the price.

There is a second pricing risk, which is more difficult to analyse. That is, the possibility that the replacement swap provider may itself have to find a new counterparty if it gets downgraded beyond the second trigger level. This replacement valuation adjustment (RVA) would need to be priced into any replacement costs otherwise the replacement counterparty could find itself in the same position as the original counterparty in the event that it is downgraded, for example, dependant on other financial institutions with higher ratings to step into the trade.

Third-Party Guarantors

An alternative to replacement is for a third party to act as a guarantor. While a guarantee could be obtained from a parent entity or a specially established DPC, in practice not many institutions are willing to guarantee the swap obligations of a third party unless

---

that could potentially arise in the event of a bank downgrade. To smooth the interest rate mismatches in the cover pool ABN Amro use a stand-by cash reserve account. It is not the first European bank to remove swaps from structured funding transaction, with Societe Generale and Credit Agricole also taking similar actions.

there is some benefit for themselves. While there has been resurgent interest in the use of DPCs to perform this function (see the sub-section on The Competitive Landscape for Third-Party Swap Providers) the collateralisation requirements to do this mean it is often more cost efficient and 'cleaner' for all parties if a replacement counterparty steps into the swap provider role rather than acts as a guarantor.

Restructuring

In the event that a sufficiently rated counterparty is unwilling or unable to step into a transaction when the second downgrade trigger has been breached, the issuer is left in a very difficult position. One option available would be to amend and restructure the swap documentation to reduce the level at which the replacement trigger is breached, but this can have negative consequences for the overall transaction. In some circumstances this may be palatable – for example, where the originator is also acting as swap counterparty and the replacement costs outweigh the benefit of appointing a replacement. Nevertheless, amendments of this type are likely to place pressure on the rating of the notes and may result in an unwanted rating ceiling on notes, which would then be capped at the rating of the swap counterparty. This can be difficult to digest and it is also likely that such measures would face stiff opposition from any trustee due to the potential detriment to noteholders.

Mitigants

Estimating the costs associated with the replacement of a swap provider are a little like picking a number from thin air. While it may be possible to construct a model that can assign the probability of a downgrade estimating those costs is far more difficult to quantify. This means that a swap provider should always be alert to the possibilities of a downgrade and be prepared to pre-empt or pro-actively manage replacement in order to minimise costs. For example, it is possible that in the event of the downgrade of a swap provider there may be a correlation with the decline of market conditions more generally. It would be prudent for a swap counterparty to be alert to the possibility of novating swaps early, or at least before they are forced to for breaching the second downgrade trigger, in order to avoid potentially inflated replacement costs.

Another possibility may be to structure for replacement risk at the beginning of the transaction. We have previously discussed the operation of standby swaps in the section on Standby Swaps in Chapter 4. A standby swap arrangement involves a third-party swap provider that intermediates between the swap provider and the issuer in the event that the swap provider defaults or fails to meet its obligations. While these arrangements can be expensive to maintain, they do provide a greater level of certainty that a replacement swap provider will be available to step into the trade upon the second downgrade threshold being crossed.

CHAPTER 8

Deal Management

In preparing for battle, I have always found that plans are useless but planning is indispensable.

– Dwight D. Eisenhower

Chapters 5–7 dealt with the pricing, structuring and risk management of specific risks in isolation. In this chapter, we assemble all the building blocks and explain how a securitisation swap transaction is put together from start to finish.

One key aspect of securitisation swaps is that, despite their complexity and the skill and effort required to competently close a deal, they are just one component of a much larger transaction: the actual funding trade itself. For third party swap providers, it pays to engage with clients as far as possible in advance of any potential trade. When the issuance process is underway, often within tight timeframes, discussing the finer points of an esoteric derivative risk factor is far from ideal. Equally, in the event that a third-party swap provider comes into a transaction late, they may find themselves under pressure to understand all of the risks inherent with the particular trade within the required timing for closing the issuance.

PRICING

The Total Swap Cost

The total cost of a securitisation swap, expressed in basis points over the mid-market level ('mid swaps'), is simply the sum of all the risk charges and other costs incurred by the swap provider. This is equally true for all swap providers (whether they are a third party or the originator). Table 8.1 lists the various components.

TABLE 8.1   Total securitisation swap costs assembled from the component charges.

Component swap charge	Basis points
Execution	[A]
Standard XVAs:	
▪ CVA ▪ FVA ▪ Others	[B] [C] [D]
Cost of capital	[E]
Sales margin	[F]
Esoteric risk factors:	
▪ Prepayment risk charge	[G]
▪ Extension risk charge	[H]
▪ Downgrade risk charge	[I]
Total fixed swap costs	**[A]+[B]+[C]+[D]+[E]+[F]+[G]+[H]+[I]**

Components [A]–[F] are present in any derivative transaction, vanilla or otherwise, although the following is worth noting:

- In the case of an originator swap provider, [F] would normally be zero.
- Different banks may have different XVAs in place depending on their accounting and auditor decisions. Newer XVAs such as KVA and MVA may or may not be included. Older XVAs such as CVA and FVA are market standard.
- For intermediated asset swaps [A] should be zero as the swap provider is hedging with the originator and not with the open market.

The total fixed swap costs are added to the mid swaps level to arrive at the 'all-in' swap cost. For a cross-currency liability swap, the mid swaps level is what the originator must pay over the domestic floating rate index to swap the bonds into another currency, ignoring all transaction costs.

EXAMPLE 8.1:

A UK-based RMBS originator is issuing three-year weighted average life (WAL) AAA-rated bonds to investors in EUR. The bonds pay 1 month EURIBOR +50 bps. In the absence of transaction costs, this swaps back to 3 month GBP LIBOR +53 bps (the mid swaps level). In other words, the swap that receives 3 month GBP LIBOR +53 bps and pays 1 month EURIBOR +50 bps has a mark-to-market (MTM) of zero at the time of pricing. If the fixed swap costs are 20 bps, then the all-in swap price for the originator is 53 bps + 0.20% = 73 bps.

The swap provider will compute the mid swaps level from two things. Firstly, there are all the component swaps that are required to manufacture the final product. For the GBP/EUR cross-currency swap in Example 8.1 there are three constituent swaps, namely, a GBP/USD cross-currency swap, a USD/EUR cross-currency swap and a 3 month/1 month EURIBOR basis swap. Secondly, the coupon of +50 bps over 1 month EURIBOR needs to be swapped back to GBP. This involves computing the equivalent fixed margin over 3 month GBP LIBOR, which has the same net present value. Many clients think that +50 bps over 1 month EURIBOR should swap back to +50 bps over 3 month GBP LIBOR, but this is not the case! As discussed in the sub-section on Vanilla Swap Pricing in Chapter 4, the *conversion factor* is required to calculate the spread on the other leg of the swap.

Pricing Transparency

Unlike vanilla derivatives, securitisation swap prices aren't live-quoted by exchanges or brokers or even disclosed to other participants in the marketplace after a trade. Even when swap documents are made public for rated transactions, the swap costs are almost always redacted. Thus the securitisation swap market is highly opaque – which is often to the advantage of third party swap providers.

In order to partially redress this information asymmetry, originator clients of third-party swap providers are well advised to ask for a breakdown of swap charges into individual components, in addition to creating price tension by engaging with multiple swap providers. In practice, clients normally do not see [E] and [F] split-out separately – those charges are deemed 'proprietary' (one can imagine that this could change in future as both practice and regulation are evolving to further increase transparency). Nevertheless, obtaining some form of price breakdown is a good way for clients to progress pricing discussions with potential swap providers, ask probing questions and ultimately achieve better pricing.

Once price breakdowns have been obtained from several swap providers, the various cost components can be compared. While there will always be some price variability, any swap provider quoting outlier pricing on a particular cost component should be questioned on its assumptions and methodology.

Another point on price breakdowns is that CVA and FVA are deeply – and inversely – connected. They are both computed from the forward MTM profile of the swap. CVA is large when the forward MTM is more heavily in-the-money to the swap provider and vice-versa for FVA. So it is unlikely that both charges can be simultaneously large. Furthermore, any structure or solution that purports to decrease one is likely to increase the other, requiring careful assessment of the merits of such arrangements.

Clients facing third-party swap providers are also well advised to seek price transparency in the mid swaps level. Each underlying swap component should be separately quoted and – ideally – compared in real time to a live quote on Bloomberg or Reuters.

Execution Charges

Originators will want to reduce the cost of every swap component in Table 8.1 to achieve the lowest possible landed cost of funds. Chapters 5–7 have discussed the numerous risk and cost mitigation strategies for the three esoteric risk factors: swap prepayment risk, swap extension risk and downgrade risk. But even something as basic as swap execution may be open to cost reduction and this shouldn't be overlooked.

Swap execution, particularly for cross-currency swaps, requires a well-planned strategy prior to execution. Time zone differences can mean that some markets are closing before others are open, so that even at the 'optimal' time for the pricing call, liquidity in one or more component swaps is scarce or even non-existent. This creates risk (and opportunity) for a swap provider that needs to warehouse market risk for a period before it can be hedged in the open market.

One way around this is to 'pre-hedge'. Pre-hedging is where the swap provider, in anticipation of an imminent issuance, begins hedging up to several days prior. When the client has consented to this practice and where pre-hedging is being undertaken for the benefit of the client (i.e. it is not front-running), this practice can be significantly cheaper than hedging the entirety of the market risk post-trade. This is especially the case for swaps with very large principal, as the risk can be drip fed into the market over a period of time in a manner that is much less likely to push rates in a particular direction. It also allows for bilateral arrangements to be made with other market participants who may be 'axed' to provide particularly favourable pricing on certain swap positions (because they have offsetting trades and/or a house view on the direction of the market).

There are numerous commercial, legal and regulatory risks to navigate when pre-hedging, but the cost savings may justify the effort. The key risks to consider and plan solutions for in advance are:

- *Unwind risk.* If the issuance doesn't occur, or occurs in substantially smaller volume from what was anticipated, who bears the swap unwind costs? If the originator bears the cost, how can the unwind cost be verified? If the swap provider bears the cost, how can it be comfortable that the originator is giving it all relevant information on the progress of the book-build in a timely manner?
- *Legal and regulatory constraints.* Do swap traders executing the pre-hedging need to be placed behind a Chinese Wall as they may be privy to private-side information? Is this sufficient or even permissible in the jurisdiction where the transaction

is occurring? At the very least, written consent from the client in advance can only be helpful to mitigating these risks.[1]

DEAL CHECKLIST FOR SWAP PROVIDERS

Securitisation swaps are complex deals, which involve more moving parts than other derivative trades. In the middle of a hectic deal situation, some tasks can easily fall under the radar, potentially creating problems later on. The following checklist contains items that should be checked well in advance of transacting a swap. Individual banks may require additional tasks to be performed.

- *Chinese walls.* Consider if a Chinese Wall needs to be set up for the deal. Engage with relevant compliance functions – it is better for the compliance department to opine that a Chinese Wall is not required than for deal staff to come to that conclusion themselves, only to be subsequently found in error.
- *Internal pricing approvals.* Numerous pricing approvals may be required. Often a central XVA desk will make the CVA and FVA price. Hurdle rates for return on equity (RoE) may need special approval for structured trades. Traders will normally quote the execution charge and may need to approve the other risk charges if they are held responsible for those risks.
- *Credit approval.* Have all the relevant credit submissions been prepared? Has the credit department been alerted that a trade is coming so that its decision can be made in the required timeframes?
- *Counterparty setup.* Securitisation swaps are transacted with SPV counterparties, not the originators. Have the SPV counterparties been setup in the relevant systems? Have all onboarding, anti-money laundering and KYC procedures been completed?
- *Limits management.* Are there sufficient market risk, credit risk and liquidity risk limits to accommodate the expected trade (also noting that some trade are upsized at the last minute)? In addition to the vanilla market risk limits, is there sufficient prepayment value-at-risk (VaR) limit, extension stress limit, contingent funding exposure limit, sub-limit and so on?
- *Product approval.* Does the swap have any particular features that require specific product approval from internal stakeholders? For example, trigger features, different underlying asset class and new jurisdiction of underlying loans.
- *Trade booking.* Can the front-office trading system book the trade? Can downstream risk systems handle the trade?

---

[1]If pre-hedging is ever deemed to be front-running, the legal consequences can be dire. See www.independent.co.uk/news/business/news/mark-johnson-guilty-hsbc-banker-fraud-case-trade-uk-energy-firm-a8015971.html.

- *Tax.* Are any tax approvals required due to the jurisdictions involved and/or proposed tax treatment of the trade?
- *Legal review and sign-off.* Have all the legal swap documents been reviewed and signed-off by internal legal counsel prior to execution?
- *Dry runs.* Have pricing call dry-runs been scheduled with the client to: (i) run through the precise sequence of execution steps; (ii) confirm alignment of rate sources; and (iii) iron out any questions in advance of pricing?
- *Back-office notification.* Has back office been notified that a bespoke trade will be executed? This may require automated confirmations to be suppressed and G20 trade reporting to be manually overridden.

CLOSING THE DEAL

The Pricing Call

Liability swaps are usually transacted immediately following bond pricing with investors so that all the market risk can be quickly hedged out. If a third-party swap provider is involved, the transaction is usually closed via a pricing call on a recorded phone line.[2] The pricing call is typically attended by one or more representatives from the originator's treasury funding team and representatives from the swap provider, usually a trader and someone from the derivative sales and/or structuring team who leads the call. The purpose of the call is for the originator to communicate to the swap provider the coupon rate and principal of bonds just issued, agree the mid swaps level, confirm the all-in swap price and re-confirm all the other terms of swap. Because securitisation swaps are complex with a long list of key terms, it is expedient to reference prior agreement, such as an email from a given date, where all the swap terms are in writing.

Immediately following the pricing call, the securitisation swap is 'live' and the swap provider has market risk to manage. It is good practice for the swap provider to send an email to the originator straight after the call with all the agreed rates in writing. The swap confirmation is usually executed upon issuance of the notes, which can occur several days later – a time lag which is unusually long in comparison to more vanilla derivative transactions. This is discussed further in the sub-section on Executing the Documents.

Arriving at the mid swaps level for a cross-currency securitisation swap typically involves a series of steps where each of the component swaps levels is agreed. The component swaps may include cross-currency swaps, single currency basis swaps and single currency fixed/floating swaps. The standard procedure for agreeing rates on a

---

[2]Sometimes the process can occur in a chat room (e.g. on Bloomberg), which is expedient if there is more than one swap provider involved and communications between the originator and the various swap providers is required to be segregated – that is, a separate chat room for each swap provider. This is easier to manage than multiple phone lines.

pricing call involves the person leading the call asking for the trader to give the prevailing market rate for each swap and then asking the originator to confirm its agreement. Because different rate sources can often vary slightly, it is a good idea to iron out any misalignments in advance by having dry-runs of the pricing call. Dry-runs also ensure that the originator understands the entire process, including aspects such as conversion factors, and isn't disputing any of the numbers. Such a dispute could delay the swap being in place in a timely manner, causing slippage while the market keeps moving (it never stops!). A clean pricing call is where the originator readily confirms all component rates read-out by the trader and agrees the all-in price. A clean call should take no longer than 10 minutes.

Executing the Documents

The signing and closing of a structured funding transaction can be an extremely complicated process with a number of moving parts. There are numerous requirements that will need to be completed within set time frames, including the completion of due diligence calls, the submission of the preliminary (red) and final (black) prospectus to the relevant listing authority, the execution of transaction documentation, the sale and transfer of the receivables, the issuance of notes to investors and the flow of funds. This process will usually be managed by the external legal counsel of the issuer in accordance with the signing and closing agenda. We do not aim to cover the operation of each of these procedures here but rather to focus on those that are relevant to the swap counterparty.

It is standard market procedure for a structured funding issuance to settle on a T + 5 basis, which means that settlement of the notes will occur five business days after the trade date. It is usual procedure for the swap pricing call to occur on the trade date but final executed documentation (namely the ISDA Master Agreement, Schedule, CSA and any confirmation) will not be available until the settlement date. This can leave the swap provider in an interesting position from a compliance perspective.

On one hand, the swap provider will act to hedge its position on the open market following the pricing call. However, on the other hand, because the swap documentation is not available until later this can cause internal compliance issues and conflict with G20 requirements, which require immediate reporting of swaps. The key lesson is to make sure that you engage with your compliance department as early as possible to avoid surprises.

Covered Bond Coupon Rounding

The covered bond market has the convention that the fixed rate coupons are rounded-down at the time of pricing to the nearest 0.125%. The difference between par and the price of the bond paying the rounded coupon is paid to the issuer as an *upfront payment*. Usually this is of no concern to the swap provider except that it has an extra cash flow to book. However, sometimes market rates can be on a knife-edge where the rounding may either be down only a tiny amount or a full 0.125%. In these circumstances, the XVA charges on the swap can be quite different depending on the outcome of the rounding.

The best way to accommodate this situation is for the swap provider to quote the originator two prices depending on which outcome eventuates. If the swap provider doesn't do this, it runs the risk of absorbing an unexpected increase in XVA costs. If the deal was finely priced, this can be an unwelcome sting!

MARKET RISK MANAGEMENT

All market risk factors should be managed within a robust, consistent and holistic risk management framework. This is especially true of more esoteric market risks such as swap prepayment risk, extension risk and downgrade risk, which are all unhedgeable. The key purpose of the risk management framework is to ensure that all business is safely conducted within approved limits.

Each of the three esoteric risks covered in this book are different. Swap extension risk is concerned with a low-probability, high-impact non-call event. Swap prepayment risk is present throughout the entire life of pass-through instruments and represents a high-probability, low-impact (hopefully) event. Downgrade risk has elements of both: the LTP payments generate ever-present XVA cross-gamma risk, but an actual downgrade event is a low-probability, high-impact event.

The key to managing these three very different, esoteric market risks is to understand how much is being taken on, ensuring it is within risk appetite and taking appropriate and timely actions based on the quantitative and qualitative information generated.

Specifically, market risk management of swap prepayment, extension and downgrade risk should ideally cover the following four activities:

1. *Measure.* Independently validated models to measure:
   - for all three risks: revaluation of pricing and stress testing;
   - for swap prepayment and extension risk: VaR; and
   - for downgrade risk: exposure limits and sub-limits, and CFVA VaR.
2. *Monitor.* This consists of quantitative and qualitative components. For the quantitative monitoring, the target state should ideally be automated daily production of the chosen risk metrics. At least as important is qualitative surveillance of the issuer's business and wider market trends to monitor the on-the-ground reality and the potential for non-call.
3. *Limit.* A governance framework with hard risk limits, informed by the institution's risk appetite settings. The current exposures should be tested against the limits within the automated monitoring process.
4. *Inform and action.* The above outputs should be integrated into forward business decisions.

Measurement

In Chapters 5–7 we described how swap prepayment, extension and downgrade risk can be priced at inception. The same calculations can be conducted throughout the life of the swap to revalue each specific risk component of swap pricing. This is a useful diagnostic for risk management, as it will reflect the impact of changes in credit and funding spreads, interest rates, foreign exchange (FX) rates and basis. It is also important for fair value accounting to ensure all trading book positions are correctly marked.

The use of VaR across all three securitisation swap risks ensures that each risk contributes to the bank's market risk capital, as every market risk factor should (stress testing can also achieve this, albeit in a different way).

Monitoring

Having independently validated models to compute the relevant chosen metrics is only part of the risk management solution. Having *automated* processes to run those models and report the results is just as important. The reasons are simple. The practical reality is that the models are complex and require voluminous inputs, so if they require manual operation to run then they are much more likely to be run infrequently, run with errors and, given the way many banks periodically restructure teams, not run at all if knowledge transfer doesn't occur. Furthermore, if a low-probability high-impact event really did occur, having reliable, pre-computed extended swap amortisation profiles upon which to quickly base a hedging decision is essential. So, while models are great, *automate*, *automate*, *automate* (without losing the critical knowledge of what is being automated).

Governance and Risk Limits

Good governance requires trading desks to have explicitly stated and approved risk limits for all risk factors. First of all, this requires deciding which metric(s) to apply limits to. No matter which metric is chosen, there will be volatility due to movement in market rates and curves. It is important to factor in this volatility (i) when sizing the risk limit and (ii) for third party swap providers especially, deciding how much new business to chase. Ideally, sensitivities would be computed to inform the business how big a market move is required for a passive limit breach to occur. This can be used to size a risk buffer and/or a limit review trigger.

The approval process for the limit is also a good opportunity to inform senior management about what each esoteric securitisation swap risk is. The various risk charges on securitisation swaps can generate decent revenue, but they do come with significant tail risk, which ought to be well understood by everyone involved.

For market risk managers, setting the risk limits at a level that triggers periodic review is one useful strategy to ensure that these risks are kept on an organisation's risk radar. It is also useful for the business to feel sufficiently scrutinised to ensure there is no creeping sense of complacency in running its book and to periodically justify why running increased amounts of risk is a good use of the firm's finite risk budget.

Inform and Act

There is always much to do managing a back-book of existing securitisation swap positions. For third party swap providers this must be done at the same time as chasing new business, while for originator swap providers there is the steady flow of new issuance to accommodate. Although everyone in the front office would like large risk limits, the reality in many institutions is that the tension between the Risk and Finance departments means there are periods of growth, and periods of constraint. Throughout this cycle, the task of effective risk management is a continuous responsibility (see Tables 8.2–8.5).

TABLE 8.2   When risk metrics are well within risk limits, approaching risk limits or beyond risk limits, a range of different responses may be required.

Status – Risk metrics	Likely actions
Metrics well within limits	Growth phase. Keep writing new business.
	Track expected future risk exposures given roll-off of back-book positions and roll-on of new business. This will indicate how long the current risk limit will accommodate the growth phase. Also track the 'run-rate' of net revenue per unit of each risk metric. Is it reasonable? Is it variable?
Metrics foreseeably approaching limits	Consider whether risk limits should be raised and/or the pace of new business needs to be reduced: ■ If so begin work developing risk committee submission. Determine how much limit is required to accommodate expected future business and the expected revenue. ■ If not, assess how roll-off of existing business will reduce expected limit usage over time so limited new business can be accommodated and client expectations can be managed. Although unlikely, also consider if certain back book positions could be feasibly novated to reduce exposure and accommodate new business.
Metrics close to limits or beyond limits	Stop writing new business unless and until limits are increased or metrics reduce well below the limit (via roll-off of existing swap positions and/or market moves).

TABLE 8.3 The range of possible responses to prepayment risk events.

Status – Prepayment risk	Likely actions
A low prepayment rate has broken a controlled amortisation schedule	Possible actions, highly dependent on the precise circumstances, are: ▪ Is the low rate due to a calculation mistake? It pays to check. ▪ Determine if the cause was a likely one-off drop in realised prepayment or if the expected average prepayment rate needs to be lowered. Will there be a compensating spike up in prepayment next period? This may involve asking the originator and other informed parties for their views. ▪ Determine a new expected principal amortisation schedule. ▪ If there is prepayment risk transfer agreement (side-letter) in place with the originator, exercise all rights under that agreement. ▪ Execute any re-hedging trades. ▪ Revalue the prepayment risk charge and update the revenue reserve. ▪ Has the originator complied with all duties of disclosure (if any) in relation to events that may have caused the unexpected prepayment rate? If not, determine what remedies may be pursued. ▪ Consider proactively communicating what has occurred to risk oversight and product control staff. ▪ Is this an idiosyncratic event, or will other loan pools and associated swaps be impacted?
Prepayment volatility and/or the expected average prepayment rate are significantly different to initial expectations	▪ As per the bullet points above, with the exception of the first two.

TABLE 8.4 The range of possible responses to extension risk events.

Status – Extension risk	Likely actions
Qualitative surveillance indicates heightened risk of non-call by a certain issuer or market subset	Possible actions, highly dependent on the precise circumstances, are: ■ Review probabilities of non-call, potentially remarking the positions to quantitatively reflect the risk. assessment and apply above actions if exposure relative to risk limit increases materially. ■ Selective avoidance of certain business. ■ Introduction of sub-limits on specific names/market subsets. ■ Attempt novation of certain positions. ■ Develop hedge strategies. ■ Execute a hedge strategy. ■ Further increase intensity of surveillance.
Actual non-call event has occurred without prior warning	Execute hedge strategy and immediately exercise all rights triggered by non-call under the swap and any related agreements. Assess whether the event is issuer-specific or wider risk management action is required across other existing swap positions. Specifically, the simplest hedge strategy is to immediately transact a reverse-polarity at-market hedging swap with a principal schedule matching the extended securitisation swap. This requires good analytics, which should be in place well in advance of such events. Exercising all rights may include some or all of the following: ■ The right to receive an increased swap spread from the SPV. This may require amending the swap booking in the trading system so that the Operations department can ensure collection of the increased spread. ■ The right to keep collateral under a *collateralised back swap* arrangement, or other similar arrangement, if any are in place. ■ If rating agencies have downgraded the bonds due to their extension or related circumstances, then the contingent liquidity obligations may have decreased. Reflecting this could reduce LTP payments to the swap provider's internal Treasury department, which in turn can lower the quantum of liquid assets required to be held.

TABLE 8.5   The range of possible responses to downgrade risk events.

Status – Downgrade risk	Likely actions
Qualitative surveillance indicates heightened downgrade risk by one or more rating agencies, e.g. negative watch or threat thereof	Possible actions, highly dependent on the precise circumstances, are: ■ Engage with rating agencies to discuss ways to forestall a rating downgrade. ■ Selective avoidance of certain business. This can be achieved by decreasing CFR sub-limits, e.g. on longer-dated swaps. ■ Stop writing new business. ■ Attempt to novate back-book swaps.
Credit rating downgrade to the first trigger	Possible actions, highly dependent on the precise circumstances, are: ■ Stop writing new business. ■ Attempt novations. ■ Ensure that collateral posted is the cheapest to deliver within the universe of eligible collateral. ■ Engage with rating agencies to negotiate alternative remedial actions to posting collateral (e.g. in the case of issuer swap providers for covered bonds, increasing the OC level may be a possibility).

Future Regulation

The Basel Committee on Banking Standards (BCBS) released revised Basel III Market Risk Capital rules in December 2017.[3] As at the time of writing, they have not yet been implemented in any jurisdiction, although there is draft European Commission legislation.[4] Should these rules be implemented as currently drafted, they can be expected to have a significant impact on both derivatives and securitisation.

The proposed regulation allows for three ways of calculating market risk capital:

■ a simplified method, which very few, if any, swap providers are expected to fall under;
■ a sensitivity-based Standardised Approach (SA), which is meant to be the 'baseline' for most institutions; or
■ by permission, an Internal Model Approach (IMA), which is based on historical simulation.

---

[3] See https://www.bis.org/bcbs/publ/d424.htm.
[4] See https://ec.europa.eu/transparency/regdoc/rep/1/2016/EN/COM-2016-850-F1-EN-MAIN.PDF.

For securitisation, only SA is allowed. While the regulation is not explicit on what this means for securitisation swaps, it is quite possible that they will also be captured by this rule. SA is prescriptive and conservative and will undoubtedly make securitisation swaps more expensive. In particular:

- There is no risk diversification across asset classes. FX and interest rate risk are computed separately.
- Swaps with prepayment and/or extension risk automatically attract a *residual risk add-on*, which adds 0.1% of the notional to the market risk capital, unless the swap is perfectly hedged.
- Any trading desk transacting securitisation swaps on SA must compute all the desk's positions on SA, including vanilla hedges, which could otherwise be treated via IMA.

As with any new regulation, market participants will likely attempt to arrange their affairs to minimise adverse impacts and contain price increases and operational costs. One could imagine new structures which split swaps into vanilla and non-vanilla components where the notional principal of the non-vanilla part is minimised in order to reduce the residual risk add-on.

ACCOUNTING

Like other derivatives, securitisation swaps operate under the prevailing accounting standards in the jurisdiction where they are booked for reporting purposes. For all major economies outside the USA and China, the national accounting standards are converging to, or use, the International Financial Reporting Standards (IFRS) developed by the International Accounting Standards Board (IASB). Domestic firms in the USA use Generally Accepted Accounting Principles (GAAP), which differs from IFRS. Hedge accounting is a complex and specialised area where standards are still in the process of evolving. Therefore, the following discussion will be confined to a high-level overview based on IFRS.

Fair Value

The most recent version of IFRS requires derivatives to be accounted for at *fair value* (IFRS 9, which replaces the previous IAS 39). Changes to the fair value of a derivative must be recognised in profit and loss (PnL) unless that derivative has been specifically designated as a hedging instrument in an eligible hedging arrangement. For third party swap providers, where there is no eligible hedging arrangement, IFRS 9 mandates *fair value through profit and loss* (FVTPL). For originator swap providers, there is a choice of accounting treatment depending upon whether they elect to apply for hedge accounting treatment. If hedge accounting is adopted, the fair value changes may be recorded as 'other comprehensive income' (OCI) known as *fair value through other comprehensive income* (FVOCI). OCI is presented separately to PnL as a special item in financial reports.

IFRS 13 defines fair value by reference to an *exit price*. This is the price at which the swap could be sold in an orderly transaction. Specifically, IFRS 13 states:

> When measuring fair value, an entity uses the assumptions that market participants would use when pricing the asset or the liability under current market conditions, including assumptions about risk.

The phrase 'assumptions about risk' has been widely interpreted, amongst other things, as including counterparty credit risk so that CVA is to be included in the exit price of a derivative (though curiously not KVA at this point in time). In the same vein, one can safely assume that charges for swap prepayment risk, extension risk and downgrade risk are also to be included. Including these more esoteric risk charges, while eminently reasonable, is not without its challenges. Specifically:

- *Opaqueness*. These charges are highly opaque. They are only ever communicated bilaterally.
- *Assumption dependence*. Computing these charges involves many assumptions, which can vary considerably – and perfectly legitimately – between different swap providers depending upon many factors including their business models, risk appetites, internal rates and revaluation policies, modelling choices, calibration methodologies, funding costs, credit rating outlook and the composition of their back-books (which can impact *incremental* risk pricing).
- *Uniqueness*. Since there is a very wide range of securitisation and covered bond structures, each deal can be very different. This may be reflected in a high dispersion of esoteric risk charges depending on the specific structure. Finding comparable deals to benchmark pricing is not always possible.

Despite these material challenges, a defensible position for third-party swap providers is revaluation based on the parameters and model pricing that won the trade at inception. This is especially defensible if the swap was won in competition with other swap providers – the inception price is then a 'market price'. Nevertheless, it is fair to say that a significant degree of judgement is required when revaluing securitisation swaps, especially if the market has moved a long way since inception and/or if there have been any material changes in the estimation of unobservable valuation inputs, such as expected average prepayment. In such circumstances, it is essential that the bank's Product Control function has sufficient understanding of the modelling.

Revenue Reserves

The three esoteric risk charges – swap prepayment risk, extension risk and downgrade risk – are often calculated with a degree of conservatism due to their unhedgeability. This means that it is likely that these risk charges will not be fully drawn down over the life of the deal. Common examples include:

- For a BGS over a controlled amortisation tranche, where the schedule is never broken by unexpectedly low prepayment rates, no re-hedging is ever required hence the entirely of the prepayment risk charge remains.
- For a BGS over a pass-through tranche, where realised prepayment volatility is low and realised average prepayment follows the expected trajectory, some of the prepayment risk charge remains.
- For any securitisation swap that doesn't extend, the entirety of the extension risk charge remains.
- For any securitisation swap where the swap provider isn't downgraded to the first trigger level or below, some of the downgrade risk charge remains (noting that the LTP component would have still been paid away to cover HQLA holding costs).

From an accounting perspective, these charges are often held as revenue reserves. This means they are not taken to PnL on day one, but can be potentially taken to PnL through the life of the transaction, if they are not drawn down. Note that reserves form part of shareholder's equity and are to be distinguished from provisions, which are liabilities.

Operationally, the simplest and more prudent way to manage revenue reserves is to only take what remains of them to PnL when the deal has terminated. This reduces PnL volatility and management of cash transfers. However, fair value accounting under IFRS 9 stipulates that the reserves should be revalued periodically to ensure that the positions are correctly marked, at least if the position is deemed 'material'. This means that revenue reserves may not eliminate PnL volatility as they may need to be topped-up during the life of the deal.

For third-party swap providers, an additional challenge when reserving revenue, but expecting to get some of that revenue back in PnL at some point, is how to compute the expected RoE of a deal at inception. This is a point of considerable importance as all banks will have minimum RoE hurdles to pass before they will enter into a transaction. Given the uncertain amount and timing of PnL drip-back from reserves, one needs to be careful to communicate what assumptions have been used when computing RoE. One possible way forward is to compute RoE based on two scenarios:

1. *Day one RoE.* Assume zero drip-back of reserves to PnL.
2. *Expected whole-of-life RoE.* Assume some ('expected') drip-back of reserves to PnL based on clear and consistent criteria, for example:
   - no extension events (as these are very rare);
   - no downgrade to the first trigger level (if appropriate, e.g. if not on negative watch and deal isn't very long-dated);

- prepayment rates follow the expected trajectory; and
- unstressed prepayment volatility and correlation parameters.

While this makes trade decisioning more complex (and it can be fraught already), it arguably provides a more complete picture of the distribution of RoEs that may eventuate.

Fair Value Hierarchy of Valuation Inputs

IFRS 9 implements a three-level valuation hierarchy as follows:

- Level 1 inputs are quoted prices (unadjusted) in active markets for identical assets or liabilities that are accessible at the measurement date.
- Level 2 inputs are inputs other than quoted prices included within Level 1 that are observable for the asset or liability, either directly or indirectly (this can include interpolated rates, implied volatilities and credit spreads).
- Level 3 inputs are unobservable inputs for the asset or liability.

Levels 1, 2 and 3 have facetiously been parodied as mark-to-market, mark-to-model and mark-to-make-believe.

Entities are required to use the highest available level of input. Valuation of securitisation swaps can involve extensive use of level 3 inputs including:

- historically estimated realised prepayment parameters;
- expected average prepayment;
- historically estimated cross-currency basis volatility parameters;
- historically estimated correlations; and
- credit rating transition probabilities.

IFRS 9 requires level 3 valuation inputs to be disclosed in financial accounts if their use is 'significant' and 'recurring'.

Glossary

ABS	Asset-backed securities
ADI	Authorised deposit-taking institution (Australian regulatory term)
BCBS	Basel Committee on Banking Supervision
BGM	Brace-Gatarek-Musiela model
BGS	Balance guarantee swap
CAF	Controlled amortisation facility
CBG	Covered bond guarantor
CDO	Collateralised debt obligation
CDS	Credit default swap
CE	Credit enhancement
CFR	Contingent funding risk
CFVA	Contingent funding valuation adjustment
CPT	Conditional pass-through
CSA	Credit support annex
CVA	Credit valuation adjustment
DPC	Derivative product company
EM	Expected maturity
ENE	Expected negative exposure
EPE	Expected positive exposure
FBA	Funding benefit adjustment
FCA	Funding cost adjustment
FVA	Funding valuation adjustment $= \text{FCA} + \text{FBA}$
FX	Foreign exchange
GAAP	Generally Accepted Accounting Standards (USA)
GBM	Geometric Brownian motion
GFC	Global financial crisis
GIC	Guaranteed investment certificate
HQLA	High quality liquid asset
IASB	International Accounting Standards Board
IFRS	International Financial Reporting Standards
ISDA	International Swaps and Derivatives Association
LCR	Liquidity coverage ratio
LTP	Liquidity transfer price

KVA	Capital valuation adjustment
LFM	Legal final maturity
LIBOR	London interbank offer rate
LTV	Loan-to-value ratio
MLE	Maximum likelihood estimation
MTM	Mark-to-market
MTN	Medium term note
MVA	Margin valuation adjustment
NCCD	Non-centrally cleared derivative
NSFR	Net stable funding ratio
OC	Over-collateralisation
OIS	Overnight index swap
OLS	Ordinary least square
OTC	Over-the-counter (a bilateral method of trading derivatives rather than via an intermediary such as an exchange)
OU	Ornstein-Uhlenbeck
Par swap	A swap with a mark-to-market of zero
PCE	Potential credit exposure
PDL	Principal deficiency ledger (a record of tranche losses in UK RMBS master trusts)
PnL	Profit and loss
PV01	Interest rate delta, defined as the change in value of a derivative due to a 1 basis point shift in interest rates
RMBS	Residential mortgage-backed securities
RoE	Return on equity
RVA	Replacement valuation adjustment
SDE	Stochastic differential equation
SMM	Single monthly mortality rate
SONIA	Sterling overnight index average
SPM	Single period mortality rate
SPV	Special purpose vehicle
SVR	Standard variable rate
VaR	Value-at-Risk
WAL	Weighted average life
XVA	General derivative valuation adjustments i.e. encompassing CVA, FVA, KVA, etc. These are added to the mark-to-market to complete the valuation of a derivative or portfolio of derivatives.

References

[AB]   Brace, A. *Mixing real and arbitrage free measures*, private correspondence 2015

[BDNT] Brigo, D., Dalessandro, S., Neugebauer, M. and Triki, F, *A Stochastic Processes Toolkit for Risk Management* 15 Nov 2007 Available at: https://ssrn.com/abstract=1109160

[BG]   Broadie, M. and Glasserman, P. (1996). Estimating security price derivatives using simulating. *Management Science* 42 (2): 269–285.

[CJ]   Chan, J.H. and Joshi, M. (2013). Fast Monte Carlo Greeks for financial products with discontinuous payoffs. *Mathematical Finance* 23 (3): 459–495.

[DJ]   Daniel, J. (2008). A variable-rate loan-prepayment model for Australian mortgages. *Australian Journal of Management* 33 (2): 277–305.

[DL]   Davidson, A. and Levin, A. (2005). Prepayment risk- and option-adjusted valuation of MBS. *Journal of Portfolio Management* 31 (4): 73–85.

[FC]   Fabozzi, F. and Choudhry, M. (2004). *The Handbook of European Structured Financial Products*. Wiley.

[JG]   Grant, J. *Liquidity transfer pricing: a guide to better practice* BCBS Occasional Paper No. 10 December 2011

[AH]   Holmes, A. *Operational Constraints on the Stabilization of Monetary Supply Growth* Federal Reserve Bank of Boston Conference Proceedings 1969. Available at: https://www.bostonfed.org/news-and-events/events/economic-research-conference-series/controlling-monetary-aggregates.aspx

[HJ]   Hull, J. (2018). *Options, Futures and Other Derivatives*, 10e. Pearson.

[JP]   Jäckel, P. (2002). *Monte Carlo Methods in Finance*. Wiley Finance.

[JM]   Joshi, M. (2003). *The Concepts and Practice of Mathematical Finance*. Cambridge University Press.

[AP]   Pelsser, A. (2000). *Efficient Methods for Valuing Interest Rate Derivatives*. Springer.

[RR]   Rudolf, F. and Rühlmann, K. (2017). *Extendible Maturity Structures: The New Normal?* ECBC European Covered Bond Fact Book.

[JS]   Staum, J. (2008). Incomplete markets. In: *Handbooks in OR & MS*, vol. 15, Chapter 12. Elsevier B.V. 511–563.

[HT]   Takehashi, H. (2005). On embedded complete markets. *Hitotsubashi Journal of Economics* 46: 99.

Index